# FREEMASONRY DECODED

## REBUILDING THE ROYAL ARCH

Kevin L. Gest

Lewis Masonic

First Published 2014

ISBN 978 0 85318 456 0

Published by Lewis Masonic

an imprint of Ian Allan Publishing Ltd, Hersham, Surrey KT12 4RG.

Printed in England by CPI Group (UK) Ltd, Croydon, CR0 4YY

Visit the Lewis Masonic website at www.lewismasonic.co.uk

*Cover image* – Hand painted apron worn by William Budd c.1818.
*The Library and Museum of Freemasonry, London*

*For Lois – thank you for your patience.*

# Contents

# Illustrations

Unless otherwise stated, all images used in the following works have been created, drawn or photographed by the author, are out of copyright due to the date of origination, have been acquired from reputable image agencies, or are available for free use in publications.

An illustration of a Lodge meeting from the early 1800s.

Examples of Second Degree tracing boards (two).

The River Thames from Richmond House, London, by Canaletto. (1747).

The west-facing front portico and the two pillars set up at the porch way, or entrance, on the south side of St Paul's Cathedral.

Spiral design used in the winding staircase.

Royal House of Habsburg – family tree.

Royal House of Bourbon – family tree.

A map of the Battle of Blenheim in 1704 (two).

The Imperial emblem of the Holy Roman Empire.

The tomb of Mary the rich, Bruges, Belgium.

3, 4, 5 Triangle provides the stair tread ratios by Vitruvius.

Medieval T-O map images.

Comparison of old embroidered apron with current manufactured style (two).

Socrates squares to double the perimeter and area (six).

Socrates square and the Apprentice apron (two).

Fellow Craft apron.

Image of man from *The Book of Kells*.

Socrates square to halve the area (four).

Master Mason apron.

Geometry in the Master Mason apron (two).

Pythagoras 3, 4, 5 triangle appears in the Masters Jewel.

Classical façade – Hampton Court Palace.

Socrates squares halving the size (several).

Socrates squares reflected in the Master Mason apron.

Typical Provincial apron and the central square geometry (two).

Diagrams: Golden ratio (two).

Diagram: Masonic progression.

Master/Past Master apron.

Symbol of Parallel lines on the Masters Apron (three).

Diagrams: Euclid's parallel postulate (four).

Diagrams: Master symbols (three parts).

Diagram: Golden ratio development.

Diagrams: Vesica development (six).

Gothic arches (three).

The house at Lyme Park, Cheshire.

Linked arch decoration in wood panelling at Lyme Park.

Left: The Mandorla in 13th-century seal, Salisbury Cathedral.

Right: The Mandorla high on the western face of Strasbourg Cathedral.

The Mandorla in ecclesiastical vestments, approx., 1450 CE, Switzerland.

Mandorla above the entrance to the tomb associated with Leonardo da Vinci.

Bishop's Mitre as a Mandorla.

Apron, pre-1800s.

A Masonic memorial featuring Vesicas.

Abbey church at Morienval (three).

Temple, Delhi showing Solomon's Seal.

Map of tribes of the Israelites.

Diagram of Constellations relating to the tribes of Israelites.

Inside a Masonic Temple showing the zodiac.

Royal Arch apron and sash.

Royal Arch jewel.

The image of circle and interlaced triangles in Chichester Cathedral.

A similar illustration in a south-facing stained glass window at Notre Dame.

Solomon's Seal and Vesica in stained-glass at Canterbury Cathedral.

Creating Solomon's Seal using the Vesica.

Solution to the Delian problem based on that developed by Sir Isaac Newton.

Royal Arch symbol.

The Tau connection with the golden ratio.

T over H illustration.

Plato's Triple Tau in Royal Arch (six).

Platonic elements.

Platonic octagram.

Platonic octagram in a Buddist temple, Malaysia.

Platonic octagram in the floor under the dome of the replica of the US House of Representatives, Havana (two).

Creating a Royal Arch Triple Tau using geometry (seven).

Royal Arch symbol.

Man, calf, lion, eagle from *The Book of Kells*.

Royal Arch regalia symbol.

Symbol: Knights of the Holy Sepulchre.

St Galls (three).

Diagrams: development of Freemasonry in England (three).

Template table.

Bishop's mitre: solution to Image A.

Abbey at Morienval: solution to Image B.

Doorway of St Paul's Cathedral: solution to Image C.

St. Gall's: solution to image D.

# Acknowledgements

OVER MANY YEARS I have called on the assistance of numerous organisations, and people, during my enquiries. Their help has extended back over 20 years, and some of the insights they provided have been incorporated in this book.

I would particularly like to acknowledge the assistance I received from the friends of York Minster and Saint Paul's Cathedral, London; the librarians and archivists at the library and museum of Freemasons' Hall, London; the library of the Royal Institute of British Architects (RIBA), London; the Goodwood Estate Company Ltd for their permission to use, and the supply of, the print of Canaletto's image of the River Thames used in the body of the book as a reference to how St. Paul's Cathedral looked in the 18th century. Equally, I thank the librarians and staff at the Abbey of St. Gall's in Switzerland, who provided a great deal of assistance through email contact prior to my visit and thereby made my short stay so productive. Very special thanks go to Professor Andrew Prescott, University College, London, formerly of Sheffield University, for permission to reproduce his lecture on the Unlawful Societies Act, and to Trinity College, Dublin, for their permission to reproduce plates from *The Book of Kells*.

A book of this nature involves not just the research and writing, but at the very least editing, planning, design and production. To Nick, Fiona, Martin, Philippa, Keith, Alistair and Rob, an enormous *thank you*.

My thanks also go to the members of the Provincial Grand Lodge of Sussex, past and present, who have given me permission to photograph and use images of artefacts held within their museum, and for access to written materials also retained by them.

I also thank the Secretary (2012) and selected members of Hemming Lodge 1512, Middlesex, for the assistance I received in locating a portrait of Dr. Samuel Hemming, one of the unsung but diligent men who made a significant difference to the development of Freemasonry 200 years ago.

And I must not forget the members of Saint Cecilia Lodge,1636, and Simplicius Chapter 8851 for permitting me to give a range of talks over several years, the feedback from which was of immense value to my thought processes.

I also convey a very special *thank you* to my wife, Lois, who accompanied me on so many of my site visits in the UK and further afield, though not always to places she would have chosen to go. And for leaving me alone to get on with the task of writing, when that phase of the book began.

To all of you – *thank you*.
KLG - December 2013

# The Opening

---

## For members of a Masonic Lodge.

*And now for something that may be controversial.*

EVERYONE WHO BECOMES A member of a Lodge does so because they get something out of it that they enjoy. It might be the camaraderie associated with being a member of a male centric organisation; escaping via membership of an old, established fraternity, from the rigours of the everyday world, being associated with and participating (even in a small way) with charitable activity; taking part in the ceremonies and delivering them as if acting in an amateur play; being dressed in the regalia which, again, transports one from the ordinary affairs of the external world. Whatever that *something* is, there are hundreds of thousands of men throughout the world who participate in such meetings.

We have for many years been led to believe that Freemasonry is probably around 1,000 years old, dating from the time of the great cathedral builders of Europe, a band of itinerant craftsmen with possible links back to the stonemasons of Rome, Greece and Egypt.

There are, and have been, many illustrious and highly qualified men who have presented commendable research about the Order, but much of this information has become a catalogue of prominent men who were members, things they did and places where they met. There is very little that attempts to explain what it is we are actually doing in our ceremonies, and where it came from.

In this book, I am presenting a very different picture.

**For those who are not Freemasons.**

*You will, I trust, have a favourable impression of Freemasonry after you have read this book.*

ONE DAY, I WAS walking along a street in London where a number of shops display and sell Masonic regalia. I heard the voice of a young lady behind me, a tourist from North America, saying, 'Hey, look at that. It's for the conspiracy guys.' I turned around and told the young lady, and her male companion, that I was one of the *conspiracy guys* she had just spoken of. I pointed out that across the road from where we stood was Freemasons Hall, the centre of regular Freemasonry throughout the world, and that there were tours of the building, a museum and library they could visit which would help them realise that we are not *conspiratorial*. And it was free. I left them as they entered the building.

Some three hours later, by chance I encountered them again, this time in Covent Garden. They said they had visited the museum, viewed a special exhibition about Napoleon Bonaparte as a Freemason, and that the tour of the building had been wonderful. They were hugely impressed by what they saw and heard, and it had changed their impression.

Over several decades, Freemasonry has provided the plot of many novels and movies, made money for those concerned, but left a very different impression of the organisation with a large swath of the public, in comparison with the reality.

I have also written this book with the non-Mason in mind, in the hope they will find it informative and correct any misconceptions they harbour.

In this book, I am presenting a very different picture.

## Chapter 1

# Mysterious background

THERE ARE FOUR BIG mysteries to solve in Freemasonry. Behind them is a peculiar code called *allegory*. Decoding this allegory, decodes the mysteries of Freemasonry.

Today, Whitehall in London is the name of a broad avenue that runs from Trafalgar Square in the east to Parliament Square in the west, flanked, for the most part, by the offices of state and parliament. The name is derived from the royal palace that once occupied the area and fronted the River Thames, a waterway that, in the Middle Ages, was also a highway for the transport of people and produce between the towns and villages established along its banks. The Whitehall Palace is said to have been the largest in Europe and, in its time, probably the rest of the known world. Built of fine limestone ashlars, it was once the London residence of Henry VIII who moved there from the Palace of Westminster, and it remained in use as a royal residence, becoming the central Court of Kings, until destroyed by fire in 1698.

Around halfway down the length of the avenue, opposite Horse Guards Parade, is a rather plain building that was originally part of the Whitehall Palace complex, and the major centre of feasting and royal revelry. Known as the Banqueting House, it was that part of the royal residence where foreign dignitaries were entertained and masque balls held. It was also through one of the upper windows of this building, facing Whitehall, that King Charles I stepped onto a scaffold on Tuesday, 30 January, 1649, where he was beheaded.

Today, this impressive structure retains its original function as a banqueting centre, boasting a wonderful ceiling, painted by Rubens, which is regarded as one of his finest early works. The scenes are an allegory depicting *The Union of the Crowns*, *The Apotheosis of James I* and *The Peaceful Reign of James I*, with the term 'Apotheosis' inferring that James I had achieved the status of divinity.

For Freemasons, the Banqueting House is a significant building in London, as it is the second that appears in a list of structures noted in the first *Book of Constitutions of Freemasonry*, in 1723. It was designed by Inigo Jones, the man at the forefront of the introduction of the Renaissance style of classical architecture to England, and completed in 1622 for James I of England (James VI of Scotland) on the site of an earlier building that served the same purpose but had been destroyed by fire, prior to that which finally destroyed the Whitehall Palace. The main hall is rectangular in shape: it is 55 feet square and 110 feet long, being in the form of a double cube, an important symbol of Royal Arch Masonry.

In the 18th century, there was what has often been referred to as a schism in English Freemasonry, when two separate groups emerged: subsequently known as the *Antients* and the *Moderns*. One claimed to be from the true stem of very ancient masonry, accusing the other of being a new innovation. Claims and counter-claims were made by each, along with no small measure of hostility of one to the other. Despite their differences of opinion, in 1813 they merged and Freemasonry in England evolved into two linked identities: that of Craft Freemasonry, and the Holy Royal Arch of Jerusalem. Following this merger it was stated that there were only three degrees, or levels, in Craft Freemasonry: the Apprentice; the Fellow Craft; the Master Mason, including the Holy Royal Arch of Jerusalem. From this, the Royal Arch, as it is known by its members, is implied to be an extension of the Master Mason degree; being very different in nature by comparison with the other three it has for many years been unofficially described as the fourth degree. The first three degrees are practised in a regular Lodge, while the ceremonies of the Royal Arch are undertaken in a Chapter – incorporating a completely different structure to that of a Craft Lodge.

In addition to the three regular degrees, the great ceremony of the Installation of the Worshipful Master (*which is not considered to be a degree*) is kept distinct and separate from the other ceremonies. It is performed at a meeting which is generally regarded as the highpoint of the Lodge year, for it is at this assembly that representatives of the Grand Master are present to carefully observe the manner in which affairs are conducted. From this, various types of reports are compiled which might affect the opportunity of a lodge member to achieve a high rank within Freemasonry in subsequent years. The Master is the person elected by all the other members of a Lodge to be the figurative head for a full year following his installation. He can be a former Master, defined as a Past Master, or must at least have held the office of Warden. There are two Wardens in a Lodge and today their roles are more akin to Masters in training. To hold an office as a Warden, one will need to have been raised to the degree of a Master Mason, while being Master, is the highest level one can achieve in an individual Lodge and, is by definition, therefore superior to any other level or office. One would therefore expect that it would be from this level of Master, or Past Master, that one would then follow on to the Royal Arch. This is not so, for the ceremony of the installation of the Master does not provide a bridging link to the Royal Arch. The only qualification necessary for a person to join a Royal Arch Chapter is that they should be a Master Mason, and furthermore they are encouraged to join a Chapter on the grounds that the ceremonies provide a *completion* of the Master Mason degree. At first view, therefore, it seems that the installation of the Master is a sideways step, an office entirely on its own, having an honorary role yet not being part of mainstream Freemasonry. How bizarre! In Freemasonry, however, everything has a meaningful purpose, nothing is there without reason, and the seemingly unusual positioning of the Master may have a very valid purpose. To define that purpose requires further background investigation.

The *Antients* and the *Moderns* had aspects of their ceremonies that were common, and some that were totally at variance. This implies that they had two separate roots from which the knowledge contained in the ceremonies was derived. Nevertheless, when the United Grand Lodge of England was formed in 1813, it required the two groups to merge, which implies that there was sufficient common ground for them to do so and to accommodate any differences. The *differences* had obviously meant a great deal to each side, and it was these variances that resulted in hostility between the two groups for several decades prior to their merger. It is therefore difficult to comprehend that either one would give up their customs to accommodate the other, as they would have wanted to see their own retained. This implies that their *separate roots* are still identifiable because there has been little change in the ceremonial structure of the Craft ceremonies for over 200 years. To get to those *differences*, however, requires yet another level of background investigation.

Then we come to the Royal Arch degree. Highly respected writers on Freemasonry have previously pointed out that this degree appeared after the first Grand Lodge was created in 1717, and that it was fully formed when it arrived. It was like a package: picked up from a shelf, once opened, the contents were revealed and a group of people, liking the look of what they saw, started working with it. As noted previously, there is nothing about the Royal Arch structure which, at first view, suggests any common link with Craft Freemasonry, everything about it is very different. So, how could that be? Where did it come from? To get answers to these questions requires yet further background research.

To put it simply, we have what are in effect four mysteries to solve:

1. Why is the Master Installation ceremony subject to exclusion and not seen as a degree?
2. What were the differences in the ceremonial contents practised by the *Antients* and *Moderns?*
3. Where did the framework that was the basis of the Royal Arch degree ceremonies originate, and what does it mean?
4. Why is the Royal Arch degree considered to be the *completion* of the Master Mason ceremony?

Could the design of the Bishop's Mitre (Image A) provide a connection with a *discarded ceremony of Freemasonry* which now forms the basis of the *Installation of the Master?*

*Top: Mitre - Image A.*

***Above:*** *Abbey - Image B.*

***Top right:*** *Doorway - Image C.*

***Right:*** *Church, central Europe - Image D.*

14

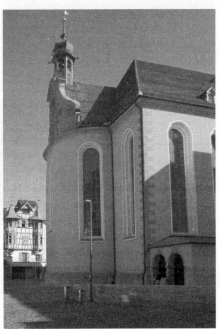

Is it possible that the building (Image B), a once proud abbey with origins dating back to the 10th century, now in ruins, is the basis for the knowledge, contained in allegorical form, of the *Antients?*

Then there is the doorway (Image C). Does it open into the world of the *Moderns?*

Could it be that the old church (Image D), situated in a mountainous area of central Europe, provided the basis for the ceremonies and legend, contained in allegorical form, of the *Holy Royal Arch?*

There are obviously answers to these questions, and in order to justify and verify those answers, we need an appropriate context to be set for each. This will be done, over the following pages.

We will also come to understand why the Holy Royal Arch is seen as the completion of the Master Mason degree.

And we will discover something else. Within the ceremonies of Freemasonry, there is an encyclopaedia of knowledge: history, logic, mathematics, astronomy, architecture, religion and geography. There is a code for life, and a structured means for encouraging every member to be a better person, an example of exemplary conduct to all those who know him.

It is all contained in the allegorical coding of Freemasonry, and the moral teachings are as relevant today as they were in the era when it was all created.

## The fifth question?

In Freemasons' Hall, London, there is a wonderful library and museum.

The library contains thousands of fascinating books and papers, most in English but a few in other languages. The one thing that really stands out is the immense dedication that has been shown by past generations of Freemasons in researching, writing and collating a vast array of factual, hypothetical and even esoteric material. There are endless works devoted to trying to prove that famous men of a bygone era, men who feature prominently in the development of the British nation, were members of the organisation. There are also thousands of items that chart the formation of individual Lodges, their history and who the members were. There are papers and documents that highlight the expansion of Freemasonry across the globe as the British Empire also expanded, from the Americas in the West to China in the East; from Sweden and Russia in the North, to South Africa and Australia in the South. There are thousands of papers and books that discuss the probable origins of the fraternity and some aspects of its ceremonies. But something is missing – there is very little material that attempts to explain what Freemasons are doing in their meetings, its significance and why they do it.

The museum has a wonderful display of memorabilia that collectively highlights a magnificent past: majestic grandfather clocks with Masonic symbolism engraved on the clock faces; furniture specifically handmade at great expense, to serve the functions of a Lodge; regalia, portraits and occasional exhibitions devoted to a specific event, to note but a few. Amongst the regalia is a range of wonderful Masonic aprons from the 18th century, all obviously handmade by the member, or perhaps their spouse, but in any case by someone who was extremely proficient in needlework through many hours of dedicated labour. No two such aprons seem to be the same, except in the display of certain symbols, such as a ladder – perceived to be Jacob's ladder of biblical mention, linking earth with heaven. It is as if these old aprons were communicating a level of knowledge and understanding that the wearer had achieved. Then in the early 19th century the individuality vanished, replaced by a standard system of designs and styles that illustrate where the member fits within the hierarchy, as opposed to, the knowledge one might have gained. Instead of being lovingly made by hand, the regalia has become a commodity, easily replicated in a factory-type environment by a range of specialist suppliers.

To the four main questions already stated, we now add another. Was anything lost in making this change?

# Chapter 2

# Opening observations for Freemasons and others

*Now every mason has taken several very solemn obligations not to divulge [their] secrets; and the way in which the promise has been kept by the hundreds of thousands of brethren who are spread all over the world is not only a credit to the Order but commands the respect of all right-minded people.*

*From a popular London magazine, 1888*[1].

**GREETINGS, ONE AND ALL.**

The paragraph above is a quotation from a widely-circulated London-based magazine published in the late Victorian era, which carried a short account of the ceremonies of Freemasonry. Since that item appeared, there have been many *disclosures* that claim to reveal the secret knowledge of Freemasonry, including television programmes that have re-enacted parts of ceremonies; so many in fact, that if there ever were any secrets, they'd have long since been exposed.

Freemasonry is a very British institution, having probably started in England and transferred to other parts of the world as British colonial interests expanded. It may never have existed had it not been for the actions of Henry VIII leaving the Holy Roman Empire and establishing a Protestant-biased Church of England. Yet, within its ceremonies there is a great deal of ancient knowledge and wisdom presented in allegorical form. In this book, I explore what the ceremonies of Freemasonry are trying to convey, what the imagery may reveal, and the origins of Masonic regalia that may claim our attention.

One of the first things a new member is told is that Freemasonry is a 'peculiar system

of morality veiled in allegory and illustrated by symbols'. Sadly, the meaning and origins of these allegories are rarely understood or even recognised today. Members learn the words and actions of the short playlets that are called ceremonies, but the performers have little idea about what they actually mean. This book is intended to open their eyes to what is beneath that allegorical layer, and thereby to reveal a fascinating world that is not immediately obvious. In so doing, I appreciate that I have an obligation to refrain from revealing all. This is not because there are deep secrets that will rock governments or destroy established religions, but simply because there is a mystique about the Order that we wish to preserve.

Freemasonry is an organisation that can boast an impressive pedigree and a unique history that extends back for at least 3-400 years. With a membership that is measured in millions, it is global in its reach and attracts persons from almost every strata of society. Although *regular* Freemasonry has, for at least the past 300 years, been restricted to male membership and is likely to remain so for the foreseeable future, for over 100 years a similar organisation, solely for the membership of women has also existed. Yet despite this impressive pedigree, discussions about Freemasonry create mixed emotions.

Those who are members gain a great deal of friendship and support from their involvement, enjoying the ceremonies and the company of friends and acquaintances, along with the joviality that invariably accompanies a meal together after a meeting: a tradition reflecting the age old practices to which most Lodges and Chapters still subscribe. Joining Freemasonry is voluntary, as is the opportunity to discontinue and resign, so every member gains something from their membership otherwise they would not continue with it. This is perhaps underlined by the impressive number of Masons acclaimed for having been members for in excess of 40 or 50 years. Freemasons believe their organisation helps to make people more just, well-balanced and moral individuals within society, and further believe that, through its charitable activities, Freemasonry is playing its part in helping the wider community of which every member is an integral element. Every aspect of the ceremonies of Freemasonry underscores the ideals of living an honourable, honest, temperate and moral life, of being a person who can be trusted, a person of integrity not only in a financial sense but in every aspect of life. These, many would argue, are the exact qualities that one would expect to find in a magistrate, a judge, an officer in local and national government, or at a high level within a company, or military service.

There are, of course, sections of society that are hostile to Freemasonry. This may stem from some past family belief, something they have read in magazines, a comment passed by a disaffected individual, hype and scaremongering that has periodically been the domain of politicians and the mass media, or through the bias of individuals who were simply seeking to gain publicity for themselves. Added to this mix must be the uncertainty and confusion created about the institution by the plotlines of movies and books of fiction, wherein it has been cast as a secret society attempting to establish a new world order, portrayed as the holder of secret knowledge that would destroy the main religions of the Western world, or as the purveyor of symbols which, when defined and viewed in certain patterns, will lead to a horde of long lost buried treasure of immense value.

Whether you are positive about Freemasonry, a practitioner, or person who is confused by what it is and what it does, it is suggested that you approach the contents of this book with an open mind.

## What Freemasonry is, and what it is not

Freemasonry is not a secret society, but like many other social organisations, it has procedures and activities that are restricted to its members. It is an organisation that has a global reach from Australasia to the Far East; from North America to South America and the Caribbean; through many of the larger countries of sub-Saharan Africa and the Indian subcontinent, and most of Europe. In many of these countries, Masonic halls are easily identified and labelled; subject to the location in which they exist, they may be used as community centres, childcare or child health clinics, or meeting places for social groups and the elderly. Some Masonic halls are large and elaborate, others are small, plain and simple; some are in the heart of major cities, others are in very small towns, along a dusty road in India, on the slopes of a mountain in Hong Kong, a village in Cuba and even in a small community on the far southwest coast of Australia, close to where the Indian and Southern Oceans meet.

**Top:** *Classical architectural design - Singapore.*

**Above:** *A small lodge centre - rural Cuba.*

*Top:* Masonic Centre Rural South West, Australia

***Above:*** *A modern Masonic Centre - Sydney, NSW*

Freemasonry is not a religion, neither is it a substitute for religion. There are no particular religions from which membership is encouraged, and none that are denied.

Freemasonry is one of the foremost charities in the world, not only providing services and help for its own members, but contributing to services in the global community as a whole, such as supporting and financing medical research and providing valuable assistance in the event of a natural disaster.

## How old is Freemasonry?

There is a history traceable back to around 1691 CE. Beyond that there are specific and isolated positive references back to about 1640 CE, and further possible links back to approximately 1620 CE, but beyond that there is nothing of any great certainty. Freemasonry was given organisational form in 1717, which makes it 300 years old at the least. It was reorganised from a series of fragmented and competing Lodge systems in1813, from which the global organisation that now exists is derived. From the mid-1700s, the British Empire grew as its trade and political influence around the world evolved. Men who were Freemasons represented commercial and administrative interests around the world, and developed their own local Lodges, with the result that, over time, Freemasonry has become a global institution.

# How did it begin?

Again there is much uncertainty. It may well have existed well before the 1600s as a religious guild, just as most of the great Livery Companies of London started. Documents used in the past as evidence to support the notion of descent from the stonemasons who built the great medieval cathedrals of Europe, are now doubted, both as a direct link to Freemasonry and *Old Charges* previously used to substantiate such earlier assertions. Yet within Freemasonry there is a range of esoteric knowledge that the early stonemasons would have needed to know to be able to design and build many of the stately edifices that we still see today. Investigating that esoteric knowledge, where it came from, how it was used, and its relevance in freemasonry, is what this book is about.

History can be a crusty old subject, being little more than a catalogue of the past. It is, however, useful in indicating how we have come to be where we are in our human development. Such information has usually been written by the victors of war, or from the perceptions of those who considered themselves as the great and good of their times. Some of it is pure propaganda and some of it is a trusty record. The difficulty arises in knowing which is which.

Faith is not fact! Fact is supported by indisputable evidence, itself the result of a rigorous gathering and application of comprehensive data that has been tested and proven to be reliable. Alas, there is very little real and tangible historical evidence within Masonic records to support some of the theories presented in the past about the origins of the organisation, especially about the ceremonies. Yet there is supporting evidence outside of Freemasonry. Some of this is recorded in the following pages, so that the reader can see how conclusions have been determined. Hence some of the observations presented in this book may seem a little *off the wall*, perhaps even contentious, by comparison with past ideas.

You are invited to be the judge.

I have been a member of the Masonic movement for approaching 30 years (at the time of writing). In my early years of membership, information was presented to me about the history and procedures of Freemasonry as if it was factual and supported by irrevocable evidence. After a few years, however, I began to question some of what I had been told, but in the absence of anything constructive to present as an alternative view, I had to accept what was imparted to me. As I have reported in earlier books, I approached senior members of our organisation expecting them to clarify my misgivings, only to find that they didn't know the answers to my very basic questions. This was, I confess, something of a revelation. How could they be in such senior positions without knowing the answers, or at least, knowing where to find them? It was at a time when, on the one hand, we were encouraged to perform ceremonies without great deviation from established principles, and on the other, there was talk of changes to the structure of ceremonies, and rumours that the degree known simply as the Royal Arch was to be floated off from the United Grand Lodge of England, to form a different stand-alone structure. If the hierarchy of Freemasonry do not know what the ceremonies are about, then any structural change to the ceremonies, even simple words or phrases, could totally undermine the objectives and purposes that are contained in the Masonic culture and have been passed down to us over the past few hundred years. We might be losing insights or information that was of value within our ceremonies because of ignorance about what they mean. And if we kept on doing it, there was no telling what may be lost forever.

Freemasonry is not the only major institution to face the prospect of losing its core knowledge. Some years ago, I read that the Jewish Torah may have suffered the same effect. It was apparently first written down around 600 BCE; then successive generations over the next 500 years began to question whether specific words or phrases in the customs, made any sense, so the scribes and hierarchy of the time changed or deleted them. Then, around 40 BCE, a stop was put on any further changes on the grounds that there was a danger that, if they continued to alter what was already in place, there would come a time when nothing of the original was left. There is a risk of the same thing happening in Freemasonry.

So in the absence of evidence to support what I was being told, I was left with no option but to try and unravel the mystery of Freemasonry myself. As I questioned some of our activities and suggested alternative views about their origins, or what they could mean, I soon became very aware that I was presenting ideas that just did not fit with opinions that were deeply entrenched in the psyche of the institution. That entrenchment wasn't surprising. In the previous 100 years there had been many eminent men – graduates of some of the finest universities and educational establishments, men with aristocratic titles and connections, educated in the classics and the most significant literature deemed necessary to obtain a degree, the law, economics and colonial administration – who had presented papers and theories in respect of the history of the organisation and its proceedings, and that information was promulgated and accepted as fact and reality. In addition, there were various groups of these individuals who formed themselves into research lodges, which gave their opinions yet further credence.

It is not my intention to be critical of the works of these eminent men, or the hierarchy of the organisation. Far be it for me to do so. It is unrealistic to expect the hierarchy to know everything. Freemasonry is an international organisation that requires individuals at its heart who can deal with issues in a diplomatic manner. There are legal issues with which the organisation must comply; our charities and charitable activity must be undertaken within strict guidelines and governance because large sums of money flow through the organisation every year to support all the charitable commitments it has entered into. It needs people at the top who can therefore provide expertise in all of the appropriate financial, legal and charitable fields. With those qualifications above, it is nevertheless sad to note that there appear to be very few that seem to have any overt grasp on the meaning of the ceremonial contents, yet these are the same people that will dictate the progress and promotions within the organisation. This lack of awareness is a pity because there is a great deal of fascinating information within the ceremonies.

So little of the earlier works and theories by these eminent men of the past, however, provide any plausible explanation that defines three key elements:

1. What we are doing?
2. Why we are doing it?
3. Where did it come from?

With respect to *where did it come from?*, there are a few existing documents that stem from around the 1720s, but there is very little conclusive or reliable evidence that exists prior to the mid-1700s. Prior to that there are a few occasional references, but not much more, which leaves the door open for considerable speculation. From around 1750, there are minute books from a few individual Lodges and Grand Lodges, and the range of documents increases thereafter, all of which have been thoroughly scrutinised. It is only from around 1810 that a comprehensive set of documents survives, but even they throw little light on *what are we doing?* and *why are we doing it?* They merely say that this is the hierarchical structure and ceremonial content every member is expected to observe, along with a designed regalia; despite the intervening passage of time, there has been little change in the last 200 years.

## Mark and side degrees

In addition to the mainstream degrees of English Freemasonry there are a series of *side degrees*. Amongst the most significant of these, in England, is the degree known as *Mark Masonry*. Mark has ceremonies that refer to the patterns of marks made on stones by stonemason craftsmen, particularly in the medieval period, as a form of identification. They were like a signature and enabled a stone to be traced to a single operator.

During the process of reconciliation between the two main Grand Lodges, the *Antients* and the *Moderns,* and the formalisation of the Holy Royal Arch, Mark Masonry was not included in the official structure, despite having a traceable pedigree that extended back to the mid-1700s. It was left to continue as an entirely separate organisation, while following the basic principles of operation of the newly formed United Grand Lodge. Mark Masonry was, however, included in the structure of both the subsequent Irish and Scottish Grand Lodge Constitutions.

In this book, only the degrees declared by the United Grand Lodge of England in 1813 are specifically considered. I trust those readers who derive much pleasure from their involvement with Mark Masonry will therefore not be affronted.

## And one other thing

Throughout the book there are a number of images that illustrate the background to items and symbols in Freemasonry, as part of the process of considering where it came from and what connections might be discerned. Some of those images I have also used in other books. They are not repeated here just to flesh out the number of pages, but to further illustrate a different aspect of the ceremonies and symbols to which the same illustration might apply. The same may also be true of several instances where similar lines of text are used to reinforce a point, ever mindful that I am naturally unaware as to what readers of this book may already know. In some cases a fairly detailed history is presented about the background to an event, especially where a proposition is at variance with long established Masonic mythology. This is necessary so that the reader fully appreciates the background to the origin of the thesis.

Be prepared for some interesting revelations.

## Caution please:

Some of the contents of this book reflect on the early years of the formalisation and development of Freemasonry. This took place at the end of a prolonged period of intense religious conviction that permeated almost every aspect of life across Europe. It was at a time of political turmoil and struggles for power between competing families organised in groups through selective marriages, who defined themselves as *Royal Houses*. It was an era of great change when science and religion were often in conflict; religion based its views on *faith,* and at least 1,500 years of reliance on scriptures that it treated as incontrovertible fact, while science demonstrated through logic, observation, experimentation and measurement a very different set of incontrovertible, repeatable facts that both challenged and undermined the rigorously-held religious *faith*

perspective. In addition, developments in the ceremonial contents of Freemasonry took place against the background of the early phase of the Industrial Revolution, and the expansion of trade that led to the creation of the British Empire.

Observations made in the following pages mention forms of religion and, in some cases, the officers of those religions. Such comments and observations are based on historical facts as recorded in a variety of encyclopaedia and textbooks. They are not, and should not be construed as reflecting, the opinions or bias of the author unless where otherwise stated.

Because formalised Freemasonry was developed against the background of this period of turmoil, it has been necessary to mention issues that, in the second half of the 20th century, some people would perhaps have preferred to sweep under the carpet. They are brought to the fore only to illustrate the difficult background and circumstances against which the organisation of Freemasonry not only developed, but became a highly respected institution with an international reach.

KLG

*Chapter 3*

# Freemasonry's fearful foundations

MUCH OF THE PAST writing about Freemasonry, while having some merit, centres predominantly around who did what at which time. Therefore, much tends to reflect the background to the administrative structure of the organisation, the so-called great and the good who were members, and to which lodges they belonged. In the case of the latter, one can almost gain an impression of an attempt to give the organisation credibility, thus enabling it to stand head and shoulders above any other similar society while also inferring a level of uniqueness. Masonic archivists in London now believe that the *Old Charges,* first published as an association with Freemasonry around 1723 and used to illustrate a connection with the former craft of the stonemasons of the medieval period, were in reality little more than a public relations exercise by the medieval guilds. The current belief is that they were concocted to give the stone-mason's guild of old, from which Freemasonry was supposedly descended, a level of pedigree and credibility to support a quest for a charter to give them some standing as a guild, through which they would receive higher levels of pay. So, in that sense, earlier eminent men were doing much the same *public relations* exercise as Masonic researchers when writing about the great and the good, but perhaps unconsciously. Yet despite this, very little has been written that attempts to explain

what Freemasons are actually doing in their meetings, or the meaning of the symbolism which decorates their banners and ritual materials.

Part of the problem rests in the fact that there is no definitive record as to how the organisation actually came into being, especially prior to 1723. There is frequent mention of the year 1717 when four Lodges, having met the previous year, came together to create one Grand Lodge to administrate over them. The reality is that we know little more than that, although one can conclude that there were obviously lodges in existence prior to 1716, and possibly in some number, to develop a need for a single body of authority over them and hence the creation of the first Grand Lodge. From 1723, surviving records become more numerous but still throw little light on what went on prior to 1717. One of the foremost archivists produced a book in the 1980s with the title *The History of English Freemasonry*. In the chapter headed 'Theories of Origins', he states in the last paragraph:

Whether we shall ever discover the true origins of Freemasonry is open to question……If [Dr] Anderson is correct in claiming that many manuscript records were deliberately burnt in 1720 'by some scrupulous Brothers that those papers might not fall in to strange hands' it may be that the vital evidence we seek has already been lost.[2]

The fact that records were burnt is generally accepted as fact, on the basis that few records of the early 1700s survive. Yet, there seems to be little evidence that anyone actually considered what motivated those 'scrupulous brothers' to burn those records. Was it just because they wanted to protect the so-called secrets of Freemasonry and thereby create an organisation with an aura of mystique? And what did Dr James Anderson mean by 'fall in to strange hands'?

The era in which organised Freemasonry is considered to have commenced, was one of fear. There were political and religious hostilities on the one hand and a liberating era with great strides in science, exploration and trade, on the other. When James Anderson wrote his *Constitutions* in 1723, Britain had faced a 200-year period of turmoil and it still was not over. It was a period when politics, science and religion were in intense conflict; yet as the forces that defined those conflicts subsided, so the world we now know began to emerge.

To set the scene for some of the observations made later in this book, in the following pages of this chapter we will look at a few of the higher profile issues that underscore this period of conflict, including just a few that extend back beyond it.

*Author's Note:*

*There are comments made in the following pages that draw attention to one particular religious belief and dogma. The observations should not be considered as a bias of the author, but are based on facts recorded in historical sources.*

*In addition, the following pages set out the paths of the religious and political conflicts that occurred over the 200-year period prior to 1717. They are by no means complete but are included to ensure all readers have the same basic information, without making assumptions that every reader is already fully conversant and aware of the facts that are presented.*

## Religion in conflict

During the Middle Ages only one religious dogma was tolerated in Europe, that of the Roman Catholic faith. The Vatican was ruthless in ensuring obedience, thereby maintaining its power base, authority and prestige. To do so, it even sanctioned acts of homicide against groups of people who held an opinion that was at variance with that which it promulgated. In the early 1200s a small sect based in the Languedoc region of southwest France, known as the Cathars, held political and religious views that the Catholic authorities deemed heretical, and they thereby became the focus of Vatican attention. A campaign against the Cathars was instigated with the objective of the total elimination of the sect and its beliefs. Nobles in France were offered the opportunity to increase their wealth and influence by being awarded the lands and property of the Cathars if they would mount military activity and eradicate the sect. This resulted in horrendous acts against the people of the region, whether they were Cathars or not.

Throughout the area of Catholic influence, the Inquisition had the power to arrest, try, torture, judge and sentence individuals that held or uttered, what it considered to be heretical beliefs. The penalty was often death. Nobody was exempt, even influential bishops fell foul of the Inquisition and were put to death. Fear permeated life in Europe for around 600 years. New knowledge was slow to emerge and science was best kept out of sight of the religious authorities, becoming almost an underground movement like the alchemists.

The 16th and 17th centuries were perhaps amongst the most turbulent eras, and provide the main backdrop to the creation of organised Freemasonry. Science from these two centuries can be detected in Masonic ceremonies.

## Opening the path to religion for all

The universal language in the Middle Ages, for both official religious and secular matters, was the Greco-Roman dialect of Latin. While members of the ecclesiastical establishment were well versed in it, many rulers of the various countries and regions across Europe and their administrators were not. They had their own local languages and often required the services of personnel from within the Church to translate documents for them and provide advice on how to deal with what such documents might request. In an era when the vast majority of people could not read or write, the Roman Catholic establishment was the sole authority on the text of the Holy Bible, what could be included in it, and interpretations of what the text meant. While that situation remained, the Church held ultimate religious power and authority over Europe. The idea that the Bible, and other religious works, should be translated into the language of ordinary citizens was vehemently opposed. If ordinary people could read the biblical texts for themselves and draw their own conclusions as to their meaning, the power and influence of the Church would be undermined. This, however, did not stop some learned men from embarking on the venture of translation. When discovered, the Church was brutal in its retribution, not only to ensure harsh punishment for the offender but as a warning to those that might seek to follow the same path.

In 1382, John Wycliffe was a teacher at Oxford University and thereby a learned man of his time. He is also acknowledged as probably the first scholar to translate the New Testament into English. The Catholic Church was so incensed by his actions, along with his outspoken criticism of the Church hierarchy and his advocacy of Church reform, that he was expelled from his position at Oxford. It is believed that two years later, on the last day of 1384, Wycliffe died, an event which did not prevent the church from taking its final retribution, some 40 years later. In 1428, on the orders of the Pope, Wycliffe's remains were disinterred and burnt, the ashes being cast into a local river so that no trace of such a vile wretch should remain. Others carried on secretly to satisfy the same objective pursued by Wycliffe. One such person was William Tyndale, who in turn had been inspired by Martin Luther.

Luther himself had committed to a life of religion, and to the Catholic Church. He had achieved a Master of Arts degree and embraced a monastic life where he studied theology, with great credit. From there he was appointed to the newly-formed University of Wittenberg, where he was ultimately to rise to the position of professor.

The Roman Catholic Church raised money for some of its expenditure through a system known as *indulgences*. The Church taught that faith alone was not the only means of redemption from one's sins, but that man could improve his lot by donating money for charity – as well as to the church, whereby it would dispense such remission. Hence by paying an indulgence one could receive absolution from sin. So in or near a cathedral, for example, a priest might set up a table, receive money and enter the name of the giver into a ledger. Put crudely, it was a system whereby one could sin today, pay money to the church tomorrow, and the church would see to it that the deity turned a blind eye to the sins committed. The venture of selling indulgences was no small undertaking. The Vatican even had a position of *Papal Commissioner for Indulgences* to oversee the collection of the cash. Academics note that one saying associated with giving indulgences, attributed to the era in which Luther lived, was, 'As soon as the coin in the coffer rings, the soul into heaven springs.'

In the early 16th century, the Pope was faced with meeting the financial cost of building St Peter's basilica in Rome, and to improve the financial situation he offered indulgences in exchange for money. The idea that one could buy off one's sins by purchasing an indulgence was an issue to which Martin Luther was hostile. There were also other aspects of the organisation, conduct and dogma of the Church that he felt needed to be changed. This led to a confrontation between Luther, the Church and, in particular, the Pope. Luther listed 95 issues which he felt should be addressed, and pinned a list of those issues to the door of a church in Wittenberg, the town in which he lived, preached and taught. *The Catholic Encyclopaedia* records the events as follows:

It is not denied that a doctrine like that of the indulgences, which in some aspects was still a disputable subject in the schools, was open to misunderstanding by the laity; that the preachers in the heat of rhetorical enthusiasm fell into exaggerated statements, or that the financial considerations attached, though not of an obligatory character, led to abuse and scandal. The opposition to indulgences, not to the doctrine – which remains the same to this day – but to the mercantile methods pursued in preaching them, was not new or silent. Duke George of Saxony prohibited them in his territory, and Cardinal Ximenes, as early as 1513, forbade them in Spain.

On 31 October, 1517, the vigil of All Saints, Luther affixed to the castle church door, which served as the 'black-board' of the university, on which all notices of disputations and high academic functions were displayed, his 95 Theses. The act was not an open declaration of war, but simply an academic challenge to a disputation. 'Such disputations were regarded in the universities of the Middle Ages partly as a recognised means of defining and elucidating truth, partly as a kind of mental gymnastic apt to train and quicken the faculties of the disputants. It was not understood that a man was always ready to adopt in sober earnest propositions which he was willing to defend in the academic arena; and in like manner a rising disputant might attack orthodox positions, without endangering his reputation for orthodoxy'. The same day he sent a copy of the Theses with an explanatory letter to the archbishop. The latter in turn submitted them to his councillors at Aschaffenburg and to the professors of the University of Mainz. The councillors were of the unanimous opinion that they were of an heretical character, and that proceedings against the Wittenberg Augustinian should be taken. This report, with a copy of the Theses, was then transmitted to the pope.[3]

Luther was in no mood to back down. In January 1521, he was excommunicated (banished) from the church and the Emperor of the Holy Roman Empire branded him as an outlaw. Being excommunicated in this era was considered a draconian punishment, meant to imply a measure of such severity that the individual was going straight to hell. After the proclamation of his excommunication, Luther translated the New Testament from Greek into German, an act also considered to be heretical. His attacks on the Pope became ever more theatrical. He wrote and published several anti-papacy pamphlets, including one in 1545 entitled *Against the Papacy established by the Devil*. Knowing that literacy levels among the ordinary citizens were not high, he even resorted to highly animated caricatures of the Pope to get his message across.[4] Luther died in February 1546, but the genie was out of the bottle and the foundations for Protestantism had been well and truly advanced. This challenge to the doctrine and authority of the Church and the Pope resulted in the Council of Trent (Trento in Northern Italy), which was a Catholic Church Council that dealt with major reforms within the Church as a counter to the growing Protestant movement.

In England, William Tyndale had obtained a copy of Luther's translation of the New Testament. England at that time was still a country dominated by the Roman Catholic Church and, after Wycliffe's translation attempts, the owning of a copy of any part of the Bible in a language other than Latin was illegal, so having a copy of the translation in German would have been regarded as heresy. Tyndale was a well-educated man with enviable linguistic skills. Knowing that if he translated the New Testament into English he would be in trouble with the Catholic authorities, he travelled to Wittenberg where Martin Luther had been a lecturer at the university. Tyndale met Luther, and whilst there he translated the New Testament into English. There had been a relatively new invention called the printing press that was becoming widely used, so Tyndale had copies printed, first in two other towns but eventually in Antwerp. From there, copies

were sent to England – the first printed copies of the New Testament in English. As was predictable, the Catholic Church was incensed. Copies were hunted down and burnt which we must assume only left those who witnessed such events curious as to what was included in the books that the Church was so vehemently against. Although he was absent from England, Tyndale was branded a heretic. The Church had a very long arm. He was arrested in Antwerp in 1535 and a year later put on trial for heresy, found guilty, and as was the case in nearly all such convictions, sentenced to death by being burnt alive at the stake.

The Protestant reform movement gathered pace in Europe following Luther's confrontation over the indulgences and the translation of the New Testament into German. Two years prior to the execution of Tyndale, in 1534 Henry VIII broke with the Catholic Church and the authority of the Emperor of the Holy Roman Empire, establishing the Church of England based on the Protestant religion.

After so much death and agony, within just the span of a lifetime, the King James Authorised Version of the Holy Bible was published and printed in the vernacular of the ordinary people of the country that James I (VI) ruled – the first authorised version in English in 1611. Scholars assert that a major portion of both books is based on Tyndale's earlier translation.

Every Masonic Lodge in England has, for at least 200 years, had a copy of the Bible open during their ceremonies. In more recent times, copies of the primary religious texts of other faiths have also been on display when required. The Bible, as translated into English, forms part of the furnishings of the Lodge and Chapter. The majority of such Bibles are the King James Authorised version.

## The earth constantly rotating on its axis in its orbit around the sun

According to tradition, around 4,000 years ago the people of the ancient city state of Sumer identified the patterns of the 12 groups of stars that appear to encircle the earth and sink into the eastern horizon as, on each new day, the Sun rises above it. Astronomically, they are known as the Great Belt. Later, the Greeks gave the name *zodiac* to distinguish these same 12 star groups. It is believed that in the period between the era of Sumer and the Greek Empire, the Egyptians were well aware that the earth was a round ball, but it took a Greek astronomer and mathematician to calculate how big the ball really was – Eratosthenes, who lived around 200 BCE.

Eratosthenes was born and raised in a town named Syene, today known as Aswan. This town is directly beneath the Tropic of Cancer.

A well is by its nature, vertical, thus when the sun shone down the shaft of the well at Syene and reflected on the water below, the sun was at its highest point in the sky – the summer solstice and would not return to that point for another 366 days. Later in his life, Eratosthenes moved to Alexandria and – with the knowledge about the well, and knowing the distance of Alexandria from Syene, on the day of the summer solstice he used the shadow cast by a stick pressed into the ground to measure the angular position between the two towns. He then used that information to calculate the circumference of the earth, which he did with great accuracy. Although this gave unmistakable credence to the idea that the earth was indeed a ball, it did nothing to dispel another theory, that the earth was at the centre of the universe and that the sun, moon and stars orbited around it. In the opening verses of the Old Testament book

of Genesis, it states that God first made the earth and then made the heavens and the stars in the firmament above. Thus, for religious bodies like the Catholic Church, it seemed obvious that the earth had to be at the centre of the universe. So powerful was this concept that it remained the core belief of the Catholic Church for hundreds of years.

It is well known in the western world that Nicholas Copernicus was not only a committed theologian within the Catholic Church, but also an astronomer and mathematician. From his observations – and those made some 500 years earlier by an Islamic astronomer and mathematician, Al Battani – he developed a theory that the earth was not at the centre of the universe with the sun and stars revolving around it known as 'the geocentric system', but instead it was the earth that rotated around the sun – 'the heliocentric system.' He published his findings in a book entitled *De revolutionibus orbium coelestium* (*The Revolutions of the Celestial Spheres*). Copernicus was still quite young when he first developed his theory, but he is alleged to have withheld publishing the full details for fear that the Church would brand him a heretic, so he was well aware of the fate that would befall him. The book is believed to have been finally published when he was literally on his deathbed, in 1543. His ideas became known as *Copernican theory.* The Catholic Church discounted this theory, but others recognised its value. One such person was Giordano Bruno.

Bruno was born in Nola, near Naples, Italy, in 1548, and was named Filippo. In his late teenage years, he entered a Dominican monastery in Naples and changed his name to Giordano. He had a very enquiring mind, and any study of him suggests he was someone of high intellect. He not only studied the theological ideals of the Catholic faith and became a priest, he also studied the works of Plato and other great philosophers of antiquity, mathematics and the works of the Islamic astronomers. Bruno had been born just after the publication of Copernicus' theory that placed the sun at the centre of the universe, with the earth orbiting around it. From his astronomical studies Bruno suggested that the universe was infinite, that the sun was a star and that throughout the universe there may well be other planets with people just like us. This, and his attempts to acquire books that were forbidden by the Catholic Church, brought Bruno to the attention of the Inquisition. Having been made aware that the authorities were about to summon him to appear before them, he decided to depart from Naples and did so by slipping out of the monastery, removing his monk's habit and putting as big a distance between him and the Inquisition that he could. Bruno headed for France and eventually arrived in Paris. He had developed a system of memorising various facts and demonstrated it with great skill. This brought him to the attention of the French king, Henry III, who was interested in his ideas and eventually encouraged Bruno to provide lectures on his technique, receiving handsome payment in return. After a few years in the comfort of Paris, Bruno moved to England armed with letters of support from the French king. England was by then a Protestant country, where he could feel relatively safe. He sought a lecturing post at Oxford, but was turned down. Although Bruno was away from Catholic ideology, entrenched views led to him being pilloried by members of the clergy attached to the Church of England for supporting Copernican theory.

Bruno's time in England coincided with the era of Elizabeth I. She was very open-minded in her approach to religion but, in the background to her reign, there was constant fear of plots against her. Some were even supported and encouraged by the Vatican, with the objective of inciting her assassination and securing the re-establishment of the authority of the Catholic faith in England. With Elizabeth out of the way, it would have provided the opportunity for a staunch Catholic supporter to ascend the throne of England: Mary Stuart, Queen of Scots. Against the background of such turmoil, Bruno left England towards the end of 1585 and returned to France before travelling on to Germany, where he obtained a teaching post in Wittenberg, the town in which Martin Luther had undertaken much of his own studies and been a lecturer at the university. Bruno stayed in Wittenberg for two years before moving on to Prague, then one of the major centres of learning in Europe, and a key city within the Holy Roman Empire. After a few years he moved on again, this time to Venice, where he was denounced to the Inquisition and arrested by the Venetian authorities in 1592. After a short trial he was transferred to Rome, to be dealt with by the full force of the Inquisition. The charges levelled against Bruno included support for Copernican theory, along with the additional notion that the universe was infinite and contained many worlds and suns that were seen as stars, and holding religious views that were contrary to the beliefs defined by the Catholic Church. In January 1600, Pope Clement VIII declared him a heretic and the Inquisition passed a sentence of death. A few weeks later, with his tongue clamped so that he could not shout to the assembled crowd, Bruno was taken to a market square in the centre of Rome,

Campo di' Fiori, where he was burnt at the stake and his ashes cast into the River Tiber. All of his writings were placed on the Catholic list of prohibited reading.

Today, a monument to Bruno as a *Martyr of Science,* stands in the centre of the market square where he met his death. His ideas about the infinity of space, the potential for other worlds and suns, along with Copernican theory and the heliocentric system, would be picked up by others. Among them was Galileo Galiliei.

Galileo was around 36 years of age when Bruno was executed by burning. They were, in many respects, contemporaries. At one stage in their lives they had both sought to be appointed to a vacant chair in mathematics at the University of Padua. Bruno was unsuccessful and Galileo was appointed some months later. He studied medicine originally, but is best known for his work in mathematics, physics and astronomy. When he was in his early forties, a new invention came to the fore: the telescope. Galileo realised its potential and made a series of design adjustments to it. Using his modified device, he was able to observe the sun and planets as nobody had previously seen them. Some 10 years after Bruno had died in the flames, Galileo observed the moons of Jupiter, the rare event of the transit of Venus, and in 1612 discovered the planet Neptune as a very dim moving star. Galileo was making his telescopic observations as the controversy surrounding Copernican theory was reaching a climax. Most astronomers held to the view espoused by the Church, that the Earth was at the centre of the universe – the geocentric universe, though whether or not they held that view because they feared the Inquisition and the same death as Bruno is uncertain. From his observations,

Galileo produced a book in 1632 which was titled *Dialogue Concerning the Two Chief World Systems* and discussed the merits of both the heliocentric (Copernican) theory and the geocentric (Church) concept. With the publication of the book, Galileo was ordered to go to Rome for investigation by the Inquisition, their main concern seeming to be his alleged support for Copernican theory. His trial started in February 1633, with judgement being passed in June. He was found to be *suspected of heresy* and of believing that the sun was at the centre of the universe and not the earth, therefore contrary to the teaching of the Church. As a consequence he was initially sentenced to imprisonment for a term that was 'at the pleasure of the Inquisition', but this was later changed to house arrest, in which state he remained for the rest of his life. His book and all his other writings, were added to the list of prohibited reading. Galileo died in 1642 and is credited with recognising mathematical associations with the laws of nature; he wrote a further book called *The Assayer* in which he describes the laws of the universe as being written 'in triangles, circles and geometry.'

Needless to say, there were many other astronomers and philosophers who supported the concept of the heliocentric system of the universe who died, or were imprisoned, for their knowledge and scientific conviction. From the earliest days of Freemasonry, the relationship between the Earth and the sun has been noted, as observed by Copernicus, Bruno and Galileo, through the ceremonial statement '.. the Earth constantly revolving on its axis in its orbit around the sun'. In addition, *triangles, circles and geometry* also signify the key knowledge contained in Masonic ceremonies and symbolism.

# Celestial and terrestrial globes

At a time when Copernican theory was just emerging from the printing workshops, another development that would lead to charges of heresy was unfolding in Flanders.

There had been an explosion in global exploration in the 150 years prior to the publication of Copernicus' work on heliocentricity – that the sun was at the centre of our solar system. Knowledge about the geographical world had grown and maps were needed to aid navigation. With the earth being spherical it made map-making a difficult task, and one of the foremost cartographers of the mid-16th century was Gerardus Mercator.

Flanders had been part of the territory of the Dukes of Burgundy. One such Duke, Philip III the Good – held a vast area of what is today, Belgium and the Netherlands, and with that territory went an equally vast array of titles. He was one of the wealthiest individuals in Europe, including in his territorial holdings the Port of Bruges, where he founded the Most Illustrious Order of the Golden Fleece in 1430. When Philip died his wealth, land and titles transferred to his son, Charles the Bold, who shortly thereafter died on the battlefield fighting against the French king. Charles the Bold had a daughter and his demise made her the most wealthy woman in Europe, and the focus of many potential suitors. Eventually she married a member of the Habsburg family, and the great estate of the Dukes of Burgundy became part of the Habsburg empire. By the time Mercator was born in 1512, Flanders was firmly under their control and an integral part of the Holy Roman Empire.

Mercator's parents came from a town which today is in Germany, close to the border with the Netherlands. When he was born his name was Gerard Kremer, which was later Latinised to Mercator (merchant). His formal education was at the University of Leuven, Belgium, after which he became a designer and manufacturer of mathematical and scientific instruments. Although his fame is based on his innovations as a map-maker/cartographer, he was also a highly skilled engraver, specialising in copper plates. Mercator was in his mid-twenties when he assisted in the making of a terrestrial globe, and it was his involvement with this project that seems to have opened his eyes to new possibilities because two years later, in 1537, he was draughting his own maps.

Mercator's early claim to fame was in making cylindrical maps. Keeping in mind that the earth is spherical, if one draws lines between the poles at intervals of 15-degree separation (360 degrees/24 hours = 15 degrees = one hour) and lines of latitude around the sphere parallel to the equator, then the resultant segments towards the poles are small and irregular in shape. The segments around the equatorial area are large by comparison, but also an irregular shape. If one prints a map based on the circular configuration, there is an illusion that the central area – the equatorial zone – has been stretched, or that the polar regions have been compressed. Mercator's cylindrical maps kept the size of the grids in equal portions.

This was an era when merchants were exploring far-flung areas of the world in search of silks, spices and precious metals to form the basis of trade. Using a globe on a ship to provide a means of navigation wasn't practical, but Mercator's cylinder maps could be laid out flat on a table, making them far more useful and manageable. Maps produced in this way became known as *Mercator projections*. His interests also extended into producing globes detailing terrestrial and celestial images. Often sold as a pair, Mercator globes became very popular in the homes of the merchants, aristocracy and landed gentry.[5]

*A pair of Mercator's celestial and terrestrial globes, as displayed at the Ducal Palace in Urbania, Italy.*

Not everything went well for Mercator. As his reputation grew so did the interest of the Catholic Inquisition. Mercator had started his map-making ventures in the era of great religious turmoil in Europe and just a few years earlier, Martin Luther had been excommunicated; Tyndale had died in the flames; Henry VIII had broken with the Catholic Church and Holy Roman Empire and established the Protestant Church of England. The regional area in which Mercator lived and worked was still very strongly tied to the Roman Church and the Emperor of the Holy Roman Empire. To produce his maps, Mercator needed to travel, gathering up old maps and information wherever he could. The Inquisition took a particular interest in him, concerned that he was promoting Copernican theory and

was thereby a Protestant sympathiser. Thus, in 1544 he was arrested and imprisoned on a charge of suspected heresy; yet within a year he was released, and no further action against him was taken.

The symbolism based on Mercator's globes was then interpreted in several other devices, such as a lectern for use in a cathedral, where on the top of the globe was perched an emblem of an eagle. The eagle was meant to represent the carrying of the *religious Word* to the most northerly reaches of the globe, to bring *religious light* to the darkened places where paganism abounded.

In St. Patrick's Cathedral, Dublin, there is a wonderful pulpit in which the lectern was designed to replicate a pillar surmounted by a globe, on which is perched an eagle. It was made in an era when the cathedral was used as a centre of Protestant belief, not long after the Union of the Grand Lodges.

*For image, see colour section plate 1*

Masonic ceremony contains the statement:
Those pillars were further enhanced by two spherical balls on which were delineated the terrestrial and the celestial globes, and were considered completed when a network…was thrown over them.

The network referred to is a representation of the longitudinal and latitudinal grid of Mercator projection. In Masonic terms, the early fathers of the institution in the 18th and 19th centuries probably used the pillars and representations of the globes to make several statements relative to their era: the two pillars of Church and State; Heaven and Earth; Monarch and People – noting that many of those at the head of the organisation were closely associated with the affairs of state and the establishment, especially during this period of trade expansion and the development of the British Empire.

In the late Victorian era, several atlases were produced in which, on the inside front cover and page, was printed a map of the world using Mercator projection. On either side of the map would be placed two pillars, one surmounted by the terrestrial globe, the other by the celestial globe.

## Political and religious turmoil

Christianity came early to England. Constantine the Great, who later became the catalyst for the development of the Roman Church, as the main religion of Europe, in addition to later founding his new city at Byzantium, observed it when he was stationed with his father at York in 305/306 CE. Academics also note that he was probably actively involved in the persecution of Christians under the rule of the Emperor Diocletian, prior to coming to England, but that he observed a peaceable Christian community during his stay at York.

*A statue in York, commemorating Constantine's time there. Photograph by J. Pooley, York.*

By the Middle Ages, Roman Catholicism was well established throughout England, with a vast network of monastic communities and bishops to oversee all religious matters. The bishops even had their own courts and prison system. Anyone could be summoned to appear before a bishop for any acts or utterances that might be considered blasphemous, heretical or sacrilegious, and punishment for the guilty was severe.

Then, in 1534, Henry VIII broke England away from the Roman Catholic faith, established the Church of England and opened the door to Protestantism. Monastic houses, priories and abbeys were closed and demolished, and practise of the Roman Catholic faith was outlawed; the Pope and the Catholic Church were outraged. For the next 70 years England lurched between Protestantism and the Catholic faith, depending on who the monarch was at the time. When Protestantism was the prevailing religion in England, many Roman Catholics were hunted out and frequently tortured or burnt, converting Catholicism into an underground movement. When a Catholic monarch was on the throne, it was Protestants who were oppressed and suffered in a similar manner. During the reign of Protestant monarchs, the Vatican and the Emperor of the Holy Roman Empire, supported by kings and nobles in France and Spain in particular, conspired to invade England and return it to what had become known as the *old religion*. These great oscillations in faith promoted a background of fear among the people. At various times, the prevailing customs and expectations that were enshrined in the rule of England could result in citizens acting in accordance with those rules and leading blameless lives, only to find themselves in a different political/religious environment a few years later, when, their deeds might be considered retrospectively in an entirely different and threatening light.

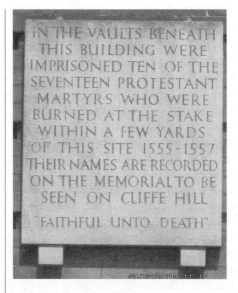

*A plaque on the wall of the town hall, in Lewes underpins the horrors of the oscillations in religious belief in England.*

At the same time, books and other published material prohibited by the Catholic Church began to appear in England and other Protestant areas of Europe. Because of the culture of fear that permeated society, some of the knowledge contained in such material went underground, especially if it fell into the esoteric category which might have been branded by the Church as witchcraft or the work of the devil. It was a time when new ideas, no matter how well-founded, were dangerous.

## Protestant v Catholic monarchs

For some 350 years prior to the 16th century, there had been a revolution in building techniques. It was the age of great cathedral building and the use of the pointed arch known as gothic architecture. Large castles, fortified houses, churches and cathedrals had existed from the

10th century, but with an architectural style known as Romanesque. After the 12th century, as they needed to be expanded, or were damaged in storms or fire or collapsed walls and towers needed repair, the Gothic style was used as the replacement. There was a steady amount of work for stonemasons and carpenters, and associated with these trades were the guilds that managed them, while guilds also flourished among merchants and other traders. Fear that small gatherings of people might become a source of conspiracy and a threat to the establishment eventually led to the Catholic faith in England being proscribed; the guilds were likewise forced to cease operating, except those which were based in London, like the merchants, at the centre of commerce. Having formerly been known as guilds, they now became London Livery Companies.

Towards the end of the 1500s, the monarch was Queen Elizabeth I, the daughter of Henry VIII and Anne Boleyn. After her mother was executed, Elizabeth, then a small child, was branded as illegitimate, which would have affected her rights in the line of succession to the throne. Nevertheless, after the death of her half-sister Mary 'Bloody Mary', who had ruled as a Catholic queen, Elizabeth acceded to the throne by virtue of her direct descent from Henry VIII and his father Henry VII. She ruled as a Protestant queen from 1558.

Mary, Queen of Scots was also seen as a contender to the English throne. She had a legitimate claim but it was not as strong as that of Elizabeth, whose claim was direct through the line of English kings. Mary's was through a line to Henry VII, a common ancestor of Elizabeth, but then via the Scottish crown. Even Mary's second husband, father of the later King of England and Scotland, had a line of descent back through the common links of Mary Tudor and Henry VII. As Elizabeth had not married and had no children as heirs, Mary's son had an indisputable claim to the throne as James I of England and James VI of Scotland.

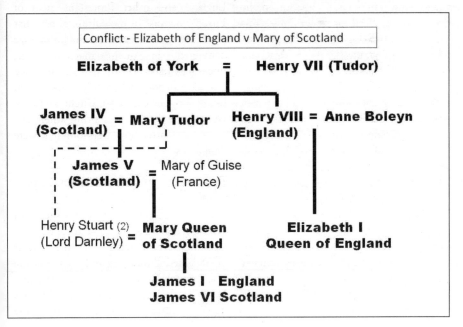

There was a further significant factor in the threat that Mary posed to Elizabeth and the crown of England. By her descent from her mother Mary of Guise, who had close connections to the aristocracy in France, a marriage was arranged between the young queen and the Dauphin, heir to the French throne, when both were still small children. With that arrangement agreed, Mary, although she was Queen of Scotland, was sent to France in order to become fully conversant with the language and affairs of the French court, getting married at the age of 16 to the Dauphin who was then 14, an arrangement cleverly contrived in France. A year after the marriage, the Dauphin became King of France as Francis II, but died just 18 months later. Through his marriage to Mary, Francis was uniting the crowns of Scotland and France, had he lived, he would have also had a solid claim to the throne of England upon Elizabeth's demise. This would have been a reversal of Elizabeth's situation which carried the title of Queen of England, France and Ireland. To gain some idea of the strength of this arrangement, through the union of these two young persons, had it lasted and they had outlived Elizabeth, their titles would have included:

King and Queen of England, Scotland and France, Naples, Jerusalem, Chile, both the Sicilies and Ireland; Defenders of the Faith, Princes of Spain and Sicily, Archduke and Archduchess of Austria, Duke and Duchess of Milan, Duke and Duchess of Burgundy, and Brabant, Count and Countess of Habsburg, Flanders, and Tyrol.[6]

Thus their territorial claim would have been very substantial. The second threat was that Mary, who was a staunch Catholic bolstered by her supporters in France, and those disaffected believers in England, posed a distinct threat of revolution within the British Isles and invasion from outside, the possibility of a return to Catholic religious domination remaining present throughout Elizabeth's reign. The failure of the Spanish Armada in 1588 gave a welcome respite, while Mary was forced to abdicate and seek the protection of her cousin Elizabeth, spending time travelling through some of the large estates in the north of England where members of the aristocracy were known to be supporters of her cause and of the old religion.[7]

Following the coronation of Mary's son, as James I of England in 1603, religious conflict subsided, especially as his queen, Anne of Denmark, was also a Protestant. The failed attempt of Catholic conspirators to blow up Parliament and the king with it, by the insurgents Guy Fawkes and Robert Catesby in 1605, gave ready proof that Catholic ambitions had not totally subsided.

The whole saga was reignited again when Charles I became king in 1625 and married Henrietta Maria, who was the daughter of the French King and Marie de' Medici. Henrietta Maria was a committed Catholic and was very open about her faith. Her father, the King of France, had insisted that she have a large group of French servants to assist her, all of whom were staunch Catholics, she being quite lavish in her expenditure. The financial cost of her extravagances and of her household, were so great that Charles had this group of servants physically removed from court and sent back to France. She also ignored all English laws that applied to Catholics and had an expensive chapel erected for her own use. She even indulged in, and encouraged, conversions to the Catholic faith, acts which infuriated the Protestant English nationals to the point of absolute hatred. There are reports of citizens being arrested and flogged for saying negative things about her, being imprisoned for life for writing less than glowing comments about her, or being mutilated by such punishments as having their ears cut off.

Some historians note that Henrietta Maria seemed to have had an uncomfortable political hold over Charles I, and was perhaps a key figure in bringing about events that ultimately led to the English Civil War. When the war started, she fled from England to Holland, from where she sought to raise funds to support Charles' war in England. She later returned and is reputed to have met with Stuart supporters in the north of England, organising an army to march from Scotland. As the Civil War progressed and the Parliamentarians gained further successes, she moved to the West Country from where she again escaped, this time to France. Charles, being short of money and materials, sent letters urging Henrietta Maria to raise money and elicit foreign troops to come to his aid. It was the capture of such correspondence between Charles and his wife, by Parliamentarian forces, that ultimately led to his execution in 1649, on the grounds of treason.

Throughout the English Civil War, the country was again in fear. Being on the wrong side at the wrong time meant almost certain death, not just in battle but depending upon whether one was a Royalist supporter or a Parliamentarian, Catholic or Protestant. Yet again, religious conflict played its part.

Following the Civil War, and for the next 100 years, puritan attitudes were the cornerstone of the English Protestant religion. Decoration in churches was removed; the King James Bible was *the* national religious book; attending church on a Sunday was mandatory and being late for a service was a sin viewed as only one step short of adultery.

The Restoration of the monarchy resulted in Charles II being crowned king in 1660. He kept a low profile as far as his religious views were concerned, but when his brother James inherited the throne it was back to the business of religious conflict.

James became James II of England and Ireland, and James VII of Scotland when he was crowned in 1685, following the death of Charles. James had been in his early teenage years during the Civil War; in disguise, he had fled from England to Holland before moving to France and joining his mother, Henrietta Maria. He lived in France for several years and even joined the French army. When Charles II, his brother, was restored to the throne of England, he invited James to join him. In the following years James acquitted himself well, even taking charge of firefighting during the Great Fire of London. He was married twice; his first wife was Anne Hyde whom he married secretly when she was about seven months pregnant, much to the displeasure of the English Court and Parliament. They had several other children, but only two survived, one of whom was later to become Queen Mary, who ruled jointly with her husband William, and the other, Anne, who ruled after the death of her brother-in-law. Charles II was annoyed by the secret marriage and insisted that Mary and Anne should be brought up as Protestants.

The Anglo-Dutch wars had resulted in the pride of the English navy being destroyed, seized as prizes or badly damaged, in a raid on the River Medway, Kent, and the dockyard at Chatham in 1667. Several other conflicts occurred in the next few years but English forces were stretched, so Charles entered into a treaty with the King of France for support. In return, among other conditions, was a pledge by Charles that he would convert to Roman Catholicism and reintroduce the Catholic faith back into England. Accordingly, in 1672, Charles introduced a Declaration of Indulgence that excluded Catholics from certain penal laws. Charles undertook the conversion just before he died, in full view of those gathered at his bedside.

During his time in France, James had converted to Roman Catholicism which, like his marriage to Anne Hyde (who died in 1671), he had kept secret. Two years later, James married an Italian princess, Mary Beatrice, whose father was the Duke of Modena. She was a committed Roman Catholic, and as a result, Parliament became concerned that, as James had also converted to Roman Catholicism, this would result in an increase in Catholic influence in England. The concern grew after Charles II issued the Declaration of Indulgence. The next year, 1673, Parliament forced Charles II to withdraw the Declaration he had issued the previous year, but at least, as far as Charles was concerned, he had made good his promise to the French king. Parliament next issued an Act that required the taking of certain oaths and excluded Catholics from any official office. Concerned about the line of succession, Parliament tried to introduce a bill that would exclude Charles' brother, James, from becoming king, but after several attempts the bill was defeated. Thus, when Charles died in 1685, his brother was crowned James II King of England and Ireland, and James VII of Scotland. Two years later, in 1687, James issued his own Declaration of Indulgence, again exempting Catholics from certain penal laws. In a confrontation with the Scottish Parliament, he declared that Protestantism was a false religion and that he would not show preference to it.

He then attempted to appoint known Catholics to every major position of state and contrived to have a Parliament that was favourable to him, and would repeal the original Act that excluded Catholics from public office.

Concern at James' actions reached new heights when Mary of Modena gave birth to a son, James Francis Edward (later to be known as the *Old Pretender)* which would have resulted in a Roman Catholic being in line to the throne of England. Thus, in 1688, several English nobles and prominent Protestants, knowing that James' daughter Mary, by Anne Hyde, had been brought up as a Protestant, approached her husband, William of Orange, to raise an army and invade England. William did so, and shortly thereafter several supporters of James defected to him. Even James' other daughter Anne, also by Anne Hyde, deserted her father and sided with her brother-in-law, William. James decided to flee from England, and was permitted by William to reach France, as James was, after all, his father-in-law. William met with Parliament who decreed that by fleeing from the country, James had abdicated and declared his daughter Mary as Queen Mary II, to rule together with her husband, William III.

James made an unsuccessful attempt to regain the throne by mounting an attack through Ireland, supported by troops from France. This resulted in James having an army that was substantially of the Catholic religion, while that of William of Orange was Protestant. A final battle took place across a river along the east coast of Ireland and has passed into history as the Battle of the Boyne. The memory of this battle in 1690, of which William III was victor, has been a source of antagonism between Catholics and Protestants in Ireland, even through to the late 20th century.

After his defeat on the Boyne, James returned to France and lived out his life there. When he died, his son by Mary of Modena, James Francis Edward – the old Pretender, was deemed the rightful king of England, Ireland and Scotland by the French, and styled as James III of England, James VIII of Scotland. When news of this reached England, the Old Pretender and his descendants, were legally stripped of all titles inherited from his father and excluded from the line of succession to the thrones of England and Scotland. The Old Pretender made several attempts to visit Scotland with the intention of gaining support in the hope of being crowned King of Scotland at Scone, the traditional place for the coronation of Scottish kings. It was in 1715 that he mounted military action from Scotland in an attempt to regain the throne of England, but the rebellion was quickly put down. The Old Pretender left Scotland and never returned. The grandson of James II, Charles Edward Stuart, better known as *Bonnie Prince Charlie* or the *Young Pretender*, made a further attempt in 1745 when he marched with an army south from Scotland towards London. He turned back after reaching Derby, believing that London would be heavily defended. Historians note, however, that had he continued his progress he could probably have taken London, as the royal entourage was out of town and London was lightly defended. The conclusion of this quest for power came with a defeat of his army at the Battle of Culloden, after which, Charles went into hiding in the Highlands of Scotland, supported by clans sympathetic to his cause, until after five months on the run he returned to France. All support for him subsequently diminished. Since that time there have been no major attempts to restore the descendants of the Stuart line to the thrones of England and Scotland, and the Jacobite cause evaporated.

***Top and above:*** *In Chichester Cathedral is a handcrafted panel illustrating all the monarchs that had reigned during the period from when the cathedral was built until the House of Hanover assumed the throne. One single panel illustrates the era from the restoration of Charles II. An image of Charles II, William and Mary, Anne and George I, are shown. The panel for James II (top right) is blank.*

## The Act of Union: Settlement, Bill of Rights

When James I became King of England in 1603 it represented a *Union of the Crowns* of England and Scotland. It was the start of the reign by the Stuart dynasty in England; Scotland had, and still has, its own crown jewels.

A political movement commenced shortly after James II fled from England in 1689. The objective was to ensure the reinstatement of the Royal House of Stuart to the throne of England, replacing William of Orange and his wife Mary. The men involved became known as the Jacobites, which academics record is a word derived from a Latin/Catholic version of the name James. The Jacobites were not only supporters of the Stuart cause, but mostly Catholic and very active throughout the period that Freemasonry was first formed (1717 – 1750).

The Stuarts, along with other European monarchs at that time, believed in the *divine rights of kings*. When James II fled to France, and his daughter and her husband became Queen and King respectively, a set of rules was drawn up in 1689 to define the process of future governance. It has become known as the Bill of Rights, and sets out the powers that are available to the monarch and to Parliament, exercising freedom of speech, and the process of regular elections.

The coronation of Mary and William, both Protestants, and the desire to effectively exclude any future opportunity for the Stuarts or any Catholic claiming the throne of England, inferred that a means of settling the future line for accession needed to be agreed. In this settlement it was determined that with the passing of Mary, who was childless, her sister, Anne, should be the next in line. Although Anne did in due course succeed to the throne, her only child who survived early childhood, and

would have duly succeeded to the throne, died during her reign. Anne had reached such an age that she was unlikely to have further children, and thereby the recognised line of progression came to an abrupt end. This situation resulted in the necessity to retrace the line of succession from James I to achieve an acceptable solution. His eldest daughter, known as Elizabeth of Scotland, had become Queen of Bohemia, which today is known as the Czech Republic with its capital in Prague. For many centuries Prague was the centre of the Holy Roman Empire, so the Queen of Bohemia held an impressive position. She had a daughter, Sophia of the House of Hanover, who in turn had a son, George Ludwig. In the line of succession, it was therefore resolved that Sophia should succeed Anne, but Sophia died a few weeks prior to Anne. Thus George Ludwig became King George I, and the era of the Hanoverians had commenced.

At first, the Scots were unhappy about the Hanoverian succession. Anne had succeeded to the thrones of England, Ireland and Scotland, but the Scots had created their own Act known as the *Claim of Rights in Scotland*. When the line of descent from James I/Elizabeth of Scotland was agreed, Scottish objections declined and the path was cleared for the Hanoverian inheritance of the two thrones. This led to an agreement between the parliaments of England and Scotland to unite the crowns of their two countries and create one single kingdom – the United Kingdom of Great Britain. In 1707, the Act of Union was completed and Queen Anne, daughter of James II, became the first monarch upon whom that title was bestowed.

There were many nobles in Scotland that had supported the Jacobite cause of the late 17th century with hard cash. Many had also invested money in a Scottish colony, a misadventure that has become known as the *Darien scheme*. The Kingdom of Scotland had, with the abdication of James VII in 1689, sought to build a colonial empire and ensure their independence through trade to compete with that being achieved in England. This resulted in the establishment of a colony known as 'New Caledonia' in 1690, in the area now known as Panama. Establishing the colony required that around a quarter of the entire Scottish wealth was invested, and most of that wealth involved the noble families of Scotland. New Caledonia was not a success and many of those that had ventured there, with the hope of establishing a new home and the creation of wealth, died due to fever, poor crop harvests and irregular or spoilt supplies sent from Scotland. Eventually the colony had to be evacuated in 1700, the Scottish adventure having been a complete failure. In consequence, the impoverished state of Scotland and its nobles, due to the downfall of the New Caledonian colonial enterprise, is cited by prominent academics as a major reason why the Scots ultimately agreed to the Act of Union in 1707.

## The Jacobites and the Cheshire Gentlemen's Club (c.1690–1745)

When James II/VII finally returned to exile in France after his defeat on the Boyne, attention of the Jacobites then turned towards his son, James, by Mary of Modena. At the time of the death of his father, James II, the young James was in his early teenage years, but that did not stop the French king acknowledging him as James III of England and James VIII of Scotland (later known as the *Old Pretender*), an acknowledgement supported by Spain and other Catholic states connected to the Vatican. Although there were perceived to be many Catholic sympathisers who would have preferred to see the return of the Stuarts to the thrones of

England and Scotland, it was not until 1715 that the first real Jacobite rebellion arose in Scotland, passing into history known as 'The fifteen'. A substantial army had been raised in Scotland to support the Old Pretender, and was involved in several military conflicts with Union troops, but none resulted in an overall victory that would underpin their cause. James had arrived in Scotland, but without a decisive victory in his favour around which to rally further support, he left Scotland and returned to France. Further attempts by the exiled Stuarts to regain the throne by military force were not made until 1745, a campaign that ended with the Battle of Culloden.

At the conclusion of the English Civil War, many prominent and aristocratic families that had supported Charles Stuart, had their lands and property confiscated and titles renounced. Needless say that most were reinstated again when Charles II was restored to the throne. When James II fled from England and his daughter, Mary II and her husband William III, succeeded to the throne, there were many descendants of Catholic participants in the Civil War Royalist regiments that were prepared to fight against the Protestant queen and king.

It has already been mentioned that when Mary Queen of Scots was first given protection by her cousin, Elizabeth I, she spent time visiting a range of houses and estates in the north of England that were sympathetic to her plight. One such house and family was that of the Leghs at their estate of Lyme Park, just outside Stockport in Cheshire. A number of the landed gentry from Cheshire, Lancashire and the surrounding areas, were supporters of the Jacobite movement whose objective was to ensure the reinstatement of the Stuarts to the throne. Some historians allege that one Peter Legh was a primary motivator of the Jacobite cause. Indeed, during a visit to Lyme Park today, one will invariably be shown one particular room where, it is further alleged, that the *Cheshire Gentlemen* met to plot their strategy. Although William III enjoyed considerable success on the battlefield, there were several plots to overthrow or assassinate him and restore James II to the throne. One such event is known as the *Lancashire Plot* of 1694, but the most prominent was the plan by Sir John Fenwick to assassinate the king.

It seems that Sir John had served under William, Prince of Orange, in Holland, and it is alleged that on one occasion Fenwick was reprimanded by the Prince in full view and hearing of several onlookers, in consequence of which, from that time, Sir John developed a deep hatred of the Prince. Thus, when William arrived in England, Sir John began to plot against him, but was caught, tried found guilty and beheaded in January 1698. He had a favourite horse called White Sorrel, which, along with other possessions, was confiscated when he was found guilty. William took a liking to the horse and was out riding his acquired mount near Hampton Court Palace when White Sorrel apparently stumbled, with a foot caught in a mole hole; William fell from the horse and broke his collarbone. Complications set in and he was struck down with pneumonia, dying in March 1702.

As mentioned earlier, in the grand house of the Legh family, on the Lyme Estate in Cheshire is a room in the heart of the building believed to have been the meeting place of a group of men from prominent Cheshire and Lancashire families, who have since become known as the *Jacobite Cheshire Gentlemen*. They commenced meeting around the year 1690 and continued until after the failed attempt of Bonnie Prince Charlie to regain the throne in 1745, a period of over 50 years when Jacobite activity was on-going. It only ceased when information apparently received from Vatican sources advised them to abandon their quest.[8]

In a number of the main rooms of the house at Lyme Park, the walls are clad with wood panelling which features a decorative design, in the form of a symbolic key to be found within the knowledge of Freemasonry and closely connected with Catholic symbolism – the Vesica.

*Top: Lyme Park, Cheshire*

*Above centre: Wood panelling at Lyme.*

*Above: The same interlinking circular pattern that is found in the wood panelling at Lyme Park is also found in the masonry of Romsey Abbey and some of the cathedrals of England.*

## Science and religion

As we have seen, science and knowledge were periodically in conflict with the dogma and doctrine of the Catholic Church. Once that influence was removed by the formation of the Protestant ethos, the pursuit of knowledge and understanding became more acceptable. During 1660, Charles II, a man brought up amid strong Catholic influence, was restored to the thrones of England and Scotland. Shortly thereafter, Sir Robert Moray[9], a known Freemason and confidant of the king, became a champion of scientific endeavour that resulted in the formation of the Royal Society in November 1660. Fifteen year later, at the king's behest, the Royal Observatory at Greenwich was founded in 1675, now regarded as one of the most important historic scientific sites in the world. These two organisations were at the forefront of much of the understanding of the physical world and the universe at the time Freemasonry was formalised. Yet with the possibility of a return to Catholic religious dominance, especially in the reign of James II, the experimenters and sky watchers must have felt a degree of unease.

## Freemasonry emerges

From all of the foregoing reflection of history as it applied to England and Scotland, and its relationship to the religious doctrine and dogma of the times, along with the struggles for power, one gets a sense of the climate against which formalised Freemasonry came into being. The following brief timeline highlights that position:

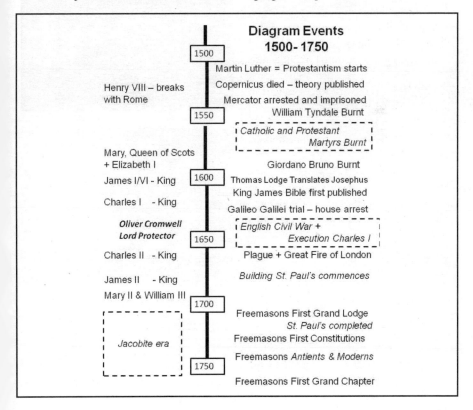

| | | Diagram Events 1500-1750 |
|---|---|---|
| | **1500** | |
| | | Martin Luther = Protestantism starts |
| Henry VIII – breaks with Rome | | Copernicus died – theory published |
| | | Mercator arrested and imprisoned |
| | **1550** | William Tyndale Burnt |
| | | *Catholic and Protestant Martyrs Burnt* |
| Mary, Queen of Scots + Elizabeth I | | Giordano Bruno Burnt |
| James I/VI - King | **1600** | Thomas Lodge Translates Josephus |
| | | King James Bible first published |
| Charles I  - King | | Galileo Galilei trial – house arrest |
| *Oliver Cromwell Lord Protector* | **1650** | *English Civil War + Execution Charles I* |
| Charles II  - King | | Plague + Great Fire of London |
| James II    - King | | *Building St. Paul's commences* |
| Mary II & William III | **1700** | |
| | | Freemasons First Grand Lodge |
| | | *St. Paul's completed* |
| *Jacobite era* | | Freemasons First Constitutions |
| | | Freemasons *Antients & Moderns* |
| | **1750** | |
| | | Freemasons First Grand Chapter |

All the above also demonstrates how, for a period of around 200 years, the Catholic Church, using others as agents, plotted continuously to secure the reinstatement of the Catholic faith in England, not only as a system of religious belief but also as a political instrument. To meet the threat that the Protestant opponents saw at various times in their conflict with the Catholic Church, they suppressed the Catholic religion and denied positions of power and influence to anyone of that faith. It was a 200 year period when religion became the focus of conflict in politics and created an undercurrent of fear. And it was against that backdrop of prolonged political and religious oscillation that formalised Freemasonry emerged.

In the period between the first, or Premier Lodge, being formed in 1717, and the United Grand Lodge of England being created in 1813, the United Kingdom of Great Britain and Ireland, faced still further trials.

## Masonic Memory Review 1

1. As mentioned in the previous chapter, there is some evidence that Freemasonry can be traced back as far as about 1621. The period between then and the formation of the Premier Grand Lodge in 1717 is that in which there was considerable turmoil surrounding both religion and the House of Stuart. Within the historical detail associated with this chapter, it is observable that, it demonstrates that in the early 18th century, England, Britain, and most of Europe had been subjected to a long period of turmoil and uncertainty.

2. Once the arguably more tolerant Protestant religion came to the fore, science and the age of enlightenment began. Progress rolled forward.

3. Within Masonic ceremonies, there are echoes of the great struggle by the *science martyrs* and their understanding of the heliocentric system of the universe. Among them are Copernicus, Giordano Bruno and Galileo Galilei. In ceremonies, all perambulation of the Lodge follows the path of the sun on its daily journey across the sky, East to South to West, when viewed in the northern hemisphere where these early observations were made. There are no ceremonial activities that take place in the North of the Lodge because the sun does not shine or visibly traverse that section of the globe. The heliocentric system explains how the sun rises in the East to bring light to the world and sets in the West to close that day, hence the Lodge is opened in the East and closed in the West. It also explains that the movement of the sun is an illusion of nature created by the earth rotating on its axis in an anti-clockwise direction; the sun is stationary, it is the earth rotating from West to East that creates the reverse effect we see.

4. Mercator developed his cylinder maps and made Celestial and Terrestrial globes. Their reference in Masonic ceremony has them mounted on the top of pillars. It is as if in so doing, the early Masonic fathers were making several statements relative to their era: the two pillars of Church and State, Heaven and Earth, Monarch and People, all under the canopy of the deity. Mercator projection also resulted in the production of maps that were useful for navigation, that in turn led to greater exploration of the planet and the trade opportunities that arose from it. Britain gained a great deal of wealth and political influence from that trade. Even in the mid-20th century, maps were still being produced complying to the principles of Mercator projection.

Chapter 4

# Influence from Ireland

REGARDING THE DEVELOPMENT OF Freemasonry in England, previous writers and researchers have made mention of a possible connection with Ireland. The theme occurs periodically in reference to both the *Antients* and Royal Arch, but surprisingly, this possible link does not appear to have been systematically researched; it is as if one or more researchers noted the comment from a previous era and have merely restated it without any further background investigation. Yet its connection with Freemasonry should not, in this writer's opinion, be underestimated.

The Grand Lodge of Ireland was formed in 1725, and as such, is the second oldest Grand Lodge in the world, which is not surprising. During the 18th century, when organised Freemasonry was finding its feet through the establishment of the Premier Grand Lodge, Ireland had been ruled from England for around 500 years, and Dublin was the second largest and most important city in the United Kingdom of Great Britain.

English dominance over Ireland can be traced back to a period of Norman rule about 100 years after the Norman Conquest of England in 1066. Ireland had, for several centuries, been ruled by a small group of kings that divided the island between them and seemed constantly at war with each other.

An Englishman, by the name of Nicholas Breakspeare, who had lived in Hertfordshire, became a monk and rose to high ecclesiastical office in France. He was later elected Pope as Adrian IV. He was aware of the conflicts amongst the Irish kings, which he wanted to stop, as well as gaining greater control and influence over the Church of Ireland. He therefore encouraged the Norman King of England, Henry II, to invade Ireland and effectively suppress it, making it a papal possession or state. (Such possessions were originally an estate donated to the Vatican which ultimately held title over it, and received income by way of rents.) Henry was not against the suggestion, as he already held the territories of Normandy, Brittany, England and Wales, so adding Ireland to his charge would greatly enhance his empire. Pope Adrian died in 1159, but it was another eight years before Henry was in a position to make his move, when he finally landed in Ireland in 1171. After capturing Dublin and securing the support of the Kings of Ireland, he then created the Lordship of Ireland ruled over by Kings of England. To ensure effective control, the land was divided between a series of barons and knights that had supported Henry, and thus the basis for aristocratic rule of Ireland was established. The Lordship lasted from 1171 – 1542, when Henry VIII broke from the Holy Roman Empire and papal dominance. Over the next 60 years, Ireland, like England, was forced to lurch between Protestantism and Catholicism, which process continued until Oliver Cromwell's military campaign suppressed the country again.

Despite the influence of the mainly Protestant overlords, the country remained substantially Catholic-oriented, while in the more rural settlements the Celtic language and traditions continued.

While all this was going on there were grand structures being built in Ireland, many for ecclesiastic purposes, which incorporated the principles of Gothic architecture as can be seen in the very fine St. Patrick's Cathedral in Dublin, which was raised from a church to cathedral status in 1220.

When William of Orange finally defeated his father-in-law, James II, at the Battle of the Boyne, the kingship of Ireland appeared settled. When James' daughter, Anne, ascended the throne in 1702, she did so as Queen of England and Ireland. Five years later, with the Union of the Crowns with Scotland, the United Kingdom of Great Britain was created.

Thus at the time the Premier Grand Lodge was created in England, so Ireland continued to be ruled by a collection of aristocratic families, many of whom had estates in England and Ireland. They were just the types of individuals to have found an interest in Freemasonry.

Suppression and control of Ireland did not cease with the Battle of the Boyne. The American War of Independence was finally concluded at the *Treaty of Paris* in 1783. One can only conclude that, in the resultant atmosphere, there was concern about the possibility of Ireland going the same way. Thus in 1783, during the reign of George III, an Order of Chivalry was developed and was named *The Most Illustrious Order of St. Patrick*. The members were chosen from families of gentlemen and aristocracy that could demonstrate three generations of noble descent, with estates in Ireland. The consecration of the Order was undertaken at St. Patrick's

Cathedral, Dublin, which remained its spiritual home until Irish Independence in 1922. The seating for the knights at the rear of the choir stalls on both sides of the central aisle can still be seen, together with the remnants of the decaying emblems of the last knights.

*(For image, see colour section plate 2.)*

The Order gradually ceased to function, as knights died, but it is still recognised, with the monarch of England retaining the sole control. At the time of writing, its official status is described as 'dormant'.

As the Industrial Revolution gained momentum, so some of these wealthy families invested in new inventions and transported ideas back to Ireland. This led to a general migration of individuals from the countryside to the main cities, Dublin in particular. It is believed that this migration also resulted in the influx of men from Ireland to London that later had a considerable influence on the development of the *Antient* Grand Lodge.

As a consequence of being a papal possession, Ireland became a firm centre for Roman Catholicism, but prior to the mid-seventh century it was also the centre for the development of Celtic Christianity and many of their traditions fused with those of Catholic dominance. Monastic communities flourished; they retained copies of the works of the great philosophers after these works were presented to the Arabic leaders in Baghdad by the Emperor in Byzantium; they retained a working knowledge of the Greek language; they gathered and copied numerous documents from which legends have been derived, including those that originated in the fourth and fifth centuries in Byzantium; they went out across Europe, founding other monastic communities as part of their missionary work with which they retained contact and exchanges for centuries. And it was in such monastic communities in Ireland that they commenced the process of illuminated script that is very Celtic in its origin, as a means of decorating pages they were copying. Some of the earliest decoration can be found in *The Book of Mullings*, a copy of the four Gospels that were copied, bound into book form and carried in leather satchels by monks as they travelled. The seventh-century monk, St. Gallus almost certainly carried such a copy when he travelled with St. Columba across France to Rome, establishing monastic communities enroute, finally settling on Lake Constance in modern Switzerland. The most famous books of all were *The Book of Kells,* and *The Book of Armagh,* at a time when there were still close connections with Constantinople and the writings issued by the ecclesiastical authorities based there. All this was happening prior to a division from Byzantium by the Vatican in 800 CE to create what we now call 'the West', when Charlemagne became the King of the Romans, which in turn provided the origins for the creation of the Holy Roman Empire.

*The Book of Kells* is believed to have been compiled over a period of 200 years between the sixth and ninth centuries by Celtic monks based at Iona, but, due to Viking attacks, was transferred to an Abbey at Kells, about 50 miles north of Dublin. Apparently, the book was stolen in the year 1007, but found in a ditch a few months later, minus its jewelled cover. It remained at Kells until the Reformation in the reign of Henry VIII, when it was secured by the Catholic Church. The actual relevance of *The Book of Kells* in the Royal Arch will become apparent in due course.

Trinity College, Dublin, was founded during the reign of Elizabeth I in 1592, yet by the time the Premier Grand Lodge was formed, Trinity was a major centre of learning from which many highly acclaimed writers, poets and philosophers would emerge. One such individual was James Ussher who later became Bishop of Armagh, the highest ecclesiastical office in Ireland, and Vice Chancellor of Trinity College. His fame rests on the fact that he calculated the origins of the world based on time intervals indicated in the Bible, and came to the conclusion that the world was created in 4004 BCE. His calculations ultimately became the basis for the dating system used in Freemasonry until the late 20th century, when it was deemed *unreliable.* Bishop Ussher arranged for *The Book of Kells* to be donated to Trinity College, where it remains to this day. Ussher died in 1656, so his gift of the book was well ahead of the Premier Grand Lodge formation.

In some Masonic images produced in the past, key features have been a rainbow arch with green open countryside in the background, the arch supported on two pillars. In 'Revelation' Chapter four verse three, it states:

> And he that sat was to look upon like a jasper and a sardine stone: and there was a rainbow round about the throne, in sight like unto an emerald.
>
> *King James Authorised Version*

Ireland is one of the wettest countries in Europe, and rainbows are quite prolific, which infers that it is very green in the rural areas, and is known as the Emerald Isle. Is it possible that the Masonic imagery used in England and mentioned above originated from Ireland?

Jonathan Swift, author of *Gulliver's Travels,* is often cited as having become a Freemason. He was born in Dublin, graduated from Trinity College and became the Dean of St. Patrick's Cathedral, dying in 1745.

The Duke of Wharton, who became the Grand Master of the Premier Grand Lodge in 1723, succeeding the second Duke of Montagu who had been Grand Master at the time of the publication of *Anderson's Constitutions,* founded the first Masonic Lodge in Spain in 1728. He also acquired the title second Marquess of Catherlough of Ireland, with a seat in the House of Lords in the Irish Parliament.

In 1743 there was a newspaper report in County Cork, Ireland, of a Masonic procession preceded by the Royal Arch, carried by 'two Excellent Masons.'[10]

The following year, 1744, saw the publication of a book entitled *A serious and impartial enquiry into the cause of the present decay of Free-Masonry in the Kingdom of Ireland,* by one Fifield Dassigny.[11]

The first officially recognised exaltee in the Royal Arch in Ireland was in 1752. A Lodge was operating in Coleraine, County Derry, in 1741 and is believed to have been working Royal Arch ceremonies around that time[12].

Laurence Dermott, who would later write *Ahiman Razon,* a book that claims that ancient Freemasonry was much older than that worked by the Premier Grand Lodge, was the Secretary of the *Antient* Grand Lodge. He was born in Dublin and joined a Lodge there in 1741.

Cadwallader, seventh Lord Blayney (1693-1732), Baron of Monaghan, was the first recorded member of the family carrying that title who is known to have been a Freemason in Ireland. He is recorded as having attended a Masonic function in 1731, and it is claimed that his membership predated that by some years.[13]

Cadwallader, Lt-General, ninth Lord Blayney, Baron of Monaghan, (1720 –1775), Grand Master of the Premier Grand Lodge and later of the *Excellent Grand and Royal Chapter.* The family estates were at Castleblayney, Ireland, and with the titles came an entitlement to take a seat in the Irish Parliament.

Earl Moira, Francis Edward Rawdon-Hastings, 1st Marquess of Hastings, (1754 – 1826), was born at Moira, County Down, Ireland, and spent his early years in Dublin. Earl Moira is a title in the Peerage of Ireland. Moira was particularly active on behalf of the Premier Grand Lodge in trying to resolve difficulties that arose from the early drafts of the Unlawful Societies Act.[14]

The above short list of Masonic connections with Ireland, in the period up to the mid-1700s, is intended solely to demonstrate that in the era prior to the first Grand Chapter of the Royal Arch – the *Grand and Royal Chapter or Excellent Grand and Royal Chapter* being formed in 1766, the first in the world – there were many connections with Ireland wherein traditions that were not acknowledged to be part of the ceremonies of the Premier Grand Lodge may well have fused with those of the *Antients* and Royal Arch. The consequences of this will become apparent in the ensuing chapters.

There is also one last point worth noting: Ireland, and Dublin in particular, has many fine stately buildings that are indicative of the architectural style developed in the period known as the Renaissance, influenced by the design concepts described by the Roman engineer Vitruvius.

## Chapter 5

# The Grand Union, the spy and the teacher

WE SHOULD PERHAPS REMEMBER that, within Freemasonry, most of the ceremonial content has existed in a structured manner for at least 200 years, since being promulgated by the United Grand Lodge of England following its creation as a centre of ultimate authority for regular Freemasonry in the year 1813. Furthermore, there are trails of evidence that show that substantial elements of the ceremonial contents of Masonic ceremonies extend back much further in time, by probably at least another 100 years, to the formation of the first or Premier Grand Lodge in England in 1717, and whatever preceded it.

In the period between 1720-1800 there were several Grand Lodges operating within the British Isles, each with their differences, common ground and own brand of Freemasonry. There was the Grand Lodge of England, formed in 1717 and centred on the City of London and Westminster, the same area for which the London Company of Masons had been granted a Charter of Incorporation by Charles II just 40 years earlier in 1677. There was the Grand Lodge of Ireland, constituted in 1725; the Grand Lodge of Antient Free and Accepted Masons of Scotland, founded in 1736; the Grand Lodge of All England at York, which some believe may have existed prior to 1705 and which later issued a warrant to William Preston, a prominent Freemason of the late 18th century, who named this new entity *The Grand Lodge South of the River Trent*.[15]

By around 1735 a separate group of Lodges had formed, mostly in London, and grew to such prominence that by around 1751 they challenged the supremacy of the Premier Grand Lodge of England. They are believed to have mainly comprised a group of disaffected individuals that had been refused admission to the London-based Lodges although they may have been members of the organisation through other Grand Lodges. This additional Grand Lodge became known as the *Most Antient and Honourable Society of Free and Accepted Masons according to the Old Institutions*. The development of this new Grand Lodge resulted in two competing entities which have passed through Masonic history, known simply as the *Antients* and the *Moderns*. By the time the Grand Lodge of the Antients had been formed, the two groups had become extremely hostile to each other, a hostility that lasted over 50 years. Within this mix of competing Grand Lodges developed Royal Arch Chapters, which, it seems, are traceable to the 1720s/30s, but evolved more solidly in the mid-1750s.[16] There is some doubt as to the origins of the Royal Arch, with speculation, in the absence of any positive knowledge, suggesting it started in Ireland, Scotland or France and then transferred to England. Early researchers note from available records that both the *Antients* and the *Moderns* Grand Lodges worked the ceremonies of the Royal Arch from around 1750, until they merged with the creation of the United Grand Lodge of England.

So just who were the *Antients* and *Moderns?* It is a subject that many Masonic researchers have repeatedly analysed. In short, current research suggests that, following the development of the Industrial Revolution that commenced around 1700, there had been an influx of workers to England from Scotland and Ireland who had been Freemasons under the Grand Lodges of both those countries. These were not just manual labourers, but people with skills in what we might refer to as *the professions*. A number of these men joined, or sought to join existing Lodges under the Premier Grand Lodge of England. For whatever reason, a significant number were turned away, so they formed their own Lodges and, eventually, their own Grand Lodge. Once these new *Antients* Lodges were established, it is believed that a number of those who had migrated to London and joined Lodges operating under the Premier Grand Lodge of England then joined them, either by leaving the older Lodges and joining the new ones, or by becoming members of both. Equally, there were a number of members who joined a Lodge under one Grand Lodge and treated this as an authority to visit the other. This resulted in edicts being issued that members of one Grand Lodge could not visit the other without having been initiated into it. Indeed, to quote one respected writer on the subject, the following observation was made by the Deputy Grand Secretary of Ireland:

> A Modern Mason cannot or ought not to be admitted into a Lodge of Antient Masons without passing the courses again as if the same had never been performed – their mode and ours being so different.[17]

These newcomers in the *Antients* Grand Lodge professed to be working with ancient ceremonies that were the original sources of Freemasonry, hence the term by which they were known. The *Antients* accused the Premier Grand Lodge of introducing innovations and, as a counter to the use of the word *Antient*, the members of the latter have become branded ever since as the *Moderns*.[18] Their separate titles became more generally known as the *Grand Lodge of England* and the *Antients Grand Lodge*.

The situation only changed with the creation of the United Grand Lodge of England, to which both Grand Lodges subscribed. Although there seems to have been a desire over some years on the part of various individuals for a merger between the two groups, nothing of any consequence happened. Talks started, followed by long periods of inactivity. The two may well have remained separate Grand Lodges had it not been for momentous changes that took place around the start of the 19th century.

## The Duke of Sussex and the formation of the United Grand Lodge of England

The United Grand Lodge of England and its sister organisation – the Supreme Grand Chapter – were both created against the background of the French Revolution that erupted in 1789 and the wars that resulted, especially after the rise of Napoleon Bonaparte 10 years later, in 1799.

Freemasonry had been well established in France for some 70 years prior to the revolution. There is speculation that the first Lodge in France was created long before the Premier Grand Lodge of England was formed, having transferred there when James II fled to France and a number of his Catholic supporters, some of whom had Masonic interests, followed him. Notwithstanding this, there is real evidence to support the existence of

Freemasonry in France from around 1725. There is even evidence that Bonaparte himself was a Freemason.

The French Revolution was a popular uprising against a harsh aristocratic regime that was still organised along feudal lines, plus a system of government wherein the monarch held absolute power and political legitimacy under the concept known as the *divine rights of kings*. This concept was based on the notion that kings derived their power directly from the deity and therefore they had a divine right to rule. It went further by establishing a philosophy that any attempt to overthrow a king was against the will of the deity and therefore a sacrilegious act, punishable by death. In view of the religious element to this concept, over the centuries it led to a cosy relationship between the monarch, the Church and the aristocracy. A similar situation had existed in Britain until the arrival of William of Orange, 100 hundred years prior to the French Revolution.

The revolution in France commenced in Paris in May 1789; by August of the same year, so much had changed that a *Declaration of the Rights of Man and of the Citizen* had been drafted and issued. During the next few years, the role of the French monarchy was changed from one of absolute power to a *constitutional monarchy* wherein the monarch is the head of state, but operates within the framework of a constitution and thereby has no effective political power.

In the years following the initial uprising, several attempts were made to form governments as an alternative to the monarchical system, but each failed. Eventually in 1792, a republic was declared and King Louis XVI was executed by decapitation under the guillotine. Much of the aristocracy of France suffered a similar fate.

The revolution in France and the American revolution – the War of Independence that had started in 1772 and finally ended with the Treaty of Paris in 1783 – both took place within a short period of time; with the signatures on the Treaty of Paris barely dry, shockwaves were sent through the royal courts across Europe. Aristocrats and monarchs feared for their own lives lest some of their citizens followed the French example – which they did. In Britain, the aristocracy concentrated their joint efforts and resolved to retain power and thereby preserve their privileges, but it was not an easy time.

With the rise of Napoleon Bonaparte and the moulding of a powerful French army, within a few years the territorial expanse of the French Empire included most of continental Europe. Even before Napoleon's rise, plans had been laid for French invasions of England, but it wasn't until 1803/4 that a very large army was assembled on the French coast at Boulogne, with the potential to mount such an invasion. It was the success of the British navy against French ships that thwarted those plans, and an invasion was postponed indefinitely. Most of the royal families of Europe gathered together armies and, under the command of the Duke of Wellington, Napoleon was finally defeated at the Battle of Waterloo in 1815. Until that outcome was secured, the survival of the monarchy and aristocracy in Britain was by no means assured.

During this time there had been concern for the health of the British monarch, King George III. In 1788, a year prior to the French Revolution, George had entered a bout of his so-called *madness* but had recovered by the time the revolution in France was well underway. In May 1800, there was an attempt to assassinate him when he attended the Drury Lane Theatre, London. It has always been asserted that this was not motivated by political objectives but by a man with a mental illness, working alone. In 1809, the madness reappeared in George III and greatly affected the working of Parliament for the whole of 1810. In early 1811, his eldest son and heir to the throne, George, Prince of Wales, was appointed as Regent to rule in place of his father. It was a situation that existed until the death of George III in 1820, the time of the key campaigns against Napoleonic forces, the Battle of Waterloo and the period immediately thereafter.

The established political interfaces of Europe had also changed. In 1807, Napoleon Bonaparte, who by that time had established a French Empire that extended across much of mainland Europe, abolished the Holy Roman Empire that had existed for around 1,000 years, demanding the resignation of the Emperor and casting himself as new Emperor of the French Empire.

Economically, Britain was in poor shape. The loss of the American Colonies had resulted in reduced trade, with manufacturers badly affected. This in turn led to high unemployment and horrific conditions of poverty. Trade continued to be affected by a controversy over the value of gold bullion and thereby the exchange rates that might apply. As George III plunged back into ill health, a severe economic depression settled on Britain, with the situation becoming so acute it led to riots in several of the major industrial towns across the country, particularly in the North of England. It was against this background that the Prime Minister, Spencer Perceval, was assassinated in the lobby of the House of Commons on the evening of 11 May, 1812. The killer was John Bellingham, a former merchant who harboured a grudge against the government; as Perceval entered the lobby, he stepped out in front of him, drew a pistol and shot him. The murderer did not attempt to flee the scene and was duly arrested, tried (without offering a plea), found guilty, and hanged within a week of the assassination.

Throughout this period, the ruling classes were constantly concerned about the fermentation of possible revolt in Britain, through the gatherings of groups of individuals into a range of societies over which they had no direct control. This concern was particularly acute during the first few years following the revolution in France. In Ireland, a group called *the United Irishmen* was quickly established as a movement that aimed to bring about independence for their homeland from the rest of Britain. They even made contact with France to gain support for their cause, and in response the French sent a small expeditionary army to Ireland but it was quickly removed. Other groups similar to the United Irishmen were formed in Scotland and England. Their cause was underlined by a small booklet which saw wide circulation in 1792, just three years after the Paris uprising. The booklet was by Thomas Paine and called *Rights of Man, being an answer to Mr Burke's attack on the French Revolution*, which in simple terms set out the idea of everyone having the right to vote for Members of Parliament, rather than just the so-called elite of society.

As a measure to block such a revolt in Britain before it began, William Pitt issued a bill which has become known by its shortened title *The Unlawful Societies Act 1799*. It was an Act that might have stopped Freemasonry from developing further. To ensure that this Act of Parliament is considered in an appropriate context along with the implications for Freemasonry, the full text of a lecture on this subject, is presented below.[19] I am indebted to Professor Andrew Prescott for his permission to reproduce the text of his lecture in full. The only modification of the original has been the omission of references:

# The Unlawful Societies Act of 1799

On 2 April 1799, the M.P. for Southwark, the wealthy banker and evangelical philanthropist Henry Thornton, wrote to the under-secretary in the Home Office, William Wickham, passing on information given to him by a Battersea distiller named Benwell. One of Benwell's employees had recently been asked to join a society which met at Wandsworth. If he joined, he would have to swear a secret oath. He would 'get a shilling for every attendance at the society, of which he would have to expend 6d at the place of meeting'. He would receive a further 2s 6d for every new member he introduced to the society. Thornton and Benwell were convinced that this was a cell of the subversive organisation known as the United Englishmen. Thornton had urged Benwell to work with a local magistrate to find out the names of all the members of this mysterious Wandsworth club. Thornton ended his letter to Wickham by assuring him of his willingness to assist in 'detecting the secret societies which may infest the parts around us'. Wickham passed on Thornton's information to the Home Secretary, the Duke of Portland. The Duke thanked Thornton for this intelligence, since the Home Office was uncertain of the exact strength of the United Englishmen. The news that money was being offered as an inducement to join was particularly interesting. The Duke suggested that Benwell should encourage his employee to join the group, so that he could give the Home Office information about it.

This exchange encapsulates the atmosphere of late 1798 and 1799, when seditious societies bound by secret oaths, the harbingers of a French invasion, were seen round every corner. This atmosphere created a groundswell of support for the passage in July 1799 of one of the most sweeping of the legislative measures introduced by Pitt's government to forestall the threat of revolution. This act, 'An act for the more effectual suppression of societies established for seditious and treasonable purposes; and for the better preventing treasonable and seditious practices', to give its full name, was, almost by accident, to form the mainstay of the relationship between Freemasonry and the state in Britain for nearly 200 years, until its repeal by the Criminal Justice Act of 1967.

One of the most important of the radical bodies which emerged in Britain in the wake of the French Revolution was the United Irishmen, a 'United Society of the Irish nation; to make all Irishmen citizens – all citizens Irishmen', which was established in 1791. Its initial aims were Catholic emancipation and radical parliamentary reform; by 1796 it had become an avowedly republican movement. The United Irish sent embassies to France to seek support for an uprising and independence, but the French and United Irish failed effectively to coordinate their efforts. In 1796, the French landed at Bantry Bay, but did not give the United Irish any advance warning; two years later, the French were in turn caught by surprise by an Irish rebellion and failed to provide adequate military support. The arrests of United Irish leaders which had helped precipitate the rebellion and the fierce repression of the rising left the United Irishmen a much diminished movement.

In England, the most prominent of the radical bodies which sprang up after 1789 was the London Corresponding Society. In 1794, a number of its leaders were arrested and tried for treason. These trials were unsuccessful, but subsequent legislation and internal difficulties had by 1797 reduced the influence of the L.C.S. From this time, an increasingly close alliance developed between Irish republican movements and those on the British mainland, with the formation of societies of United Englishmen and United Scotsmen on the Irish model. Some of the remaining members of the L.C.S. played an important part in the United movement in Britain. Further impetus was given to the United societies by Irish migrants active in Manchester and other parts of the north-west.

Despite the great blows suffered by the republican movement in 1798 as a result of the arrest of much of its leadership and the failure of the Irish revolt, Pitt's government remained uncertain of the real strength of the United bodies and was worried that they were regrouping. Shortly before Christmas 1798, the opposition Whigs accused Pitt of justifying repressive measures by scare mongering. Pitt responded by declaring that, if need be, the truth of his allegations could be proved. The following month, parliamentary committees were appointed to examine secret evidence held by the government and to report back to parliament on the nature of the threat. The House of Commons secret committee reported on 15 March 1799. It declared that, from the documents shown to it by the government, it had found the 'clearest proofs of a systematic design, long since adopted and acted upon by France, in conjunction with domestic traitors ... to overturn the laws, constitution and government, and every existing establishment, civil or ecclesiastical, both in Great Britain and Ireland, as well as to dissolve the connection between the two kingdoms...' The secret committee went on to state that, 'The most effectual engine employed for this purpose has been the institution of political societies, of a nature and description before unknown in any country, and inconsistent with public tranquillity and with the existence of public government.'

The report described the various United bodies and their connections with the London Corresponding Society. It emphasised their use of 'an oath of fidelity and secrecy' to 'form themselves, under the eye and in defiance of government, into one body, compacted by one bond of union'. The report described how these societies 'principally carried on their intercourse by agents, who went from place to place, and were recognised by signs, which were frequently changed'. The documentary appendix of the report included examples of membership certificates issued by London divisions of the United Irish, certifying that the bearer had passed various tests. Equally alarming to the committee was the organisational structure of these groups. The elaborate hierarchy of the United Irish, with their overall executive directory and subordinate baronial, district and county committees, was described in detail. The appendix reprinted the rules of various United groups in full. In the view of the secret committee, a sinister feature of these organisations was that the forms of election used meant that the membership as a whole did not know the composition of the executive committee.

The report noted how previous legislation had restricted subversive lectures and meetings, but added that 'many of the debating societies, which subsist at the present time, appear, to your committee, to be, in great measure, directed to the same pernicious objects, and to require further animadversion and correction'. Likewise, the committee was concerned about 'the establishment of clubs, among the lowest classes of the community, which were open to all persons paying one penny, and in which songs were sung, toasts given, and language held, of the most seditious nature'. The secret committee also called for further restrictions on the press, which it considered excessively licentious.

The trustworthiness of the information in the secret committee's report has been hotly debated for a long time. The most trenchant criticisms were made in the 1820s by the radical and former member of the L.C.S., Francis Place, in his autobiography. Place singled out as particularly ludicrous the claims of the secret committee that there were 40 divisions of United Englishmen in London. In Place's view, the United Englishmen in London amounted to no more than a few disreputable hot-heads, egged on by government spies. However, Place was anxious to demonstrate his own respectability and to show that the L.C.S. in its early days was a force for moral improvement. Moreover, he was based in London and was not well-informed about conditions in north-western England, Scotland and Ireland. Whatever the truth of the allegations of the secret committee, its political consequences can be more easily established.

On 19 April 1799, the House of Commons debated the report of its secret committee. Pitt rose to announce the measures proposed by his government. The suspension of Habeas Corpus was to continue, and powers would be sought to move prisoners about the country as the government sought fit. Pitt continued: 'we must proceed still farther, now that we are engaged in a most important

struggle with the restless and fatal spirit of Jacobinism, assuming new shapes, and concealing its malignant and destructive designs under new forms and new practices. In order to oppose it with effect, we must also from time to time adopt new modes, and assume new shapes.' Not only should the societies mentioned by name in the secret committee's report, the L.C.S., the United Irish, the United Britons, the United Scotsmen and the United Englishmen, be suppressed, but all societies of this type should be made unlawful. Pitt described the characteristics of the societies he wanted to outlaw: 'These marks are, wicked and illegal engagements of mutual fidelity and secrecy by which the members are bound; the secrecy of electing the members; the secret government and conduct of the affairs of the society; secret appointments unknown to the bulk of the members; presidents and committees, which, veiling themselves from the general mass and knowledge of the members, plot and conduct the treason – I propose that all societies which administer such oaths shall be declared unlawful confederacies...' Noting the remarks of the secret committee about debating clubs, Pitt also proposed that all meetings where money was taken at the door should require a magistrate's licence.

The final part of the measures proposed by Pitt were major new restrictions on printers. All publications should in future bear the name of their author and publisher. A general register was to be established of all printing presses, including those owned by private individuals.

George Tierney, the effective leader of the Foxite opposition in the Commons who in the previous year had fought a duel with Pitt, replied. He criticised the report of the secret committee, declaring that he 'never saw a report made to this House that was so little supported by the evidence'. He complained that the proposed law would give undue power to the crown, and breed an army of spies and informers. He pointed out that the effect of such a bill would be 'to pull down every club in the country', since most clubs took some kind of money and would come within the scope of the proposed legislation. Tierney's greatest concern, however, were the restrictions on printers, which he thought worse than an imprimatur. He could never support such measures: 'I had rather be subjected to the most bitter reproaches and malicious statements for the remainder of my days, than have the press limited to the extent to which this goes.'

Despite Tierney's opposition, a motion was passed to bring a bill to implement these measures, and the bill was duly published the next day, receiving its first reading in the Commons on 22 April. This bill outlawed the L.C.S., United Englishmen, United Scotsmen, United Irishmen and United Britons by name. It also defined as an unlawful combination and confederacy 'every society, the members whereof shall ... be required or admitted to take any oath or engagement ...' Societies were required to admit members 'by open declaration at a public meeting of such society'. Every society was required to keep a book containing the names of all its officers, committees and members, which was to be open to inspection by the entire membership. Membership or support of any society which breached these regulations would be a criminal offence. Magistrates acting on the word of a single informer could impose summary fines on offenders; where offenders were indicted

by jury and tried in a higher court, the punishment was transportation.

Any premises on which public meetings or lectures were held (apart from universities and properly constituted schools) required a magistrate's licence, even if the premises in question consisted of an open field. Similar licences were also required by Reading Rooms which charged for admission. The most elaborate provisions of the bill were the restrictions on printing. Anyone possessing a printing press or even type was required to register with the Clerk of the Peace, who would forward the information to the Home Office. Vendors of printing presses and type had to keep full accounts, open for inspection by a Justice of the Peace. The names and addresses of printers were to appear on the title and end papers of all books. Printers were to keep an archive of all their publications. The sellers of publications which breached these regulations could be summarily arrested. It was these restrictions on the press which attracted most criticism of the bill when it came to its second reading in the Commons on 30 April.

Such wide-ranging legislation was bound to create problems by inadvertently catching in its net harmless and respectable activities. Many of these difficulties became apparent when the bill came to committee on 6 May. The restrictions on lectures created difficulties for such places as the Inns of Court and Chancery, and exemptions for these were added to the bill. Exclusions from the restrictions on printers were inserted for the King's printer and the two University presses. The kind of absurd situation to which the bill could potentially give rise was illustrated by one exchange in which an M.P. asked 'whether astronomical lectures came under the exempting clauses, as the Justices were not compelled, but only allowed to grant licences. Pitt replied that such occasions 'might be made a cloak for seditious lectures'. The M.P. was not convinced, but the government was adamant that no such exemption could be permitted. When the bill came to receive its third reading on 9 May, it was belatedly realised that Parliament itself could fall foul of the regulations on printers, and a clause was hastily added 'by way of Ryder, declaring that the Provisions of the Bill shall not extend to Papers printed by Order of either House of Parliament'.

One major difficulty which had become apparent was the position of Freemasons. The provisions of the bill against the use of secret oaths in societies potentially placed Freemasons in a difficult position, although arguably these oaths were outside the scope of bill since they were not seditious. More problematic was the requirement that initiations should take place in a public meeting. The Grand Lodges must also have been uneasily aware that they did not have a comprehensive register of members of the sort required by the bill, and that the compilation and distribution of such a register would have been an enormous undertaking.

The two English Grand Lodges and the Scottish Grand Lodge had quickly taken action to try and deal with these problems before the bill got to committee. On 30 April, the day on which the bill received its second reading, Pitt received a request for a meeting with Masonic representatives, and a delegation went to Downing Street on 2 May. The Masonic representatives included Lord Moira, Acting Grand Master of the Grand Lodge of England, the Duke of

Atholl, Grand Master of the Antients' Grand Lodge and Past Grand Master Mason of Scotland, as well as other Grand officers. The most important official record of this meeting is a note in the minute book of the Hall Committee of the Modern Grand Lodge, reporting that the Prime Minister had 'expressed his good opinion of the Society and said he was willing to recommend any clause to prevent the new act from affecting the Society, provided that the name of the society could be prevented from being made use of as a cover by evilly disposed persons for seditious purposes'. William White, Grand Secretary of the Moderns, afterwards recalled the meeting in similar terms, recalling that Pitt 'paid many compliments to the Society and said there was no imputation against its conduct, and that it was only wished to adopt some regulations to prevent the name of our Society from being perverted by bad people to a cover for their machinations against the government'. Lord Moira also subsequently recalled how 'I have pledged myself to His Majesty's ministers that should any set of men attempt to meet as a Lodge without sanction, the Grand Master, or Acting Grand Master (whomsoever he might be), would apprise parliament'. Pitt himself reported to the House of Commons that the Freemasons 'were very ready to acquiesce in any security the legislature would require from them for the tranquillity of the state'.

However, it seems that Pitt probably also pointed out that the government had worrying information which suggested that the Masons needed to be more vigilant. Among the documents which had been shown to the secret committee was a letter sent to the Home Office by John Waring, a Catholic priest at Stonyhurst, who described how an Irishman named Bernard Kerr had told him he was 'a Freemason, a Knight Templar, and belonged to a society of people who called themselves United Englishmen'. Kerr had shown him the printed rules of the United Englishmen, which he kept in a large portfolio together with his papers of admission as a Knight Templar. These concerns about connections between the United bodies and Freemasonry were not idle. Many of the United Irishmen were Freemasons and many features of their organisation, such as the use of oaths and secret signs, were drawn from Masonic models.

Moreover, the problems were not restricted to Irish Masons. On 17 April, shortly before Pitt met the Masonic deputation, James Greene, a Freemason and lawyer staying in Leeds, wrote to the Home Secretary, describing a meeting of a Lodge at Leeds. 'Being no stranger to the disaffected principles of too many in this place and especially among the lower class of Freemasons', he wrote, 'I made it a point to visit a Lodge of that class; and tho' politics are never introduced while the Lodge is sitting, it became a topic out of the Lodge when a part of the fraternity withdrew from the Lodge room to supper, when a shrewd sensible fellow began to inveigh against the measures of the government, and spoke in very high terms in favour of the Cannibalian government in France, to which I exhibited a seeming pleasure. After the Lodge was over, and since, I got a great deal of information from him by seeming to be one of that infernal class, and being desirous to obtain more, I begged to see him as often as he could make it convenient to talk matters over. He called upon me several times at my lodgings, and having given credit to the seeming sincerity of my attachment to that they call the cause, and confiding in my secrecy as a Free mason, produced a letter from one of the leaders among the United Irishmen, dated Dublin the 31st of March ult[im]o.'

This letter referred to a major United meeting which was to take place, under cover of a Masonic gathering, at Paisley in Scotland. Greene concluded his letter as follows: 'Now my Lord, if your Grace will approve of it, as I am in the higher orders of Masonry, and as I have every reason to believe that I can be of signal service in this matter, I will very readily undertake to conduct matters as occasion may serve so as to nip the evil in the bud, or let it run to such a length as may come to a riper maturity, and tho' there are too many rotten of the Craft fraternity, I can with great truth aver that the general part of the mass are strictly loyal'.

The aftermath of Pitt's meeting with the Masonic delegation suggests that he gave them the gist of the information received from Greene. Although it seems that the Lodge in Leeds was not an Antient lodge, it was the Antients who took these concerns most seriously, perhaps because of their greater strength in the north-western industrial towns, where the United groups were strongest, and their closer connections with Irish Masonry. Immediately after the meeting with Pitt, the Grand Officers of the Antients met at the Crown and Anchor Tavern in the Strand. They agreed to recommend two emergency measures. The first was 'to inhibit and totally prevent all public Masonic processions, and all private meetings of Masons, or Lodges of emergency, upon any pretence whatever, and to suppress and suspend all Masonic meetings, except upon the regular stated Lodge meetings and Royal Arch Chapters, which shall be held open to all Masons to visit, duly qualified as such'. It was also agreed 'that when the usual Masonic business is ended, the Lodge shall then disperse, the Tyler withdraw from the door, and formality and restraint of admittance shall cease'. These two measures were formally approved on 6 May at a Grand Lodge of Emergency, with the Duke of Atholl himself in the chair.

The actions of the Antients and the assurances given to Pitt convinced him that the Grand Lodges were determined to ensure that Freemasonry could not be used as a front for radical activity, and at the committee stage of the bill Pitt himself accordingly introduced amendments to exempt them from the act. He proposed what was essentially a system of self-regulation operated by the Grand Lodges. The relevant clause read as follows:

...nothing in this act contained shall extend, or be construed to extend, to prevent the meetings of the Lodge or society of persons which is now held at Free Masons Hall in Great Queen Street in the County of Middlesex, and usually denominated The Grand Lodge of Freemasons of England, or of the Lodge or society of persons usually denominated The Grand Lodge of Masons of England, according to the Old Institution, or of the Lodge or society of persons which is now held at Edinburgh, and usually denominated The Grand Lodge of Free Masons of Scotland, or the meetings of any subordinate Lodge or society of persons usually calling themselves Free Masons, the holding whereof shall be sanctioned or approved by any one of the above mentioned lodges or societies.

The amendment envisaged a system whereby the Grand Secretaries would each year deposit with the Clerks of the Peace a certificate containing details of the time and place of meeting of all approved Lodges in the county, together with a declaration that the Lodges were approved by the Grand Master. All Lodges were to keep a book in which each member was to declare, on joining, 'that he is well affected to the constitution and government of this realm, by King, Lords, and Commons, as by law established'. This book was to be kept open for inspection by local magistrates. The Grand Lodges were thus to be made responsible for policing Freemasonry; Lodges whose names did not appear on the return made by the Grand Secretaries would be criminal conspiracies.

It was in this form that the bill went to the House of Lords, where it received its first reading on 10 May and its second on 3 June. The bill went into committee in the House of Lords on 5 June. The debate was lead by the Foreign Secretary, Lord Grenville. Much of the debate consisted of a detailed consideration of the regulations for the control of printing types and the effects of the legislation on Catholic and non-conformist schools. A number of amendments were passed, the most notable of which was that the Gresham College lectures should enjoy the same immunity as the Universities and Inns of Court.

No amendments were made to the clauses concerning Freemasons, but concern was expressed about them in the course of the debate. Lord Grenville himself observed that, 'With respect to the clause adopted by the other House of Parliament for exempting societies of Freemasons from the operations of the bill ... though he did not mean to propose setting it aside, yet it did not appear to him to be fraught with that clearness and certainty which he could wish. He was free to express his belief, that whatever the conduct of Masonic societies in foreign countries might be (where in some instances designs of the most destructive tendency were brought to perfection) these societies in this country harboured no designs inimical to the state, or suffered or entertained such in their Lodges. Yet what the clause provided was of an anomalous nature, and new to the functions of Parliament. The officers, & c., of the subordinate Lodges were to be approved by the Grand Master and others of the principal Lodges before they could be entitled to hold their meetings. Now, how such officers, who were to have the licensing power, were to be constituted and appointed, that house, as a legislative assembly, knew nothing. It was not his own intent to propose any specific amendment to the clause; he only threw out the observation, in order that other lords, more conversant in such matters, might if they were willing, come forward and suggest something...'

Grenville thus felt that the idea of self-regulation raised serious constitutional difficulties; it seemed to him inappropriate that Grand Officers should be given statutory authority effectively to license Masonic Lodges when Parliament itself had no control over how those Grand Officers were appointed. The Duke of Norfolk, declaring himself to be a Mason, expressed some alarm at Grenville's remarks and 'deplored the idea of setting aside the exempting clause, as tending to their annihilation'. Grenville assured Norfolk that he was not proposing removing the clauses, just asking for

a better method of regulating Lodges. Norfolk was unable to suggest a new formulation and proposed instead that the act last only for a year, which was unacceptable to Grenville. The clauses concerning the Freemasons survived the committee stage in the House of Lords, but the concerns raised by Grenville were soon to resurface and present a serious threat to Freemasonry

On 20 June, the bill came up for its third reading in the House of Lords. The first speaker in the debate was the pedantic and cantankerous Earl of Radnor, who proposed an amendment to drop the exemptions for Freemasons. He said that, 'Not being himself a Mason, and having heard that they administered oaths of secrecy, he did not know, whether in times so critical as the present, it was wise to trust the Freemasons any more than any other meetings.' He went on to add that 'their meetings were, in other countries at least, made subservient to the purposes of those illuminati who had succeeded in the overthrow of one great government, and were labouring for the destruction of all others. This he conceived to have been proved in a work some time since published by a very learned Professor (Dr Robison), and he was desirous to guard against any similar practices in this country.' It seems that this was the first point at which Robison's famous 1797 anti-Masonic work was mentioned by name in the course of the discussion of the 1799 legislation.

The Duke of Atholl responded to Radnor, and, in the words of the report in *The Senator* 'defended with great earnestness and ability the institutions of Freemasonry'. The fullest account of his speech is in *The Senator*, and is worth quoting at length:

The Noble Duke contended, that the imputations thrown upon Freemasons by the Noble Earl, on the authority of a recent publication, however justified by the conduct of the Lodges on the continent, were by no means applicable to those of Great Britain. His Grace avowed, that the proceedings in Masonic Lodges, and all their obligation to secrecy simply related to their own peculiar little tenets and matters of form. There were no set of men in the kingdom, and he had the best opportunities of knowing, having had the honour to preside over a great part of them in England as well as in Scotland, who could possibly be more loyal or attached to the person of their sovereign or the cause of their country. There was nothing in the Masonic institution hostile to the law, the religion or the established government of the country; on the contrary, they went to support all these, and no person who was not a loyal or religious man could be a good Mason.

Of those well-established facts perhaps the Noble Earl was ignorant in consequence of his not being a Mason, but they were strictly true: added to these considerations, the Masonic system was founded on the most exalted system of benevolence, morals, and charity, and many thousands were annually relieved by the charitable benevolence of Masons. These very laudable and useful charities must necessarily be quashed did the bill pass into a law, as recommended by the Noble Earl. The very nature and foundation of Freemasonry involved in them the most unshaken attachment to religion, unsuspected loyalty to sovereigns, and the practise of morality and benevolence, in the strictest sense of the words. To such regulations as went to prevent the perversion of their institution to the purposes of seditious conspiracy, he could have no objection, and as a proof of the readiness with which they would be acceded to by the Masonic societies, he need only mention that this subject had occupied their attention for several years past...

The Bishop of Rochester, Samuel Horsley, who produced a famous edition of Newton's works and was a former secretary of the Royal Society, spoke next. He declared that he was 'a member of the branch of Masonry which existed in Scotland' and agreed with everything the Duke of Atholl had said: 'the innocence of these [Masonic] institutions was unquestionable, and other objects which it embraced were of the most laudable nature.' However, this applied only to genuine and regular Lodges in Britain and was not, in his view, true on the continent. There was a risk that continental influences could affect Freemasonry in Britain: 'As secrecy was absolutely necessary, no person could say that the doctrine of innovation, which had diffused itself on the continent, had not found its way into this country.' The Bishop reminded the House that Robison had calculated that there were no less than eight illuminated Lodges in Britain. He felt torn between his loyalties as a Mason and his duty as a legislator, but in the end his obligations as a member of the House of Lords required him to support Lord Radnor, since, 'By the bill as it then stood, the meetings of such Lodges were sanctioned, or were approved by persons appointed they knew not how, or by whom; by individuals, however respectable they might be as such, of whom they, as a House of Parliament, had no cognizance.' In other words, the Bishop felt, as Grenville had earlier, that a responsible parliament should not countenance a system of self-regulation by the Grand Lodges.

What happened next is not clear. According to one account, Radnor's amendment was passed, and Freemasonry in Britain was within an ace of becoming a criminal conspiracy. Whatever the exact sequence of events, the day was saved by Lord Grenville. Grenville proposed substituting the clause implementing a system of regulation by the Grand Lodges with others, 'the effect of which his Lordship stated in substance to be, to require that the objects and purposes of such Lodges as should be permitted to meet, should be declared to be purely Masonic, and only for the avowed objects of the institution, the principal ends of which he conceived to be those of charity and benevolence; that the mode of certifying should be, that two members of the Lodge should make affidavit before two or more magistrates of the particular place where the Lodge was held, and of the number and names of its members. That these accounts should be transmitted to the Clerk of the Peace, who should, once a year at least, furnish a general account of the whole within his district, to the magistrates sitting in quarter sessions, who should be empowered, in case of well-founded complaints against any particular Lodge, to suppress its meetings.' The onus for regulation was thus to be shifted from the Grand Lodges to the Justices of the Peace, who would rely on certification by local Lodges. All specific mention of the Grand Lodges in the bill would be removed, and it would refer only to 'the societies or Lodges of Free Masons'.

The Duke of Atholl agreed to accept Grenville's compromise, and amendments in this form to the bill were passed, although Radnor still felt it necessary to enter in the Journal of the House of Lords a formal protest against the exemptions for Freemasonry. The convoluted story of this piece of legislation was still, however, not concluded. When the Lords' amendments were communicated to the Commons, it was found that, by passing Grenville's new clauses, the Lords had exceeded their authority. The Speaker observed that these amendments imposed new burdens on the people, which was an exclusive privilege of the House of Commons. The only way of dealing with this problem was to shelve the old bill and bring forward a new one incorporating the revised clauses on Freemasons, which would have to go through the entire parliamentary procedure again. The new bill was therefore brought forward later that day, and its process expedited, so that it received the royal assent on 12 July.

The Grand Lodges energetically circularised secretaries of Lodges reminding them of their obligations under the Act and providing pre-printed forms for the necessary declarations and returns. Chapters of the Royal Arch also received similar circulars. One odd side-effect of the hasty way in which the amendments had been passed was that only Lodges which existed before 12 July 1799 were protected by the legislation. This meant that the Grand Lodges could not authorise new Lodges, and had to resort to the expedient of giving Lodges the warrant and number of extinct Lodges. The measures of the 1799 act were extended and refined by further legislation against subversive clubs in 1817, and it was assumed that this resolved the problem about new Lodges, but many years later this was found not to be the case.

The 1799 act was largely an exercise in closing stable doors after horses had fled. The United Irish were already regrouping into an even more secretive and militaristic organisation. London radicals resorted to holding informal tavern meetings which fell outside the scope of the legislation. Even on occasions when the 1799 act might have been useful, other legislation was used. For example, the 1799 act would have been applicable in the case of the Tolpuddle Martyrs, who used oaths and rituals of initiation, and who sought to organise their 'General Society of Labourers' as Lodges under the jurisdiction of a Grand Lodge. However, the Tolpuddle Martyrs were prosecuted under the 1797 Unlawful Oaths Act, not the 1799 legislation. Likewise, when prosecutions were brought against radical printers such as Richard Carlile (who wrote his well-known *Manual of Freemasonry* while imprisoned at Dorchester), charges of seditious libel or blasphemy were usually preferred. Later, the 1799 and 1817 acts were easily circumvented by chartist organisations, which distributed advice on how to avoid prosecution under this legislation.

The main legacy of the 1799 act was the various returns made to the Clerk of the Peace. The returns of printers, continued until 1865 when the restrictions on publications and reading rooms were lifted, are a vital source of information on the history of provincial publishing. The returns of Freemasons, continued up to 1967 and still preserved in county record offices, have been little used as a source of Masonic history. The returns are probably fuller for the earlier 19th century than later; in 1920 the London Clerk of the Peace estimated that only half the Lodges made returns. However, the 1799 act seems to have been appreciated by the Grand Lodges, which perhaps felt that it gave them some standing in law and also provided a potential means of proceeding against Lodges acting irregularly. In 1920, Grand Lodge circularised Lodge secretaries reminding them to make their returns, prompting the secretary of a Lodge in Clapton to write to Lloyd George urging him to repeal the old act.

A more serious problem arose in 1939, when the Deputy Clerk of the Peace in Essex wrote to Lodges pointing out that only those founded before 12 July 1799 were entitled to exemption under the act. Counsel's opinion confirmed this view. The United Grand Lodge of England sought to promote a private bill creating a general exemption for Freemasons from the act. The government was, however, apprehensive about changing this legislation by private bill. A Home Office official observed that the old act could still be useful against the I.R.A. and Fascist organisations. In any case, in wartime there was no parliamentary time for legislation of this kind. A compromise was agreed whereby the Attorney General agreed not to prosecute any Freemasons' lodges under the terms of the act, and Clerks of the Peace were asked to accept returns without comment. Consequently, it was not only until the major criminal law reform of the 1967 Criminal Justice Act that the 1799 Unlawful Societies Act was finally repealed.

One can see from the text of this impressive lecture that the implications of the French Revolution were far-reaching, not only in the Napoleonic era but for 150 years thereafter. One can therefore well imagine that those involved with the amalgamation, reconciliation and promulgation of the new Masonic structure that emerged in 1813 would have been very careful not to provide any reason for the organisation to be the subject of investigation under the law, or indeed for themselves to be deemed to have been associated with any act that might lead to their own prosecution. As Professor Prescott's lecture points out, there was not only the Unlawful Societies Act to contend with, but also the Unlawful Oaths Act, not to mention the risk of prosecution under laws of blasphemy.

The extent of Masonic records from this period to 1813 are acknowledged by archivists at Freemasons' Hall, London, to be very limited. It is as if those involved in the reconciliation and promulgation process met quietly around a dinner table furnished by the Duke of Sussex, discussed proposals, agreed what was to be done and by whom, but without recording minutes of the meeting so as to avoid the production of potentially incriminating evidence that might later be used against them, and the organisation.

Yet, they faced the task of merging what were effectively three different Masonic orders, each with ceremonial content that was around 100 years old at the very least. This had to be done while ensuring that, when completed, the resultant structure complied with legislation but did not compromise the basic philosophy of Freemasonry, or devalue the ceremonial concepts that had been developed.

Earlier we noted that, as the French Revolution unfolded, the aristocracy in Britain were determined to ensure they had absolute control so as to avoid any similar revolutionary occurrence that might affect their own position. We have also noted, through the Unlawful Societies Act 1799, that Freemasonry was required to conform to law, albeit that overtures were made to the government to implement changes because of what was seen as the unintentional consequences for the movement resulting from legislation intended to uphold the security of the nation. Thus, in 1792, three years after the revolution in France had begun, so the first significant steps to reconcile the two feuding Grand Lodges of the *Antients* and the *Moderns* commenced. It took over 20 years to complete. It was also in 1792 that the third Grand Lodge – the Grand Lodge of All England at York – suddenly ceased to exist. The first efforts to achieve reconciliation between the *Antients* and *Moderns* gained little momentum, and a further 17 years passed before another meaningful attempt was made in 1809. Even so, another four years passed before any great progress evolved, when in 1813, HRH the Duke of Sussex became the Grand Master of the Grand Lodge – the *Moderns* – and his brother, HRH the Duke of Kent, became Grand Master of the *Antients* Grand Lodge.

> In a matter of six weeks they had concluded the negotiations, drawn up Articles of Union which were agreed by the Grand Lodges, and arranged the great Union meeting on 27 December 1813 at which the United Grand Lodge came into existence as the sole Craft authority for England and Wales and English lodges abroad." [20]
>
> John Hamill –
> *The History of English Freemasonry*

With the new United Grand Lodge in place, the Duke of Sussex became its first Grand Master. As Grand Master of the

Premier Grand Lodge, his position was viewed as the more senior of the two, especially with a proven historical origin to 1717, and thus his brother the Duke of Kent graciously acquiesced.

It would obviously have been easier to manage one organisation with all its separate cells or lodges, than two, and as the Unlawful Societies Act of 1799 came into effect it would have become apparent that there was a need for change. During the process of the amalgamation a need arose to revise the ceremonial contents of the meetings.

There were five key individuals involved in the process of amalgamating the ceremonial rituals of the *Antients*, *Moderns* and *Royal Arch,* agreeing and organising the promulgation of them:

Duke of Sussex – Grand Master of the United Grand Lodge of England.
William White – Grand Secretary
William Williams – Provincial Grand Master of Dorset
H. J. da Costa – Provincial Grand Master of Rutland – unofficial secretary to the Duke of Sussex
Reverend Dr Samuel Hemming, DD.

As mentioned earlier, the records of meetings that took place to consider how the ceremonies and primary differences of the two Grand Lodges might be reconciled are virtually non-existent. As this book progresses, we will gain some insight into the discussions that must have taken place around the dining table with the Duke of Sussex. This chapter would not be complete, however, without first commenting on the background of two of the above partners in the amalgamating process, and their influence over the development of Masonic ceremonies – the spy and the school teacher.

# Hipólito José da Costa (1774–1823)

*(Full name: Hipólito José da Costa Pereira Furtado de Mendonça)*

Da Costa was born at a time of turmoil in South America. Spain had long had a presence in that part of the world, creating great wealth for itself in harvesting hoards of gold and silver from the region. Portugal was no less effective, as it had a major foothold in the territory we know as Brazil. This led to tensions and disputes between Spain and Portugal over the occupation of the more southern area that we know as Uruguay.

One of the most significant waterways and natural harbours in the region is that known as the Rio de la Plata (River Plate). In an effort to inhibit the southern expansion of Portuguese Brazil, the Spanish built a settlement on the northern banks of the River Plate, deep into the estuary. This was countered by the Portuguese, who built fortifications closer to the mouth of the estuary. This fortification grew into a town named Colonia del Sacramento, which today is almost directly opposite Buenos Aires, the capital of Argentina, on the southern side of the River Plate. It is also approximately 100 miles (160km) west of Montevideo, the capital of Uruguay, which is also at the mouth of the Rio de la Plata. It was in the Portuguese town of Colonia del Sacremento that José da Costa was born.

Da Costa was clearly from a well-established family, and was regarded as highly intelligent, being sent from the Portuguese colony in Uruguay to study at one of the oldest universities in Europe – based in Coimbra, the old medieval capital of Portugal, about 120 miles (200km) inland from Lisbon. His arrival in Portugal coincided with the height of the French Revolution, and although he was unaware of it, it was the period when the possibility of the merger of the two main Grand Lodges in England was being actively considered. Da Costa graduated after studying Mathematics, Law and Philosophy. In addition, based on his later testimony,[21] he had a good grounding in Greek, Latin, French, German and English.

Da Costa's family clearly had good connections and he was obviously well considered, as not long after graduating he was employed within diplomatic circles on behalf of the Portuguese government in the United States. He was recruited for this diplomatic mission by the Count of Linhares, who had attended the same university as da Costa and was at the time the Prime Minister of Portugal. For most of that time it seems da Costa was based in Philadelphia, where he was initiated into Freemasonry,[22] and on the completion of this diplomatic mission he was then sent to London.

Several writers commenting on da Costa's missions in the United States and in England have referred to him as a spy. He may well have been gathering intelligence, but that is different to spying. As stated above, his university education coincided with the French Revolution, and his missions were set against the early years of the rise of Napoleon Bonaparte and the victories of his campaigns in Italy and Egypt. The French had provided support to the Americans in the War of Independence, and the treaty that sealed that independence was signed in Paris. Furthermore, American independence provided a basis for the nation's expansion, and the position of Washington as capital had not long been agreed and was still in development. Thus any nation with an eye to the future would have wanted to gain both the support of America and to gauge its reaction to the revolutionary activities taking place in Europe. By the time da Costa arrived

in England, the Unlawful Societies Act was well entrenched, as were the efforts of the aristocracy to secure their positions and defend the British interests against French incursions. England had long been an ally of Portugal, so it would have been natural for diplomatic conversations to take place.

On his return to Lisbon from England, da Costa was arrested on the instruction of the Portuguese Inquisition. The initial charge was that he had left the country without proper authority and a passport. However, it became apparent that the real motive for his arrest was based on information that he was a Freemason. In his autobiographical account of his arrest, subsequent trial and imprisonment by the Inquisition, he wrote in his opening comments:

> Three or four days had elapsed, after my arrival in Lisbon from England, in the latter end of July, 1802, when a magistrate abruptly entered my apartments, and telling me who he was, informed me, likewise, that he had orders to seize all my papers, and conduct me to prison, where I was to be rigorously kept aloof from all communications…He then shewed me a letter from the intendant-general of police. This note directed my imprisonment, the seizure of my papers, and that endeavours should be made to find upon me, or about me, some masonical decorations. The motive of this proceeding as stated in the order of the intendant-general, was, that I had been in England, without a previous passport.[23]

Despite his protestations, da Costa was taken away to prison, and eventually brought before a magistrate. Here he was interrogated on several aspects of the arrest warrant, including his membership of freemasonry. He wrote:

...amongst my papers were some that were found that gave my persecutors an opportunity of setting aside my pretended crime of a want of passports, I meant my certificate as a freemason, and other documents relating to freemasonry. Sensible of no cause for shrinking from such a confession, I did not hesitate for a moment in acknowledging, as soon as I was interrogated, that the certificate was mine, and that I had actually been admitted a freemason, in the city of Philadelphia, in the United States of America. The corregidor [civil magistrate] minutely enquired what had induced me to enlist myself in that society; to which I answered that being informed of several persecutions which some magistrates of Portugal had indicated several individuals, whom they were pleased to denominate freemasons, although they were perhaps not freemasons, and to whom, according to public report, these magistrates had imputed many crimes, of which they entirely cleared themselves; ...... these measures of the Portuguese magistrates were so much at variance with the general estimation in which masonic societies are held in America, where individuals of almost every degree of respectability, both as to rank and talents, enrol themselves as members, this opposition was the powerful motive that raised my curiosity, and induced me seek admission into the society, that I might be able to perform a personal judgement if such a difference really existed between the opinions and proceedings of two different countries.....

The magistrate was not happy at the suggestion of impropriety on the part of his colleagues and asked da Costa to give examples as evidence, but he declined. Instead, he answered that he was interested in determining which was the better way: that of the Portuguese government or all the other nations of the world. With this reply, the magistrate asked him about his method of joining Freemasonry and which eminent persons were present, to which again da Costa was not happy to provide an answer in full, but stated:

> ...As there is no law whatever in Portugal that prohibits Freemasonry, it never could have been a crime to become a member of such a society, it being a natural consequence of civil liberty, that every man should enjoy the moral faculty of doing everything that is not prohibited by law...

Thus were da Costa's protestations, but they did not serve the purpose he originally intended. It was clear that he was the subject of interest by the Inquisition, and gaol was to be his home for the foreseeable future.

Over those few years, da Costa was kept in solitary confinement in prison, only at the end of which he was brought before the Inquisition for trial. Even so, when the trial did commence he was sent back to his cell on several occasions with instructions that he should consider carefully the folly of his actions, and left for weeks without further interrogation. On each occasion da Costa answered the questions put to him, which again centred around Freemasonry. On one occasion, the chief Inquisitor noted that if he stated the names of others he knew were Freemasons, and where their money chests were hidden, his sentence might be a little more lenient. Again, da Costa was straightforward in his response:

In this examination, however, something more than usual was done, for the inquisitor told me that, as I had declared myself to be a Freemason, and to be disposed to confess this, his charity would be extended so far as to receive my depositions that day...

Da Costa's trial lasted for eight months, notwithstanding the period he was held prior to appearing before the Inquisition, and a further six months elapsed before he had any indication as to its progress – only then when a solicitor visited him, whereupon another six months passed before he was again to face the Inquisitor. Thus, after three years in the Inquisition's prison, his mind turned to the idea of escaping. His primary motive for considering an escape plan was that of his health. He felt he had done nothing wrong, nor had he broken any law of Portugal, but it did not matter whatever he said or did: the Inquisition had already made its mind up, even before he had first appeared before them, that he was guilty of heresy through his membership of Freemasonry, and nothing was going to change their minds. Thus, if he died while in prison, his friends and relatives would also consider him guilty by virtue of the fact that he had not secured his freedom.

Da Costa resolved to escape without causing injury to anyone or damaging any property, because if he was then caught, the resulting punishment would be particularly draconian. However, his lucky break came.

His cell, was one of several that were formed around a large hall, situated in the centre of the building. He happened to notice that at night the gaoler threw the keys of the cells onto a table at the centre of the hall. It was the gaoler's ritual. On the table was also a lamp that ensured a level of light. Using a piece of metal from an old plate he had in his cell, da Costa was able to form a key to the lock on his cell door. When the gaoler had retired, having made his customary deposit of the keys, da Costa managed to open his cell door and grab the bunch. To his amazement, it contained a key for every door that he needed to open in order to get outside the prison. Thus he was able to make his escape without causing injury or damage; it also seems that he was able to obtain a book placed on the table which contained a record of his imprisonment and periods of trial. After eluding search parties sent out to find him, able to sufficiently disguise himself, he escaped from Portugal and headed for England.[24]

Da Costa reached London in 1807. Shortly thereafter, he commenced writing an autobiographical account of his imprisonment, *A narrative of the persecution of Hippolyto Joseph da Costa Pereira Furtado – By Hipólito José da Costa,* which was published in 1811 and includes a scathing attack on the Inquisition's procedures, along with a second volume that sets out a number of decrees and by-laws under which the Inquisition operated. A year after his arrival in England, he started a newspaper aimed at expatriate Brazilian and Portuguese nationals, published from 1808 – 1823. During his earlier diplomatic mission to London, he had attended a couple of London lodges and it seems now that he re-established his contact with them. This led to him being introduced to the Duke of Sussex and to his ultimate destiny of assisting in the Lodge of Promulgation for the dissemination of the ceremonial contents of the three primary Craft degrees, agreed through the merger of the two Grand Lodges.

*Author's Note:*
*Cartagena, in Columbia, was once the base for the Inquisition in that part of South America. On one side, fronting what today is a rather beautiful square, stands a rather splendid building known as the Palace of the Inquisition. It was here, in the opulent luxury of the times, that the Court of the Holy Office had its base. Behind the Palace, but within its grounds, stands what used to be the prison and torture cells, now named as the House of the Dungeons. A plaque on the wall, just to the side of the doorway that would have been the entrance through which prisoners of the Inquisition were taken, tells tourists a little of its sad past. Of particular note is the last line that states that nobody that entered as a prisoner for interrogation by the Court was ever found innocent. The centre of the beautiful square that the palace now overlooks is the place where most prisoners met their end – burnt alive. No wonder da Costa was anxious to secure his freedom from the Inquisition and escape.*

## Reverend Dr Samuel Hemming DD

Dr Hemming came, it seems, from a family steeped in the traditions of the clergy. He had a good but modest education in his younger years, went on to Oxford University and graduated with a Bachelor of Arts (BA) degree, followed by a Master of Arts (MA) degree which he received in 1791. It was a further 10 years before he obtained his Doctorate in Divinity.

For nearly all young men of no great fortune, marrying well did not necessarily mean a harmonious union based on a deep and lasting mutual affection; however, to find a wife from a respected family of at least three generations standing, who possessed a good character, a sizeable fortune and a handsome income from investments made in her name was a most desirable necessity. To this end, it seems that Samuel Hemming did well and his marriage appears to have been a happy union.

Prior to achieving his doctorate, Hemming had become attached to St. Mary's Church in Hampton, Middlesex. Within the parish was a free school that was paid for from

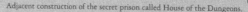

HOUSE OF THE DUNGEONS

Adjacent construction of the secret prison called House of the Dungeons.

It consisted of a total of thirteen collective cells, where all of the prisoners awaiting judgment by the Court of the Holy Office were brought.

These cells held the torture instruments of the Court of the Holy Office, including the pillory, the stocks and the weighted balance. It is said that the accused were weighed, and that the innocent should weight a kilo for every centimeter of their height over a meter. Then, every weight over or under this measurement was considered evidence of witchcraft.

The principal purpose of the Inquisition was to judge crimes committed against the beliefs defended by the Holy Church, however in all of the trials held in the city, not a single person was ever found innocent.

income from trust funds and investments that wealthy individuals had previously bequeathed. By 1800, the school had already established an enviable pedigree, having been founded some 250 years earlier, with teaching undertaken by church members with the necessary qualifications.

Hemming was thus appointed by the trustees of the school, first as a teacher, then as deputy master, and finally as master (head teacher) of the school from 1803.

Here then was a man not yet 40 years of age, well educated, married to a lady of no small income, which implies that both she, and he, were well connected, plus the accolade of being deputy master of an influential school; an impressive connection with ecclesiastical traditions and a Doctorate of Divinity to add to his stature. Such an individual would have been a well-respected member of the community and, no doubt, of unblemished character, fully conversant with the manners and expectations of that position in life. He would have been a *pillar* of the society and community of which he was a part. Thus it was that, in 1802, Hemming was initiated into Royal Somerset House and Inverness Lodge, London, one of the four original Lodges that came together to create the first Grand Lodge in 1717. One of his proposers was the Grand Treasurer of the Premier Grand Lodge, which is perhaps an indication of his connections. The origins of Royal Somerset and Inverness Lodge are unknown, but it seems to have descended from Horn Tavern Lodge, which appears in records in the late 1720s, and later from Old Horn Lodge in the late 1760s, before a series of amalgamations resulted in the prestigious Lodge into which Hemming was initiated.[25]

Hampton, Middlesex, is the location of Hampton Court Palace, some 15 miles (25km) from central London. Today, it is treated as a suburb of Greater London, but in 1802 it would have been a very different rural setting. Using a carriage and achieving a speed over unmade roads of about five miles (8km) per hour, it was a journey that took at least three hours and to do so at night was probably not to be relished, thereby demanding an overnight stay. Thus the commitment required of Hemming to regularly attend meetings in central London would have been considerable. Hence about a year later he transferred his regular loyalties to a Lodge that met in Hampton – The Lodge of Harmony – of which he became the Worshipful Master in 1808, and served in that office again on several occasions over the next 15 years. Within that Lodge he developed an enviable reputation as a fine ritualist.

Hemmings close working environment and residency close to Hampton Court Palace, and his standing in the community, led to him meeting members of the royal family, through which he also became acquainted with Prince Augustus Frederick who in 1801 was bestowed with the title by which he is frequently referenced in Freemasonry: Duke of Sussex. According to lists of lodges active in 1799, the Lodge of Harmony is shown with the number 384, and as meeting occasionally in a private room at Hampton Court.

When the process of uniting the Grand Lodges commenced in 1813, a Lodge of amalgamation was established comprising two small groups of specifically chosen individuals, of equal number from each of the *Antients* and the *Moderns* Grand Lodges. This specially created Lodge had the task of reviewing the ceremonial attributes of each Grand Lodge system and seeking a sensible means of integration.

With his connections to the Duke of Sussex, his membership of the prestigious Somerset House and Inverness Lodge, his reputation as a superb ritualist, plus his academic standing and his proposer having been the Grand Treasure of the Premier Grand Lodge, it is not surprising that Dr Samuel Hemming was invited to become a member of the new Lodge of Reconciliation. Structured like any other Lodge with regard to its officers, Dr Hemming became its first Master and seems to have played a major role in the development of the subsequent ceremonies we know today under the auspices of the United Grand Lodge of England.[26] While we can now look back and appreciate the considerable effort that was involved in the reconciliation process, in the post-promulgation analysis Hemming did receive some criticism, nearly all relating to one aspect of Freemasonry that was a theme as far back as the formation of the Premier Grand Lodge in 1717: the feast day and veneration of St. John.

There are several St. John's, but the two feast days of note in Freemasonry are that of John the Baptist (24 June), and John the (Apostle) Evangelist (27 December). The Premier Grand Lodge was formed on 24 June 1717, the nativity of St. John the Baptist, and became the main feast day in the Masonic calendar for several decades thereafter. For reasons that are not entirely clear, this feast day was later changed to that of St. John the Evangelist (27 December). The origins of both these dates are obscured by time, except that in the fourth century the Roman Church began to honour individuals that they regarded as Christian martyrs, and in the sixth to eighth centuries feast days of saints came into being when a number of the martyrs were elevated to this new status. It was at a time when the Roman Church was seeking to eradicate or Christianise pagan festivals and places of worship. The three pagan festivals that were most widespread across Europe were the celebration of the summer solstice (21 June), winter solstice

(21 December) and rebirth of the sun (6 January). It seems that 25 December was set as the Christ's nativity as a way of countering the Winter solstice, and 6 January was allocated as the 12th night after the arrival in Bethlehem of the three kings from the east, as told in the biblical narrative. To have two major feast days celebrating two separate nativities within a few days of each other was inappropriate, so the Baptist's feast day was set for the mid-summer.

At the time that Hemming was undertaking his work on the ceremonies, Catholicism was still treated as an outcast religion in Britain; continuing to champion saints or festivals of the Catholic Church probably did not fit with the ethos of the nation, the Grand Master or a man of the Protestant following. Although it is only speculation, one can imagine that these elements were removed on those grounds, and also because such celebrations bore no real relationship to the core objectives of Freemasonry at that time, especially as there was a need for compliance with the Unlawful Societies Act.

## Benefits of the involvement of da Costa and Dr Hemming

There is no official record as exactly what part these individuals played in the amalgamation and promulgation processes, but each brought an invaluable perspective to the table. Da Costa had become a Freemason in Philadelphia, under the Scottish Constitution; he was an outspoken defender of the institution, its members and its ethos in the face of the Inquisition; as a writer and journalist, he knew how to put pen to paper; he had worked in diplomatic circles and understood the necessary protocols; he had studied Philosophy and Law, and had a good grasp of several languages, old and modern. Dr Hemming, on the other hand, was a sound administrator and recognised as having an excellent grasp of the rituals of the Premier Grand Lodge, while he was also an influential rhetorician, and had a thorough understanding of ecclesiastical matters.

These two men were like two separate pillars of knowledge and life experience, but when considered together they provided no small measure of the *strength that established the institution to stand firm forever* – at or least over the past few hundred years.

Hemming apparently undertook much of the work involved in drafting the content and structure of the ceremonies that exist today. Indeed, we may credit him for the moral aspect of references to Old Testament scripture that form part of the structure of

Freemasonry, which would have found favour with the Duke of Sussex. Prince Augustus Frederick was the only son of George III who did not enter into a career in the military, as in his younger years he had apparently considered a life in the church, which gives some indication of his religious convictions. Thus, had Hemming or any other member of the amalgamation team proposed a connection with the Old Testament, it is likely to have been well received by him.

The history of the organisation suggests that Hemming may not have been the first to provide the references to religious text that are part of the ceremonies, but may have built up on or rationalised an idea that already existed. This being so, then where did the influence originate?

## Masonic Memory Review 2

Throughout this chapter it becomes evident that the turmoil generated in the late 18th century, first by the revolution in America and then by the French Revolution, resulted in the British aristocracy seeking to retain wealth, power and influence rather than losing their heads as their French counterparts had done. The fear of revolution reaching Britain led to the Unlawful Societies Act which, perhaps not intentionally, actually embraced Freemasonry.

To comply with subsequent Acts of Parliament, it became desirous to merge the competing Grand Lodges and Chapters and thereby create one single entity over which a proper administrative control could be exercised. This seems to have resulted in a hierarchical structure which became a dominant feature of the institution.

Although two major lodges were created to deal with the amalgamation – the Lodge of Promulgation and the Lodge of Reconciliation – details as to how conclusions were reached that influenced the structure of the organisation were not retained.

Thus it would seem that any attempt to understand *what we are doing* and *what it means* can only be accomplished by a process of reverse engineering, by looking at our traditions, and trying to understand their relevance in the minds of individuals associated with the creation of a new ceremonial structure two to three hundred years ago.

We should remember these two men who made such an important contribution to Freemasonry during in the period of its development, its global reach commencing in 1813 following the reconciliation of two competing Grand Lodges, resulting in the creation of the United Grand Lodge of England. They were the authors of the format and content of the ceremonies of Craft Masonry, the formal acknowledgement of the Royal Arch, and the development and style of regalia, promulgated through the Lodges that existed at that time.

*For images of Dr. Hemming and da Costa, see colour section plate 3 & 4*

*Chapter 6*

# Tracing the religious allegory

IT IS DOUBTFUL THAT anyone sat down and created out of thin air the ceremonies that each of the Grand Lodges performed just for something to do. The contents and structure had come from somewhere, or to have been inspired by something. That *somewhere or something* may not have been a single source or event but may have been derived from a range of diverse influences. Those influences may well have been almost anything of substance, such as factual historical knowledge and events that occurred long ago; legends and stories passed through the ages, repeated as folklore; historical figures that existed around the time the first Grand Lodge was created, or of whom there was a common memory in the society of the day; political activity, including that which was influenced by religion; and of course, religious ceremony and dogma as well. Therefore we need to look at what was going on in the wider world prior to the formation of the first Grand Lodge of England in 1717, and thereby any influence those events may have had on the ceremonial structure handed down with the passage of time, and to do the same again in the hundred years that led up to the formation of the United Grand Lodge of England in 1813.

It is doubtful that such ceremonies resulted from minor events that meant little or nothing in the lives of people over the centuries: it's more likely they were large scale events that had a profound effect on life – important events that needed to be recorded and passed on to later generations. To try and unravel what the inspirational events may have been requires one to look at the world that existed around two to three hundred years ago with the eyes and ears of that era. Looking with 21st century eyes could result in an entirely misleading perception of the ceremonies, that some today may consider merely colourful, distasteful, discredited or irrelevant symbolism. Three hundred years ago, that same symbolism may well have been a far more profound key component in the lives of many people by comparison with the credit given to it in our own age and environment.

In the previous chapters, we've looked at some of the turmoil that surrounded British politics in the few hundred years leading to the formation of the United Grand Lodge of England. It was a period of immense agitation and fear associated with religion. Masonic researchers and authors of the early 20th century suggest that, during the first 50 years following the formation of the Premier Grand Lodge in 1717, Masonic ceremonies went through a period of *development*. This one word alone implies that elements were discarded, added and/or consolidated. There is very little information to indicate what the changes were. Shortly after this period of development, however, William Preston published his system of Masonic lectures along with a book entitled *Illustrations of Masonry* in 1772. Preston greatly enjoyed his Masonry and had researched and gathered together much of what he considered to be the underlying principles of the institution. Great store has been placed on Preston's work over many decades, not least for the reason that it is amongst the first genuine attempts to consolidate the background history, development and ceremonial attributes of the institution.

The one element that is common across all three Masonic degrees and the Royal Arch today, and also appear in Preston's works, is the use of or reference to religious text. This raises the questions why and where did it originate?

## Religion and the allegory

In the 20th century there were several writers of note who suggested that the religious overlay and influence of the ceremonies probably originated from the medieval period, prior to the rule of the Tudors. This, they suggested, was because the stonemasons undertook a considerable amount of work for the monastic communities and would have embraced terminology that aligned with working practices in that environment. Others suggest that the larger monastic houses often had brethren attached to them who were conversant with building practices, who assisted in major works and used religious text to remember certain processes which were then adopted by the operative stonemasons. When

one considers that, in the early 20th century, most such written works were produced by prominent Masons who were members of the clergy, then this would have seemed to be a natural conclusion to them, which should not be discounted. Yet, there may be another reason.

First, we should look at early ceremonies for evidence of their religious content, and what it may have comprised.

## Masonic ceremony 1730 – Pritchard's disclosure

Exactly what Masonic ceremony may have comprised in 1717 or earlier, is unknown. The absence of records from this era is a source of great frustration to anyone, past or present, who has embarked on Masonic research and enquiry. We may have had information of value had it not been for a group of 'scurrilous brothers' who burnt a range of documents in 1720 to prevent them from 'falling into strange hands'.[27] We know that there were Masonic groups meeting in various parts of the country, but accounts of what was actually being done at meetings are somewhat less reliable. One of the main sources we have is a so-called disclosure from 1730 entitled *Masonry Dissected, being a universal and genuine description of all the branches of the original at this present time*.[28] This is a pamphlet attributed to one Samuel Pritchard, who defined himself as a 'late member of a constituted lodge' in 1730.

A Masonic reprint of this disclosure, by John T Thorpe FRHistS, adds a range of notes of which the following gives an indication of the impact of the original Pritchard publication:

The earliest 'exposure'….. was compiled and published by Samuel Pritchard in the year 1730 under the title *Freemasonry Dissected*…Such was the extraordinary demand for the work, that three editions were issued within 11 days, followed by many more up to the 30th. It was translated into French, German and Dutch, and had a most extensive sale for many years.

Just this one comment gives some feel for the way in which Pritchard's work was received. Pritchard goes on to describe the origins of Freemasonry thus:

The original Institution of Masonry consisted on the foundations of the liberal Arts and Sciences, but most especially on the fifth, viz, Geometry. For at the building of the Tower of Babel, the Art and Mystery of Masonry was first introduced, and from thence handed down by Euclid, a worthy and excellent mathematician of the Egyptians, and he communicated it to Hiram, the Master Mason concerned with the building of Solomon's Temple in Jerusalem, [and there] was an excellent and curious Mason that was the chief under their Grand Master Hiram, whose name was Mannon Grecus, who taught the art to one Carolos Marcil in France, who was afterwards elected King of France, and from where, was brought to England in the time of King Athelstone…who ordered an assembly to held once every year at York…

The Tower of Babel is today identified by archaeologists as a ziggurat built around 3,500 BCE in the ancient city state of Sumer, with its main town of Ur. Sumer was founded at the confluence of the great rivers, the Euphrates and the Tigris in the area that has often been described as the 'fertile crescent' and also suggested to be the location of the Garden of Eden. Some of this territory is now in Iran and some in Iraq. A ziggurat was a pyramidal structure, believed to have been the place where, according to the peoples of that time, a specific god lived.

The Hiram of Solomon's Temple is misplaced in this 1730 statement. The temple was probably constructed around 950 BCE, some six hundred years prior to the era of Euclid; thus Euclid could not have passed the information to Hiram.

Euclid was a Greek mathematician, credited with the title 'Father of Geometry'. He lived around 300 BCE at Alexandria, a city founded by the Macedonian warrior Alexander the Great, which is today in Egypt. This may account for the Egyptian attribution in 1730, when that city would naturally have been see as part of Egypt. Furthermore, for some 2000 years prior to the era when Euclid lived, Egyptian civilisation had flourished and their priests and magi had developed a wealth of knowledge about geometry and astronomy, plus the ability to build elaborate structures using stone. Thus Euclid, had access to the sum of knowledge that had been developed up until his own era.

The story of Mannon Grecus – referred to in other later Masonic related texts as Marcus Grecus – may be related to an early style of architecture that later developed into the Romanesque style. This development may have originally transferred to Europe around 750-800 CE from Byzantium

(Constantinople) to the Frankish kingdom in the reign of Charles II (Martel) – referred to in this extract from *Masonry Dissected* as Carolos Marcil. Martel is arguably the founder of the dynasty of Carolingian kings of which the most renowned is probably Charlemagne, credited as the first Emperor of the Holy Roman Empire in 800 CE, after suppressing most of the population of what we now know as Europe and enforcing the religious doctrine of Roman Catholic Christianity. Athelstan was Alfred the Great's grandson who united all the individual tribal areas of England to become one nation. This made Athelstan 'The first King of all the English.' These aspects are covered in greater detail in my earlier book, *The Mandorla and Tau*.

Samuel Pritchard continues:
The terms of Free and Accepted Masonry (as it now is) has not been heard of till within these few years; No constituted Lodges or Quarterly Communications were heard of until 1691, when Lords and Dukes, Lawyers and Shopkeepers, and other inferior tradesmen, Porters not excluded, were admitted into the mystery or no mystery; the first sort being introduced at very great expense, the second sort at a moderate rate, and the latter at for the expense of Six or Seven Shillings, for which they receive that badge of honour, which as they term it is more ancient and more honourable than is the Star and Garter, which antiquity is accounted...

NOTE: The inflation in the value of money over the last three centuries (from approx 1700 – 2010) is substantial. Thus, £1.00 sterling in 1700 would be worth approx £1700.00 at the time of writing, while six shillings in 1700 would be worth approximately £530.00.[29] These sums suggest that membership would have been generally only available to the wealthier members of society.

Pritchard continues his disclosure by indicating the contents of the three main degrees, which he calls the Entered Apprentice, the Fellow Craft and the Master-Mason. The ceremony is conducted in a question and answer process. The following is a short extract of each:

1. **Entered Apprentice**
   Q. What Makes a Just and Perfect Lodge?
   A. Seven or more.
   Q. What do they consist of?
   A. One Master, Two Wardens. Two Fellow Craft and two Entered Apprentices.
   Q. What form is the lodge?
   A. A long square.
   Q. How long?
   A. From East to West.
   Q. How broad?
   A. From North to South?
   Q. How is it situated?
   A. Due East and West.
   Q. Why so?
   A. Because all Churches and chapels are or ought to be so.
   Q. What supports a Lodge?
   A. Three great pillars.
   Q. What are they called?
   A. Wisdom, Strength and Beauty.
   Q. Why so?
   A. Wisdom to contrive. Strength to support and Beauty to adorn.
   Q. Have you lights in your Lodge?
   A. Yes. Three.
   Q. What do they represent?

A. The Sun, Moon and Master Mason.

Q. How are they situated?

A. East, South and West.

Q. Why are there no lights in the North?

A. Because the sun darts no rays from there.

## 2. Fellow Craft degree.

Q. How came you to the middle chamber?

A. By a winding pair of stairs.

Q. How many?

A. Seven or more.

Q. Why seven or more?

A. Because seven or more make a Just and Perfect Lodge.

## 3. Master Mason degree

The contents of this degree deal mainly with historical elements of the Old Charges, and includes reference to Euclid and geometry.

From these few extracts we can see a close resemblance to aspects of Masonic ceremonies that exist today. Although there are some religious references they are not as prolific as they later became. A study of Pritchard's disclosure, also reveals that a reasonable proportion of the ceremonial content was later rolled up and included in the Tracing Board lectures that are believed to have developed under William Preston, some 40 years after these disclosures were made. This is an issue we will return to in due course.

# Josephus in Masonry

As noted earlier, British politics were in constant turmoil for the whole of the century leading up to 1717, the year of the founding of the first Grand Lodge, and for the next 40 years afterwards, with divisions over religion that continued until after 1745. Just 100 years previously, the King James Authorised Version of The Bible was published, and became the mainstay of every church and cathedral in the land. Although in the vulgar tongue of the English, the main body text was commensurate with all forms of Christianity and, with the Old Testament based on the Jewish Torah, it could comfortably satisfy the religious doctrines of the main religious faiths operating in Britain in the early 18th century. It was therefore the ideal vehicle to be used as the template for the allegorical content of Freemasonry. But not everything is as it seems.

For example, take the references to Solomon's Temple. In Masonic ceremonial, Hiram is the Master Builder who, in the process of construction, has the misfortune to die. He is buried, but later his body is recovered and reinterred with great ceremony as would befit a man of his standing, within the temple and as close as possible to the most sacred area within the *Sanctum Sanctorum*, that which he helped to build. Yet if one reads the Old Testament text that relates to the building of Solomon's Temple, there is no mention of Hiram's death.

During the 16th and 17th century, another source was widely read for religious interpretation. Flavius Josephus, a Roman citizen and Jew, wrote a series of works including *The Antiquities of the Jews*. He records items about the building of Solomon's Temple and other events from the distant past, leading some commentators to suggest that he may have had access to records long since lost, or that they were part of a verbal tradition, or that he wrote only what seemed to make sense to him. It is from his works that much of the contents of Masonic ceremonies are drawn. The following extract is how *The Catholic Encyclopaedia* records him:

> Josephus's second work, the *Jewish Antiquities*....contains in 20 books the whole history of the Jews from the Creation to the outbreak of the revolt in A.D. 66. Books I-XI are based on the text of the Septuagint, though at times he also repeats traditional explanations current among the Jews in later times. He also quotes numerous passages from Greek authors whose writings are now lost. On the other hand he made allowance for the tastes of his Gentile contemporaries by arbitrary omissions as well as by the free embellishment of certain scenes. Books XII-XX, in which he speaks of the times preceding the coming of Christ and the foundation of Christianity, are our only sources for many historical events. In these the value of the statements is enhanced by the insertion of dates which are otherwise wanting, and by the citation of authentic documents which confirm and supplement the Biblical narrative.[30]

Although Josephus was a Roman citizen and was certainly well respected by both the hierarchy of the Jewish and Roman customs, he actually fought against the Roman army during the Jewish uprising of 66 CE, witnessing the destruction of the Herodian Temple in Jerusalem (on the site formerly occupied by Solomon's Temple) by the Romans in 70 CE. His first written work, about the Jewish wars, is based on his own knowledge of those times. According to *The Catholic*

*Encyclopaedia*, his ancestral Jewish connection went back at least five generations, with his mother claiming descent from the Machabeans.

The first translation of Josephus' works into English is credited to one Thomas Lodge in 1602, the year prior to James I/VI ascending to the English throne. A further translation was undertaken by William Whiston in 1732 and is known to have been widely available. Indeed, during the late 18th century and well into the Victorian era, it is stated that nobody of any standing was without at least one copy on their bookshelves. This latter translation was right in the middle of the period 1717 – 1750, when the fledgling formalised Masonic movement was still finding its feet.

Despite the apparent use of the works of Josephus in Masonic ceremonies, there is no mention of the death of Hiram here either. This then raises the prospect that if it is not the death of the builder of Solomon's Temple at the centre of Masonic ceremony, then who is it? Could it be that this death is an allegory for something else? And has the translator of Josephus's works, Thomas Lodge, been overlooked?

## Josephus and Thomas Lodge (1558–1625)

Thomas Lodge was well connected and highly educated, his father having been created a knight, and at one time being the Lord Mayor of London. Lodge attended Oxford University and achieved a Master of Arts Degree, and while he entered the legal profession his main claim to fame came through his writing, including that as a playwright.

*The Catholic Encyclopaedia* notes that he wrote a book entitled *Robin and the Devil* (1591) in which he possibly drew on an ancient legend that was first recorded some 300 years prior to his own work. Lodge also travelled to Brazil and other areas of South America in an era when such extensive travel was a real expedition into the unknown. After returning, he undertook the translation of Josephus in 1602, possibly during a period of self-imposed exile. He had converted to Catholicism during the reign of Elizabeth I, at a time when Catholics were being persecuted following the failed attempt of the invasion of England by the Spanish Armada, and the plot to remove the Queen with the support of France and the Vatican. He is believed to have gone to France and studied medicine a few years prior to the publication of the works of Josephus, a translation which academics suggest became very popular and was widely circulated in England.

By the skill that Lodge exercised to produce this first translation, it could be argued that he laid the foundation stone William Whiston would later build upon.

## Josephus and William Whiston (1667–1752)

Whiston's main academic achievements correspond to the era when Freemasonry as an organised institution was finding its feet. He was born in Leicestershire, England, and died in the adjoining county of Rutland. He is noted as having been a theologian who also had a considerable interest in both mathematics and history. He was closely associated with Cambridge University, and it is noted that Sir Isaac Newton had been one of his mentors. Whiston was certainly a man who held some fairly controversial opinions on both religion and astronomy, but was also well respected and frequently gave lectures at the Royal Society. One of his controversial works was entitled *A New Theory of the Earth* (1696), in which he suggests that the flood associated with the biblical story of Noah and the Ark may well have been the consequence of a comet plunging to Earth. This work was published just 50 years after Galileo Galilei had died while under house arrest for what were regarded as his contentious views of the universe and support for Copernican theory, according to the Catholic Inquisition. Whiston was subjected to a different form of inquisition for his religious views.

In the reign of the Roman Emperor Constantine the Great, at the time that Christianity was being moulded into the various forms we have known over the past 1500 years, there was a great debate that needed to be resolved for which the church leaders gathered for the Council of Nicaea in 325 CE. The debate was about the 'Arian Heresy', which centred on the views of a Bishop named Arius. His view on the Divinity of the Christ was that Jesus was not literally a son of God, but a man like any other. It was a view that threatened to tear the young Church to pieces, as some bishops accepted traditional opinions and others backed Arius. Constantine called the Council of Nicaea, in part, to agree a single doctrine. 'Arianism' was discounted, but although the Council agreed to accept the traditional opinion of divinity, Arianism never quite disappeared. It had considerable support amongst the peoples of Eastern Europe in the seventh and eighth centuries, and caused Charlemagne much trouble in his quest to create the vast Frankish kingdom he ruled over. Whiston, it seems, was sympathetic to the views that Arius had expressed over 1200 years earlier. The hierarchy of Cambridge University deemed his opinions to be heresy and he was dismissed from his position, just as Wycliffe had been from Oxford 500 years earlier.

Whiston moved to London and became a frequent preacher there and in other parts of the country. Thus it was that in 1732 he published his own translation of the works of Josephus, which it is believed to have been an immediate success.

Whiston was a contemporary of Dr Anderson, who produced the first Constitutions of Freemasonry in 1723 but then went on to produce a much larger and wider ranging edition in 1738, six years after Whiston's translation of *Antiquities of the Jews* had appeared in print.

## Josephus v Old Testament, Text comparisons

There are two books in the Bible, namely 'Chronicles' and 'Kings', in which references are made to the pillars of Solomon's Temple. Each has a slightly different text with reference to the outer shell being made from brass. Brass is a very specific alloy made from a combination of copper and zinc; the ratios of the mixture can vary to provide a range of different compositions that are good for resisting corrosion or are soft enough to construct musical instruments.

Bronze is a different alloy, comprising a mixture of copper and tin, and it is highly probable that the metal used in the pillars was bronze and not brass.

Historians note that the Bronze Age started at approximately 1,000 BCE, which is around the time that Solomon's Temple is alleged to have been built. Prior to that time, pillars are likely to have consisted of plain stonework or to have been decorated with paints and dyes, as is seen in Egyptian architecture. The use of metal cladding for the pillars probably indicates a noteworthy era of new technology. Furthermore, historians also note that the Phoenicians, mostly based in Tyre at the time of Solomon, were travelling to Cornwall and trading in the tin that was being mined there. If tin was an important trading commodity it would suggest that bronze was in high demand. Brass was known in Roman times after about 300 BCE and may have been born from a confusion between the two differing constituents of tin and zinc, thereby accidentally creating the new alloy we know as brass. The Industrial Revolution was just getting under way when Whiston made his translation of Josephus, and brass would have been a more commonly available metal by comparison with bronze. 'Brass' is the description given in the King James Bible.

The following tables show the translation of the Josephus text from *Antiquities of the Jews* by comparison with text taken from each of the books of Chronicles and Kings in the King James and New International Versions of the Old Testament, in respect of the pillars that were erected at the front of Solomon's Temple.

| Josephus, Whiston Translation 1732 | Typical biblical interpretation, King James Version, 1611 | Modern translation, New International Version post- 1970 |
|---|---|---|
| *Antiquities of the Jews* | **2 Chronicles 3, 15 - 17** | **2 Chronicles 3, 15 - 17** |
| ....made two [hollow] pillars, whose outsides were of brass, and the thickness of the brass was four fingers' breadth, and the height of the pillars was 18 cubits and their circumference 12 cubits; but there was cast with each of their chapiters lily-work that stood upon the pillar, and it was elevated five cubits, round about which there was net-work interwoven with small palms, made of brass, and covered the lily-work. To this also were hung two hundred pomegranates, in two rows. The one of these pillars he set at the entrance of the porch on the right hand, and called it Jachin and the other at the left hand, and called it Boaz.<br><br>Now Solomon sent for | Also he made before the house two pillars of thirty and five cubits high, and the chapiter that was on the top of each of them was five cubits.<br><br>And he made chains, as in the oracle, and put them on the heads of the pillars; and made an hundred pomegranates, and put them on the chains. And he reared up the pillars before the temple, one on the right hand, and the other on the left; and called the name of that on the right hand Jachin, and the name of that on the left Boaz | For the front of the temple he made two pillars, which together were 35 cubits long, each with a capital five cubits high.<br><br>He made interwoven chains and put them on top of the pillars. He also made a hundred pomegranates and attached them to the chains. He erected the pillars in the front of the temple, one to the south and one to the north. The one to the south he named Jakin and the one to the north Boaz. |

| Josephus, Whiston Translation 1732 | Typical biblical interpretation, King James Version, 1611 | Modern translation, New International Version post- 1970 |
|---|---|---|
| *Antiquities of the Jews* | 2 Chronicles 3, 15 - 17 | 2 Chronicles 3, 15 - 17 |
| an artificer out of Tyre, whose name was Hiram; he was by birth of the tribe of Naphtali, on the mother's side, (for she was of that tribe,) but his father was Ur, of the stock of the Israelites. This man was skilful in all sorts of work; but his chief skill lay in working in gold, and silver, and brass; by whom were made all the mechanical works about the temple, according to the will of Solomon. Moreover, this Hiram made two [hollow] pillars, whose outsides were of brass, and the thickness of the brass was four fingers' breadth, and the height of the pillars was eighteen cubits and their circumference twelve cubits; but there was cast with each of their chapiters lily-work that stood upon the pillar, and it was elevated five cubits, round about which there was net-work interwoven with small palms, made of brass, and covered the lily-work. To this also were hung 200 pomegranates, in two rows. The one of these pillars he set at the | And king Solomon sent and fetched Hiram out of Tyre.<br><br>He was a widow's son of the tribe of Naphtali, and his father was a man of Tyre, a worker in brass: and he was filled with wisdom, and understanding, and cunning to work all works in brass. And he came to King Solomon, and wrought all his work.<br><br>For he cast two pillars of brass, of 18 cubits high apiece: and a line of 12 cubits did compass either of them about.<br><br>And he made two chapiters of molten brass, to set upon the tops of the pillars: the height of the one chapiter was five cubits, and the height of the other chapiter was five cubits:<br><br>And nets of checker work, and wreaths of chain work, for the chapiters which were upon the top of the pillars; seven for the one chapiter, and seven for the other chapiter. | King Solomon sent to Tyre and brought Huram, whose mother was a widow from the tribe of Naphtali and whose father was from Tyre and a skilled craftsman in bronze. Huram was filled with wisdom, with understanding and with knowledge to do all kinds of bronze work. He came to King Solomon and did all the work assigned to him.<br><br>He cast two bronze pillars, each 18 cubits high and 12 cubits in circumference.<br><br>He also made two capitals of cast bronze to set on the tops of the pillars; each capital was five cubits high.<br><br>A network of interwoven chains adorned the capitals on top of the pillars, seven for each capital.<br><br>He made pomegranates in two rows encircling each network to decorate the capitals on top of the pillars. He did the same for each capital. |

| Josephus, Whiston Translation 1732 | Typical biblical interpretation, King James Version, 1611 | Modern translation, New International Version post- 1970 |
|---|---|---|
| *Antiquities of the Jews* | 2 Chronicles 3, 15 - 17 | 2 Chronicles 3, 15 - 17 |
| entrance of the porch on the right hand, and called it Jachin and the other at the left hand, and called it Booz. | And he made the pillars, and two rows round about upon the one network, to cover the chapiters that were upon the top, with pomegranates: and so did he for the other chapiter. And the chapiters that were upon the top of the pillars were of lily work in the porch, four cubits.<br><br>And the chapiters upon the two pillars had pomegranates also above, over against the belly which was by the network: and the pomegranates were 200 in rows round about upon the other chapiter. And he set up the pillars in the porch of the temple: and he set up the right pillar, and called the name thereof Jachin: and he set up the left pillar, and called the name thereof Boaz.<br><br>And upon the top of the pillars was lily work: so was the work of the pillars finished. | The capitals on top of the pillars in the portico were in the shape of lilies, four cubits high.<br><br>On the capitals of both pillars, above the bowl-shaped part next to the network, were the 200 pomegranates in rows all around.<br><br>He erected the pillars at the portico of the temple. The pillar to the south he named Jakin and the one to the north Boaz. The capitals on top were in the shape of lilies.<br><br>And so the work on the pillars was completed. |

It is apparent in this comparison table that the reference to brass in Whiston's Josephus and the King James version, changes to bronze in the more recent translations of the late 20th century.

Those familiar with Masonic ceremony will immediately recognise the similarity of ceremonial aspects illustrated by the above segments, and the inclusions derived from the Josephus text.

Thus one is encouraged to contemplate the possibility that where biblical references are made, they may stem more commonly from Josephus rather than the King James Version of the Bible, if not in whole then very probably in part. In which case, where did the link originate?

Whiston's version of the Josephus translation was published in 1732, a time early in the development of organised Freemasonry. The common links may well have been Dr Anderson and Presbyterianism.

## Presbyterian Church

The Presbyterian Church has a strong connection with Scotland. From the time Martin Luther started his protest movement and called for reform of the Catholic Church hierarchy, various other reformers also rose to the challenge. Whenever an established institution faces a challenge to its authority, it will almost always retaliate, claiming that the challengers are misguided and that their institution is the sole arbiter of responsible doctrine. In the case of the Catholic Church, there were those that had been faithful to it but saw a need for change and Luther's challenge provided the opportunity and timing for them to make that change. The result was a split between Catholicism and Protestantism. The Roman Church sought to deal with the issues raised by the challenges at the Council of Trento.

Protestantism, which did not have one single administration or centre of authority, resulted in several different strands of religious understanding, all having a common bond with the fundamental basis and principles of the Christian religion, but with slightly different interpretations.

John Calvin, a Frenchman, was excommunicated by the Catholic Church, for his beliefs. Today, being excommunicated means very little other than being excluded from certain religious practices, but in the medieval period the church preached that it meant that upon one's death, one was destined to go straight to the fires of hell, and remain there forever. For the average citizen such a prospect was terrifying, but Calvin was less than convinced by such a philosophy and, after moving to Switzerland, established a different Protestant perspective.

John Knox was a Scot and a religious reformer at a time when Mary Queen of Scots was an infant and her mother, Mary of Guise, acted as Regent. England had already become a Protestant country under Henry VIII, but Mary of Guise was a staunch Catholic. Knox therefore moved to England, but when Mary I Tudor inherited the throne of England, and revitalised Catholic belief, he moved to the continent and met John Calvin in Geneva. The reformed doctrine that Calvin advocated, had a great effect upon Knox, and he wrote a revised service which was later adopted as the Order of Service for the Reformed Church of Scotland. Knox had been exposed to the fluctuations of religious turmoil and at times was himself considered a revolutionary, as he orchestrated the demise of Catholicism in Scotland and a break with the papacy in 1560. He was once held a prisoner of the French and forced to row in the French galleys, and in later life became the champion of the reform movement in Scotland that created the Presbyterian Church. Presbyterian values were accepted and enshrined in the Act of Union between England and Scotland in 1707, which created the United Kingdom of Great Britain. Thus, Presbyterianism held a prominent place in the religious affairs of England and Scotland at the time the first Grand Lodge was formed in 1717, and when James Anderson produced the first Constitutions in 1723.

## Dr James Anderson and William Whiston

James Anderson (1680 – 1739) was born in Aberdeen, Scotland, and received his early education in that city, achieving a Master's degree. His father was a Scottish Presbyterian minister, into which calling, James followed. He first preached in Scotland before moving to London, where he became the Minister of three Presbyterian churches over the rest of his life.

Anderson was also a contemporary of William Whiston, in that they were both Presbyterian churchmen and probably circulated in similar social circles in London. Indeed, in that era, London and all the major cities of Britain abounded with a wide variety of social groups, fraternities and societies that met regularly in the fashionable chocolate and coffee houses and debated political and religious issues, as well as matters relating to science and invention, alongside financial investment clubs. Anderson had joined Freemasonry in 1721 and in 1723 published his *Book of Constitutions*. The social network that his church and Masonic links must have created, makes it difficult to believe that he was not acquainted with Whiston, especially as the latter preached and debated his religious opinions in many of the London chocolate and coffee houses. It is also difficult to conceive that Anderson, through the Presbyterian origins he shared with Whiston, would not have been aware of the Cambridge

heresy controversy. In addition, Whiston regularly gave lectures at the Royal Society in London, an elite organisation with whom many prominent Freemasons of the era were associated.

Dr Anderson is believed to have been awarded his doctorate from Aberdeen in 1731, a year prior to Whiston publishing his Josephus translations. Anderson then published a further edition of his *Constitutions* in 1738. His first, in 1723, seems to reflect on some of the materials that may have existed in the London Company of Masons at that time (the *Old Charges*), as well as a list of several well-known buildings that had been built in the Renaissance and neo-classical styles in England for monarchy, aristocracy and landed gentry, particularly highlighting the work of Inigo Jones. As such, the 1723 edition is quite modest in size, although elaborately presented to give it an appearance of importance. The 1738 edition was of an entirely different character. It was still presented in a manner that was intended to underline its importance, but its contents were greatly expanded by comparison with the earlier edition. The number of printed pages extended to over 230, and included a section relating to characters and events found in the Old Testament, including the story surrounding Noah and the Great Flood. One gets the impression, rightly or wrongly, that much of the material is based on what Anderson may have learned during his theological studies, especially those associated with his doctorate. Neither can one ignore the potential for a greatly changed and enlarged perception of the world that would have emerged during his lifetime, as the period of the *Enlightenment* gained momentum with the establishment of the Royal Society and the Royal Observatory at Greenwich, both instigated in the reign of Charles II.

In the text of Anderson's *Constitutions*, relating to events recorded in the Bible, we also see dates that form part of the chronology and dating system that was devised by James Ussher, former Archbishop of Armagh in the Church of Ireland. Ussher calculated all the time intervals recorded in the Bible and came to the conclusion that the world was created on the night leading into Sunday 23 October 4004 BCE, based on the old Julian calendar. His chronology became so accepted that it even found its way into the dating system used in Freemasonry. Because of the tradition that surrounds it, this dating system is still referred to in Masonic explanations but its significance is often minimised by a statement that notes how these dates are now considered *unreliable.*

It is therefore entirely reasonable to conclude that the actual and circumstantial evidence implies that religious overtones in Masonic ceremonies come not from former connections with pre-Tudor monastic houses, but through the Presbyterian background of Dr Anderson, intermingled with the translations of Josephus, *Antiquities of the Jews* made by his fellow Presbyterian clergyman, William Whiston.

What is more, neither of these two clergymen, highly educated in their times, would have been unaware of the earlier translation of Josephus by Thomas Lodge, and the connection between his family name and that given to the place where, traditionally, stonemasons undertook their stone-carving work – a *Lodge.*

Note: The word Lodge, it seems, does not readily appear in Masonic use until after the publication of the 1723 *Constitutions.* Prior to that time nearly all references to the fledgling Masonic organisation, or to Freemasons prior to the year 1700, use the term 'society' or 'fraternity' and the term 'Lodge' is only referred to in connection with the operative masons.

The word 'Lodge' has several meanings: a meeting place and a sheltered place. Anderson compiled the 1723 *Constitutions*, and thereby provides the first, or surviving, written connection between the *Old Charges* supposedly associated with the stonemasons of the medieval period and the Masonic movement then developing. The *Old Charges* are now largely discredited as a source for establishing the pedigree of Freemasonry, and are considered as documents that were probably written to substantiate the credibility of the stonemason's guilds in seeking higher rates of pay for the work they did, or applications for being granted charter status. Anderson would probably have been unaware of such background. Yet, the 1730 disclosure of *Masonry Dissected* by Samuel Pritchard, uses the term 'Lodge' quite freely, and makes the comment:

> No constituted Lodges or Quarterly Communications were heard of until 1691...

This was at the height of yet another oscillation in political and religious turmoil, with James II Stuart of England having fled the country and been deemed to have abdicated against the background of concern about a possible Catholic revival. It was the start of the period when Jacobites were contemplating how to restore the Stuarts to the throne.

It is my conjecture (and I stress mine alone), that there were men who were indifferent to any specific religious persuasion and adopted the Old Testament and translations of Josephus by Thomas Lodge as a way of distancing themselves from persecution, should there be another bout of religiously inspired political turmoil, while at the same time being seen to support a Christian religious sentiment. Furthermore, by concentrating on the Old Testament they were distancing themselves from the turmoil that surrounded events recorded in the New Testament.

In Pritchard's *Masonry Dissected*, the use of the word 'Lodge' is not necessarily a connection with a place where the operative masons undertook their work.

Thus, in an allegorical context, 'Lodge' would be a reference to the works of Josephus as first translated by Thomas Lodge, while in the operative sense it refers to the meeting place or sheltered place where the work was undertaken. Allegorically, therefore, it has a dual meaning.

What we can see in this is that by comparing the text of Pritchard's disclosure of 1730 and the ceremonial aspects of later years, the religious overlay in the ceremonies suddenly appears. This may be entirely due to the influence of Dr James Anderson when he compiled the enlarged *Constitutions* that was published in 1738, having received his doctorate after the publication of his 1723 edition.

## Masonic Memory Review 3

We have seen how ceremonial aspects mentioned in Pritchard's *Masonry Dissected* have a connection with Masonic ceremonies, even today. Unlike some later disclosures, this pamphlet did not set out to ridicule the *society* or *fraternity* that then existed, but appears to be a genuine reflection of ceremonies that were worked at that time. Whereas, nearly all writers up to the mid-20th century have homed in on the date 1717 as being associated with the origins of Freemasonry, Pritchard makes it clear that there was an organisation of substance in place in 1691. This is, perhaps, overlooked in favour of the time when aristocratic members became more closely associated with the ultimate development of the organisation.

The table of comparison with the text of Josephus, the King James Version of the Bible and more recent translations show that there have been quite significant text changes due to the correction of original translation errors, such as with *bronze* and *brass,* but there is a clear connection with Josephus in our ceremonies.

The Presbyterian Church was an equally significant organisation in England and Scotland in the era when the two nations came together to create the United Kingdom of Great Britain, in the reign of Queen Anne. Two of the prominent men associated with the Presbyterian Church in London around the time that Freemasonry was formalised were James Anderson, of 1723 *Constitutions* fame, and William Whiston, for his translation of Josephus. This seems too much of a coincidence.

Noting that Freemasonry is a *system of morality veiled in allegory and illustrated by symbols*, the connection between Thomas Lodge, the Masonic use of the term *Lodge* and Josephus as a source of Masonic ceremonial, also seem too coincidental. The result suggests that there may have been very little religious text reflected in Masonic ceremonies prior to 1717, but this was added to through the 1723 *Constitutions* and enlarged by drawing references from Josephus by Lodge and Whiston. Using this as a template, the more elaborate moral aspects and associated religious text references were then drafted by the Reverend Samuel Hemming.

*Chapter 7*

# Freemasonry and ancient architecture – lost and found

WE SHOULD REMEMBER THAT the organisation uses the term Freemason or *Free-mason*. The word *free* in this context is a reflection of a man in the late medieval period who was not a peasant or serf or otherwise literally owned by a lord, but a person who had completed a seven-year apprenticeship in a specific trade in order to be admitted to a guild and take on work for his own account, or someone who had bought their freedom. Being *free* also had other benefits, such as being able to take part in elections, not having to pay taxes in order to sell his wares at local fairs and so on, while the word *mason* implies a person skilled in working with stone. In the medieval period through to the era just prior to the 1700s, it was only major structures like castles, monastic communities, cathedrals and palaces that were built with stone, so masons were also builders. As such they needed to understand all the techniques that gave a building integrity, from the laying of foundations to the role of the keystone in a rounded arch or vaulted ceiling. They also needed to know how to produce the key decorative components of the various architectural styles that developed over time, some of which carried intense symbolism.

Within the ceremonies and symbols of Freemasonry, there are many references to the tools and skills of the stonemasons. Masonic Halls are often richly decorated with images taken from the architectural styles of the classical Greek and Roman periods. Noting that the first Grand Lodge of England was formed in 1717, then in all probability we are dealing with architectural perspectives in the era that preceded it and the tools of trade needed to furnish those styles that were then fashionable. The masons would also have encountered styles from earlier periods, and would therefore have needed to understand construction methodology that applied in those instances as well.

To understand how these aspects developed in Freemasonry, we need to go back to the era just prior to the collapse of Rome.

*Author's note:*
*In the following paragraphs there is a restatement of some facts that are repeated elsewhere in the book. This is intentional so that various sections are complete in themselves.*

## The legacy of Constantine the Great

By around 300 CE, the Roman Empire was not only vast in the geographical area it covered, along with the many cultures and languages that entailed, but it was also torn by internal strife and divisions. The people of Rome worshipped many gods, and to these could be added the deities and religious practices of the many other cultures in the empire. The religion that we now know as Christianity had developed in the area at the eastern end of the Mediterranean known as the Levant, and had spread northeast through Turkey where it was well established around the ancient city of Ephesus, along the Mediterranean coast of North Africa, where it crossed into southern Spain and then, tradition has it, up through Santiago de Compostella to Ireland, and thence into the border area between Scotland and England from where it fanned out throughout Britain.

Constantius Chlorus, a Roman Emperor, had come to Britain in 305 CE and established himself at York, from where he launched attacks against the Picts in the highlands of Scotland who had been raiding the settlements in Northern England and generally causing much disturbance in that area. Chlorus was joined in York by his son, Flavius Valerius Aurelius Constantine, later to be known as Constantine the Great. Chlorus died at York in 306 CE, but before finally passing he recommended his son as his successor.

Constantine realised that to cement his position he needed to return to Rome where a number of usurpers were claiming the role for themselves, which resulted in several battles between armies supporting the various claimants until Constantine rose as the victor. Rome, the city at the heart of their administration for around 600 years, was a bustling metropolis with a substantial population; streets were crowded and administrative practices were often the subject of bribery and corruption. Constantine knew that differences across the empire resulted in a lack of cohesion, and he sought a way

to rectify that situation. He decided that the administration of the empire should move away from Rome to a new centre, better equipped to deal with the its size and variety of cultures. He chose a site at the eastern end of the Mediterranean at a city known by its Greek name of Byzantion, or Byzantium in Latin. He renamed the city as New Rome, but in praise of his vision the city later became known as Constantinople. At first it was the centre of the Eastern Roman Empire, but after the fall of Rome around 450 CE it gradually became the capital of the Byzantine Empire, which in many respects was the remnants of the old Roman Empire, ruled over by an Emperor. It remained a major city of Roman inherited administration for over a thousand years, until the 15th century.

One of the other means Constantine used to consolidate his administration was by decreeing that Christianity should become the main religion throughout the empire. This led to the birth of the organised Roman Church.

As a tribute to Constantine and to commemorate the military victory that led to him becoming emperor at the Battle of Milvian Bridge, the Roman Senate allocated funds for the building of a triumphal arch in Rome. Today, this arch still stands a short distance from the Coliseum and is known as the *Arch of Constantine*.

One of the key features about the design of this triumphal arch is that it has a large opening in the centre, flanked by two smaller openings on either side. With Constantine venerated as the founding father of Roman Christianity, this concept was immortalised in the design of many ecclesiastical buildings, from cathedral doorways to windows, and simple decorative features.

**Top:** *The Arch of Constantine in Rome.*

**Above:** *The arch combination at Lincoln.*

## The creation of the West

In the seventh century, the religion of Islam had been created and established itself in the Arabian area, mainly by conquest. As its influence spread, so the domination of the Roman-Byzantium Empire shrank; then around 800 CE, several events took place that altered the course of knowledge and Western civilisation.

In Europe, a Frankish king, later known simply as Charlemagne had created a kingdom that extended from the Pyrenees and Mediterranean to the Baltic Sea, from the Atlantic and North Sea coasts of France and the low countries to the Russian border. It was a kingdom that, with few territorial exclusions, embraced the whole of both Eastern and Western Europe. He was a strong supporter of the Roman Church, and the populace of everywhere that he subdued and absorbed into his kingdom, were expected to become devout Christians. At that time, Byzantium was still officially the main centre of the empire to which both Charlemagne and the Roman Church were subservient. In a dramatic gesture of gratitude for his support, the Pope crowned Charlemagne as King of the Romans in 800 CE, which resulted in a split from Byzantine dominance based in the *East*. The Pope became the head of the Christian religion with its centre of administration remaining in Rome and Charlemagne became Emperor of a new Western Empire, with his main centre of operations based at Aachen, now part of modern Western Germany. The *West* was effectively created as well, and the foundations for another new institution, known as the *Holy Roman Empire,* were set in place. Charlemagne died in 814 CE, and over the next few centuries the peoples of the West were subjected a constant round of wars and bloodletting as various kings and nobles wrestled to gain power and territory. During this period, the works of the great philosophers were largely ignored in the West. It was the period generally referred to as the *Dark Ages.*[31]

The Emperor in Byzantium was outraged at what today we might call a *unilateral declaration of independence* by the *West,* yet despite attempts at winning back territory and regaining Rome itself, their influence was minimised and their efforts were thwarted; thus Byzantium and the West, remained two separately administered empires.

One legacy left by Constantine the Great was that Byzantium was strongly Christian with an ecclesiastical structure that evolved into what is known today as the Eastern Orthodox Church. Thus not only was the old empire divided into the two different administrative cultures, but the Christian church was also essentially divided.

At the time of the break in the empire, Byzantium was faced with the further threat of invading Islamic armies. In an effort to forge peace, the Byzantine Emperor offered to provide the Muslims with copies of the works of the great ancient philosophers and mathematicians, such as Homer, Plato, Aristotle, Euclid, Pythagoras and many others. This peace was agreed and a special study centre was established in Baghdad, where knowledge from ancient Greece was translated into Arabic. While the West stagnated in a period of internal strife and with the benefit of this vast array of knowledge obtained from Byzantium, the Islamic world went on to develop as the most sophisticated civilisation for the next 600 years, with expertise in astronomy, geometry and medicine, in particular.

Towards the end of the 11th century, Byzantium was in a fractured state just as Rome had been some seven centuries previously. A new Emperor rose to prominence as Alexis I, and found himself facing similar difficulties to those which confronted Constantine in his time. Although Byzantium would later recover under the leadership of Alexis, its armies had been heavily defeated in battles with the Islamic Seljuk Turks. Alexis feared for the future of his empire and called on the Pope and the Roman Church to support him, principally in the defence of Jerusalem – an important city for the three main religions of Christianity, Judaism and Islam. Since the victories of the Seljuk Turks, it had become increasingly difficult for Christian pilgrims to visit the Holy City, thus Pope Urban II called on the bishops and the nobles of the West to organise armies and restore access to Jerusalem and other holy places for the benefit of Christianity. This instigated the era of religious wars known as the Crusades, with Jerusalem being captured by Christian forces in the year 1100.

## Lost knowledge found

Following the conquest of Jerusalem and most of the Holy Land by the Christian armies, the works of the Greek philosophers previously translated in Baghdad, were rediscovered and sent to Rome. Over the following decades, until around 1135, the same works were translated from Arabic into Latin, including Euclid's geometrical studies. Of particular interest was the device known as the *Mandorla* created by the process of two or more interlocking circles of the same diameter, where the circumference of one intersects the centre of the other. The pattern became the basis for creating what we know as *Gothic architecture*, although in its early days it was known as the French style because it was used extensively in the rebuilding of St. Denis Cathedral, in northern France. So revered was this knowledge that it was featured in the fabric of almost every major abbey and cathedral in Britain.

***Top and above:*** *Examples of the circles that help form the basis of the pointed arch of Gothic architecture, as found in Canterbury Cathedral and the Knights Templar's round church in London.*

The *Mandorla* not only provides the basic shape of the Gothic arch, but it has many geometric characteristics that will be illustrated in later chapters. It is a very ancient symbol, and is often portrayed as the most sacred of all geometric forms. This is because the shape is similar to that of the female vulva in all human and animal life, the source of life for us all, and is therefore perceived as the source of creation. It is regarded as being so sacred that it is built into the stonework and decoration of many of the great cathedrals of Europe as well as in the stalls of Saint George's Chapel, Windsor Castle, the spiritual home of the Most Noble Order of the Garter.

***Top and above:*** *The image of the Mandorla as seen above is associated with the tomb of Charlemagne in Aachen cathedral, Germany, and (left) the great west window complete with circle to imply 'everlasting', and the seven-pointed star to signify 'creation/creator', in Chichester cathedral. Tradition has it that with the Mandorla being seen as a source of life and creation, so an image of the Christ was usually included at the centre, to imply being reborn again into the Kingdom of Heaven.*

Gothic architecture was the prominent design style in Europe from around 1135-1485 CE, when it was replaced by a more simplistic style developed in the *Renaissance*.

Just as Gothic architecture was possibly born out of the rediscovery of the works and knowledge of the ancient philosophers and mathematicians, like Euclid, so Renaissance architecture owes much to a similar rediscovery of *lost knowledge.*

Some of this *lost knowledge,* especially that associated with the Mandorla, surfaces again in Freemasonry.[32]

## Introducing Vitruvius

Some 400 years prior to Constantine the Great becoming Emperor of the Roman Empire, another Roman namely Vitruvius, set down principles of architecture that have influenced the western world for most of the past 2000 years.

Marcus Vitruvius Pollio was a Roman engineer who lived in the first century before Christ, probably between the years 80–15 BCE. Biographies, as well as his own writings, indicate that his early life was spent in the Roman army as an artilleryman. In those days, the artillery comprised mainly catapults, massive machines incorporating ropes and pulleys capable of hurling large rocks at defended positions like the walls of a city, to break them down during a siege. From these beginnings, it seems that the process of construction and the use of such machines may have led Vitruvius to take an interest in creating other types of machinery, because later in his life he developed water wheels and water-lifting screws, sundials, under-floor heating systems and a range of devices and instruments that were an invaluable aid in construction.

Vitruvius wrote an impressive work known as *On Architecture,* in which many of the terminologies used today in both architecture and construction originated.

There are several impressive translations of *On Architecture,* and the knowledge and understanding it contains still stands at the core of the study of this noble art.

It seems that Vitruvius' ideas continued to be used in both Rome and Byzantium, but gradually ceased to have any great influence through the Dark Ages in the West. Just as the works of the great Greek philosophers and mathematicians slipped into obscurity, so too the works of Vitruvius became less known. Just as those same lost works were regained and launched into a new era of understanding leading to the development of the Gothic arch style, so the rediscovery of Vitruvius' works launched yet another new era of understanding – the Renaissance.

The *lost knowledge* contained in Vitruvius' *On Architecture* was to surface unexpectedly, and have a significant influence, in Freemasonry.[33]

## Giovanni Francesco Poggio Bracciolini and Filippo Brunelleschi

After the fall of Rome around 450 CE, the knowledge and writings of many of the Greek and Roman philosophers fell into disuse. The Roman Church continued to be administered from Rome, even though the administrative centre had moved to Byzantium, and monastic communities grew across the empire. St. Anthony's monastery in Egypt is regarded as the oldest, having been founded in the fifth century. Another of the early Christian monasteries was founded around 529 CE by St. Benedict at Monte Casino in Italy, the place where the Benedictine Order was formed, to be closely followed by St. Catherine's Monastery around the year 540 CE, which still exists at the foot of Mount Sinai.[34]

By the eighth century, monasteries were numerous across the whole of the former Roman Empire. These old monasteries were centres of knowledge as well as religious devotion, and they accumulated or made copies of works of the great spiritual writers of the church like St. Bede, or produced the great illuminated religious texts such as *The Lindisfarne Gospels* and *The Book of Kells*. As time passed and the authority, dogma and influence of the Church grew, so the works of the old philosophers of Greece and Rome became less known. The manuscripts of their works sat on shelves in monastery libraries gathering dust, and the knowledge therein withered.

The Gothic style became the dominant building concept in cathedrals, monasteries, abbeys, castles and other major structures, for a period of around 400 years, towards the end of the 15th century. The dominance of the Gothic style was then overtaken by a new architectural style, that of the Renaissance. Although several prominent builders or designers were primary instigators of this change, one man, Giovanni Francesco Poggio Bracciolini, perhaps had the greatest influence, almost by accident. According to *The Catholic Encyclopaedia*, Poggio, as he is often referred to, was born in Tuscany in 1380 and died in Florence in 1459. He studied the classics and came to the attention of the Vatican where he was appointed as an Apostolic Secretary, serving several popes yet never taking Holy Orders. As a result of his interest in the classics, he began to travel and visited the libraries of several of the old monasteries, during which he discovered a number of manuscripts attributed to the ancient philosophers. Ironically, many of the monastic houses in which these manuscripts were stored had no idea they were there, the facsimiles having sat undisturbed on shelves or in cupboards for hundreds of years. As Poggio discovered them and recognised their significance, he sent them to Florence where they were translated into Latin and Italian. Poggio received great acclaim for his insight and diligence in uncovering works that had hitherto, been considered as lost forever. Among these lost works were those of Vitruvius.

Renaissance architecture was about style, proportion and the geometry of the ancient and classical civilisations. For the new Italian innovators, and others from diverse nations that would later visit Italy and study the structures created by various designers, there were many examples of forms, particularly from ancient Rome, that were easily accessible to them. Thus the styles of the pillars and the regularity of the designs – based on geometry and mathematics, incorporating rounded arches, slender supports in colonnades and hemispherical domes – replaced the heavier style of the Gothic era. Most of these structures were based on the design ideas recorded in the manuscripts of Vitruvius – *the father of architecture*.

One of the earliest innovators in the new Renaissance style was Filippo Brunelleschi, who was based in Florence where he trained in one of the art guilds and became a Master goldsmith. Fabricating exquisite items is not only about artistic interpretation but proportion and form, and for large works it is about understanding the engineering and production process to be used in order to create that item. Specialist architects as we know them today did not exist in the late Middle Ages, so what inspired Brunelleschi to take an interest in building design is something of a mystery. Maybe he saw it as an extension of an art form, but he seems to have been pursuing this interest with some vigour, even before Poggio rediscovered the lost works of Vitruvius. Several specialist architectural writers, indicate that around 1400 CE, Brunelleschi went to Rome and noted the manner and style of many of the surviving structures from the classical Roman period. It seems that the knowledge and enlightenment he gained from that visit, plus the rediscovery of Vitruvius by Poggio, provided him with sufficient knowledge to undertake several design commissions in the period 1420-1440 CE, one of which was the dome which graces Florence Cathedral. He also reintroduced pillar designs from the classical Roman period, and in so doing transformed his abilities from that of an artisan goldsmith to architect, builder and engineer.[35]

Brunelleschi was followed by many others, including Michelangelo, while Andrea Palladio is often mentioned in connection with Renaissance architecture. The person credited with introducing the Renaissance style to England, was Inigo Jones, who not only visited Italy and observed Palladio's designs but incorporated the Italian's ideas in building a number of stately homes.

The first edifice he constructed in England in the Renaissance style was the Queen's House, which today forms part of the Maritime Museum complex in Greenwich Park, London. Another was the Banqueting House in Whitehall, London. Both buildings are listed in James Anderson's *Constitutions of Freemasonry* of 1723, while Inigo Jones and Filippo Brunelleschi are also mentioned.

Aspects of the works of Vitruvius are featured in Masonic ceremonies and symbols, while the discovery made by Poggio and the circumstances of that discovery feature in a most elaborate Masonic legend. To put this into context, there are other architectural observations that need to be considered.

## Vitruvius and the First Degree lecture

At the time that Freemasonry was being regularised and promulgated, the five noble orders of architecture were Masonically defined as Doric, Ionic, Corinthian, Composite and Tuscan.

Although these five orders are quoted in the ceremony of the Degree of the *Fellow Craft*, there were originally only three and they are mentioned in the very first ceremony, that of the *Apprentice*. In the lecture that accompanies this degree, reference is made to three pillars which should form the basis of order in the world in which we live: *Wisdom, Strength* and *Beauty*. *Wisdom* entails the ability to contrive good and better ways to live; *Strength* is defined as being honest and morally steadfast, keeping going when times are difficult and the path we tread in life is rough; and *Beauty* equates with a charitable disposition and helping others so that we can be at peace inwardly, in the knowledge that we have done unto others as in similar circumstances we would wish they would do unto us. They represent an *allegorical morality* for the way we should conduct our lives on a daily basis and thereby become *pillars within our society*.

As there are no pillar designs that bear the names of *Wisdom, Strength* or *Beauty*, these attributes are represented by the three original orders of architecture, viz Doric, Ionic, and Corinthian. Indeed, in the illustration that accompanies this first lecture a Tracing Board is positioned for all of the members to see, displaying a representation of the design characteristics attributed to each. It may be remembered from an earlier chapter that, in Samuel Pritchard's *Masonry Dissected*, the three characteristics of *Wisdom, Strength* and *Beauty* formed part of the ceremony of the Entered Apprentice, and their inclusion is an allegorical reference to these three main orders of architecture.

Many of the ancient temples of Greece and Rome featured columns styled in one of the three orders of architectural design, and the place where many Masonic Lodges meet are called *Temples,* which also variously display samples of the same column designs. The definition of a temple is *a place where Heaven and Earth come together.*

In recent years, the fashion of so-called *political correctness* considered many regularly used words and expressions 'inappropriate' on the grounds that they could possibly offend others. As an example, the expression *brainstorming,* used to define a creative thinking process and used in management circles for many years, was declared *politically incorrect* by certain government authorities as it might be insulting to members of the wider community who suffered mental disabilities. During this short-lived period, the Masonic use of the word *Temple* was changed in many localities, to *Lodge Room,* because certain members of the religious establishment complained that only their organisations should use such a term and, as Freemasonry had long since declared that it was not a religion, or a substitute for religion, it had no right to it. Yet in the same era, we were encouraged to consider our bodies as *temples,* as examples of wondrous creation that we should endeavour to nurture in a fit and healthy state. Indeed, in the First Degree ceremony the new member is urged to maintain:

…a well regulated course of discipline as may best conduce to the preservation of his corporeal and mental faculties in their fullest energy, thereby enabling him to exert those talents wherein the deity has blessed him.

It's another way of describing the human body as a temple.

In his works on architecture, Vitruvius draws comparisons between the design of the human body in nature and the way in which characteristics of human and natural geometry should be used in the design of temples. Thus, on the age-old premise that a deity had designed everything in nature as well as we human beings, then by building these characteristics into the design of the structure of a temple it would indeed be a place where Heaven and Earth came together. This will be illustrated further in another few pages, but first we should look at the origins of the designs of the pillars.

Vitruvius describes the origins of the three main column styles as follows:

Corinthian columns have all their proportions like the Ionic, with the exception of their capitals. The height of the capitals renders them proportionately higher and more slender, because the height of the Ionic capital is one third of the thickness of the column, that of the Corinthian is the whole diameter of the shaft. Therefore because two-thirds of the diameter of the Corinthian columns are added to the capitals they give an appearance of greater slenderness owing to the increase in height.

Thus from the two orders, a third is produced by the introduction of a new capital. From the formation of the columns, come the names of the three styles, Doric, Ionic, Corinthian; of which the Doric came first and from early ages. For in Achaea and over the whole Peloponnese, Dorus, the son of Hellen and the nymph Phtia was king; by chance he built a temple in this style at the old city of Argos, in the sanctuary of Juno, and, afterwards, in the other cities of Achaea after the same style, when as yet the determination of the exact proportions of the order had not begun.

Afterwards the Athenians, in accordance with the responses of Apollo, and by the general consent of all Greece, founded 13 colonies in Asia at one time. They appointed chiefs in the several colonies, and gave the supreme authority to Ion, the son of Xuthus and Creusa (whom Apollo, in his responses at Delphi, had declared to be his son). He led the colonies into Asia and seized the territory of Caria. There he established the large cities of Ephesus, Miletus, Myus (of which, being swallowed up in marshy ground, the worships and vote in the League were transferred to Miletus), Priene, Samos, Teos, Colophon, Chios, Erythrae, Phocaea, Clazomcnae, Lebedos, Melite. Against Melite, because of the insolence of its citizens, war was declared by the other cities, and it was destroyed by general consent. In its place, afterwards, the city of the Smyrnaeans was received among the Ionians by the kindness of King Attalus and Arsinoe. These cities drove out the Carians and Leleges and named that region of the earth Ionia from their leader Ion, and establishing there sanctuaries of the immortal gods, they began to build temples in them.

First, to Panionian Apollo they established a temple as they had seen in Achaia. Then they called it Doric because they had first seen it built in that style.

When they wished to place columns in that temple, not having their proportions, and seeking by what method they could make them fit to bear weight, and in their appearance to have an approved grace, they measured a man's footstep and applied it to his height. Finding that the foot was the sixth part of the height in a man, they applied this proportion to the column. Of whatever thickness they made the base of the shaft they raised it along with the capital to six times as much in height. So the Doric column began to furnish the proportion of a man's body, its strength and grace.

Advancing in the subtlety of their judgments and preferring slighter modules, they fixed seven measures of the diameter for the height of the Doric column, nine for the Ionic. This order because the Ionians made it first, was named Ionic. But the third order, which is called Corinthian, imitates the slight figure of a maiden; because girls are represented with slighter dimensions because of their tender age, and admit of more graceful effects in ornament.

Now the first invention of that capital is related to have happened thus. A girl, a native of Corinth, already of age to be married, was attacked by disease and died. After her funeral, the goblets, which delighted her when living, were put together in a basket by her nurse, carried to the monument, and placed on the top. That they might remain longer, exposed as they were to the weather, she covered the basket with a tile. As it happened the basket was placed upon the root of an acanthus [a thorny flowering plant]. Meanwhile about spring time, the root of the acanthus, being pressed down in the middle by the weight, put forth leaves and shoots. The shoots grew up the sides of the basket, and, being pressed down at the angles by the force of the weight of the tile, were compelled to form the curves of volutes at the extreme parts.

Then Callimachus, who for the elegance and refinement of his marble carving was nick-named Catatechnos by the Athenians, was passing the monument, perceived the basket and the young leaves growing up. Pleased with the style and novelty of the grouping, he made columns for the Corinthians on this model and fixed the proportions. Thence he distributed the details of the Corinthian order throughout the work.

The proportions of the capital are to be arranged thus. The height of the capital with the abacus [a flat area used as a platform on top of the column as a support surface for a structure to sit on] is to equal the diameter of the bottom of the column. The width of the abacus is to be so proportioned: the diagonal lines from angle to angle are to equal twice the height of the capital. Thus the front elevations, in every direction, will have the right breadth. Let the faces be curved inward from the extreme angles of the abacus the ninth part of the breadth of the face. At the lowest part, let the capital have the diameter of the top of the column, excluding the curving away of the column into the capital, and the astragal. The thickness of the abacus is one seventh of the height of the capital.[36]

What we learn from Vitruvius is that the column sizes were based on human proportions, starting with the length of a foot being one sixth of the height of the person; that the first column style was Doric, followed by Ionic; that the main difference between the Ionic and Corinthian columns is one of height because the Corinthian has a longer capital which therefore creates the illusion of greater height and slenderness.

Although the image of the First Tracing Board is displayed in the Lodge and also in a range of books, the majority of members only tend to give them a casual glance. Yet, in the modern version of the image, we see the three architectural Orders featured in the columns shown, and the originator has cleverly pulled the Doric column to the foreground to signify it being the first, as defined by Vitruvius in the legend outlined above. With equal skill, the Corinthian column has been set forward marginally from the Ionic, to show that it is taller than the former, again as defined by Vitruvius, and to illustrate that it is tapered from the base towards the capital.

In the description by Vitruvius, mention is made of a flat supporting plate on the top of the column known as the *abacus*. Descriptions of this element note that a further derivation of the word is *abaculus*, which describes a much smaller flat component, sometimes noted as a tile. These components were frequently used in mosaics for creating a chequered pattern in a floor or a tessellated border, the flooring which is found in virtually every Lodge, and which is thereby a reflection of the building terminology associated with Vitruvius.

Another comment in the works of Vitruvius relates to perspective in design, stating that the building when drawn should be facing forward and that if a circle was described to encompass the front view, then the sides of the building diminish

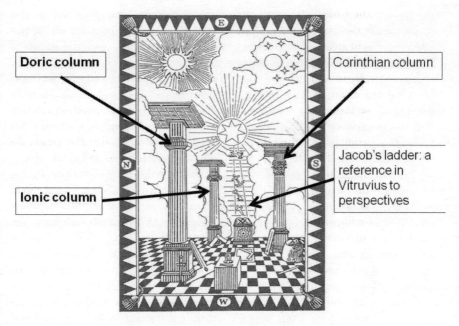

Doric column

Corinthian column

Ionic column

Jacob's ladder: a reference in Vitruvius to perspectives

*One of several patterns of design used to illustrate the First Degree Tracing Board.*

as the perspective moves backwards, to disappear into the centre-point of the circle. Thus, in the Tracing Board image we can see a representation of a block of stone on which is inscribed a circle, with the centre clearly delineated. In the background is a further image that has, in the past, often been referred to as a representation of Jacob's ladder, mentioned in the Old Testament. However, the horizontal lines in the background, often perceived to be the rungs extend unusually in an irregular fashion beyond the left and right of the supposed ladder. This illustration has more significance in a stonemasonry context, if the horizontal lines represent courses of stone blocks in a wall of a structure, while the two vertical lines imply perspective as defined by Vitruvius. Indeed, if the illustration is studied with care, then the two vertical lines, when carried downwards to the stone block which features the circle, intercept the outer diameter of the circle on the stone.

Propped against one pillar in the Tracing Board is the image of what appears to be a dagger or poniard which, as a short double-bladed dagger, was an item often carried by knights and aristocrats during the Renaissance. In consequence, the inclusion in the illustration could be an allegorical symbol which points to the era in which Vitruvius' works were discovered by Poggio. It could also represent a *Skirit,* which is a length of cord wound around a steel spike and used to mark out foundations for a building. In the First Degree ceremony, the new member is made fully aware of the importance of laying firm foundations to support the building, just as, allegorically, it is important to build firm foundations for all the enterprises one will encounter in life.

Therefore, noting that the Tracing Board image also depicts representations of a range of the tools the stonemason would use to fashion the pillars from raw stone when *setting them on their proper bases*, it is more realistic to consider the First Degree Tracing Board Image to be a reflection of Vitruvius' works, rather than Old Testament biblical imagery.

Having looked at the legends that surround the development of the three styles, as recorded by Vitruvius, there is other information that is worth noting.

The **Doric (Strength)** column/pillar was used in Ancient Greece at a very early date, probably earlier than the sixth century BCE, to support the triangular pediment that formed the entrance of a building, such as a temple. Although Doric is relatively plain in its aesthetics, it is a sturdy design that gives an impression of strength. Some books suggest that it may have been inspired by the use of tree trunks in earlier times. In the Old Testament, we learn that Solomon used trunks of cedar shipped from Tyre as structural supports for his palace, and a visit to the ancient Minoan city of Knossos on the island of Crete, shows how that was done from around 1500 BCE. Archaeologists suggest that the trunks were installed with the thicker end at the top and the ancient Greeks may have tapered their columns at the top to give an impression of greater height. Sitting directly on the pavement, slightly tapered in the length or height, and finishing with a carved smooth boss at the top, they were the main frontal support of a structure. We note from Vitruvius that their sturdy visual impact, gives the design an appearance likened to the body of a man: feet firmly on the ground, sturdy and undertaking heavy work. In the translations of Vitruvius' work (Book Four, Chapter Three), he specifies exactly how Doric columns are to be designed and the proportions applying to every part, describing the method of placing the pillars for support under a portico.

Vitruvius refers to structures of two potential widths, one with six columns in support and the other with four. It seems that in ancient Greece, the prevailing design was for six pillars (hexastyle), but in many Roman temples, there were four (tetrastyle). Dimensions are expressed in modules, not only for the pillars but also the other parts of the portico, with the module size defined by the width of the structure. In the era of 2000 years ago, a typical unit of measure was the cubit, which is used in the following examples.

If we imagine that a Roman temple is to have four pillars, then each module is 1/27th part of the width, and if it was to have six pillars then the module is 1/42nd part of the overall width. For the sake of simplicity, let us imagine that a temple is to be 42 cubits wide, then a module has a length of one cubit. The proportions of the column are defined thus:

> The diameter of the columns will be two modules, the height including the capital 14, the height of the capital is one module, the width two modules and a sixth. The height of the capital is to be divided into three parts…

Thus, in this imaginary temple, the diameter of the pillars would be two cubits, with the overall height being 14 cubits, of which one cubit will be the capital, reducing the height of the main pillar to 13 cubits. The overall width of the capital would be two modules (the diameter of the column) plus one sixth of the size of the module.

Vitruvius then goes on to define that there are to be flutes (grooves) added, and that there should be 20 of them. This is how he described the depth of the groove:

The columns ought to be fluted with 20 flutes. If the flutes are flat, the columns must have 20 vertical edges marked. But if the flutes are hollow, we must fix their form in this way: draw a square with equal sides as great as is the width of the fluting. Now in the middle of the square the centre of a circle is to be placed, and let a circle be described which touches the angles of the square; and the curve which comes between the circumference and the side of the square, will give the hollow of the flutes. Thus the Doric column will have the fluting proper to its order.

For this work, the stonemason needs a square and pair of compasses:

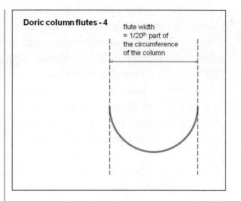

Doric column flutes - 4

flute width
= 1/20th part of
the circumference
of the column

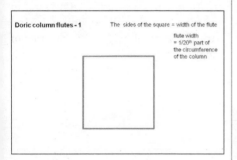

Doric column flutes - 1

The sides of the square = width of the flute

flute width
= 1/20th part of
the circumference
of the column

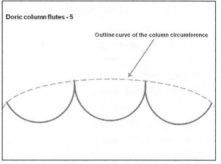

Doric column flutes - 5

Outline curve of the column circumference

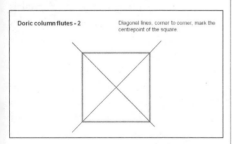

Doric column flutes - 2

Diagonal lines, corner to corner, mark the centrepoint of the square.

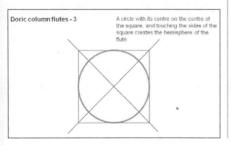

Doric column flutes - 3

A circle with its centre on the centre of the square, and touching the sides of the square creates the hemisphere of the flute

*Examples of Doric columns used in a memorial in London.*

In addition to the height and diameter, dimensions are also given to the spacing of the pillars. The architectural term is intercolumniation, which was always based on the diameter of the base of the pillar shaft, and varied depending on the style of the building. A series of words derived from the Greek language, define the spacing styles thus:

*Pycnostyle,*   *when the intercolumniation is*
                  *of one and a half diameters;*
*Systyle,*   *of two diameters;*
*Eustyle,*   *of two and a quarter diameters;*
*Diastyle,*   *of three diameters*
*Araeostyle,*   *of four diameters or more.*

Thus we now have the basic proportions and spaces that apply to the Doric column.

The **Ionic (Wisdom)** column/pillar, is arguably an improvement in aesthetics by comparison with the Doric. Wisdom, it seems, was applied to contrive and make the Ionic more attractive than the solid and sturdy Doric. It is to be noted, that Vitruvius suggests the design originated on the island of Ionia, being separately dated as having originated in the mid-sixth century BCE. More slender than the Doric version, the Ionic has a far more ornate capital which some architects attribute to eyes and eyebrows watching people as they approach. As the style developed, so the column was dressed with a series of flutes throughout the length, therefore helping to reduce the appearance of bulk. Hence, as we have noted, Vitruvius associated this slender form with the female body.

The flutes or grooves are equi-spaced around the column. In this style there are usually 24 such flutes by comparison with the 20 used in the Doric column. Although not commented on by architects, these pillars usually adorned the entrance to temples, which were centres of learning

and religious ritual to appease the gods. The possibility is that this is a reflection of known astronomical knowledge, where the column represented the circle of the earth and the flutes were a reflection of the record of time, which was measured at 15 degree intervals: 360/15 = 24. Vitruvius, however, refers to the number of these flutes, as representing the direction of the 24 winds.

*Examples of Ionic columns used in (top) a city hall in the Champagne district of France, and (above) the portal of a prestigious bank in London.*

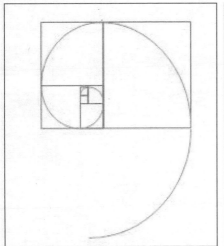

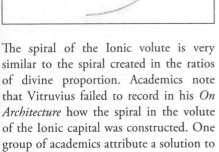

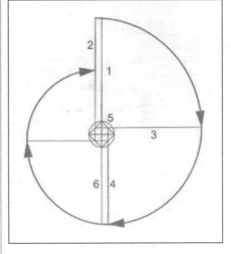

The spiral of the Ionic volute is very similar to the spiral created in the ratios of divine proportion. Academics note that Vitruvius failed to record in his *On Architecture* how the spiral in the volute of the Ionic capital was constructed. One group of academics attribute a solution to one G.P. Salviati in 1552.[37]

The **Corinthian (Beauty)** column/pillar is the most elaborate of the three, and is believed to have developed in Corinth (Greece) in the fourth century BCE. Often tall and elegant in appearance, the capitals feature the lavish decoration of leaves and flowers that protrude from the top. The columns are fluted again to reduce the appearance of bulk and are tapered towards the top and the junction with the capital, thereby creating a sense of height. They usually stand on their own square bases with a circular collar that interfaces between the shaft of the column and the base.

Vitruvius states the following in respect of the development of the Corinthian column:

...But the third order, which is called Corinthian, imitates the slight figure of a maiden; because girls are represented

with slighter dimensions because of their tender age, and admit of more graceful effects in ornament...

It is interesting to note that the proportions of most of the key components illustrated by/from Vitruvius are developed using the square and compasses.

*Below left and bottom:* Corinthian column details

*Below and bottom:* Examples of the use of the Corinthian Column in a memorial archway, London.

Vitruvius adds an association between the dimensions and form of the human body and the building of ancient temples:

The planning of temples depends upon symmetry: and the method of this architects must diligently apprehend. It arises from proportion (which in Greek is called analogia). Proportion consists in taking a fixed module, in each case, both for the parts of a building and for the whole, by which the method of symmetry and proportion is put into practice. For without symmetry and proportion no temple can have a regular plan; that is, it must have an exact proportion worked out after the fashion of the members of a finely-shaped human body.

For nature has so planned the human body that the face from the chin to the top of the forehead and the roots of the hair is a tenth part; also the palm of the hand from the wrist to the top of the middle finger is as much; the head from the chin to the crown, an eighth part; from the top to the breast with the bottom of the neck to the roots of the hair, a sixth part; from the middle of the breast to the crown, a fourth part; a third part of the height of the face is from the bottom of the chin to the bottom of the nostrils; the nose from the bottom of the nostrils to the line between the brows, as much; from that line to the roots of the hair, the forehead is given as the third part. The foot is a sixth of the height of the body; the cubit a quarter, the breast also a quarter. The other limbs also have their own proportionate measurements. And by using these, ancient painters and famous sculptors have attained great and unbounded distinction.

In like fashion the members of temples ought to have dimensions of their several parts answering suitably to the general sum of their whole magnitude. Now the navel is naturally the exact centre of the body. For if man lies on his back with hands and feet outspread, and the centre of a circle is placed on his navel, his figure and toes will be touched by the circumference. Also a square will be found described within the figure, in the same way as a round figure is produced. For if we measure from the sole of the foot to the top of the head, and apply the measure to the outstretched hands, the breadth will be found equal to the height, just like sites which are squared by rule."

Therefore if nature has planned the human body so that the members correspond in their proportions to its complete configuration, the ancients seem to have had reason in determining that in the execution of their works they should observe an exact adjustment of the several members to the general pattern of the plan. Therefore, since in all their works they handed down orders, they did so especially in building temples, the excellences and the faults of which usually endure for ages.[38]

From the proportions shown in the two images, we then get the image of

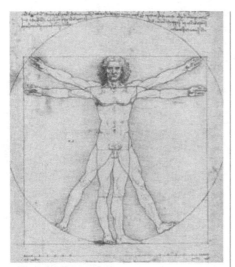

Vitruvian Man that was developed by Leonardo Da Vinci.

Having dealt with the three primary orders of classical architecture, there are two others bringing the total to five.

## Composite Column.

This is a style that does not appear in the writings of Vitruvius, but seems to have evolved about 150 years after his death, and is generally regarded as a simplified version or combination of Ionic and Corinthian columns.

Around 69 CE, there was a revolt by the Jews in Israel against Roman rule. It concluded in 70 CE when remaining rebels committed suicide at Masada, followed by the destruction of the Herodian Temple in Jerusalem. The general in charge of the campaign for the Roman Empire was Titus, who was received with great acclaim on his return to Rome, with the erection of a triumphal arch in his honour. Architectural historians note that this arch, when built around 80 CE, may well have been the first use of the Composite style.

## Tuscan Column

This style is not featured in the works of Vitruvius, which has led to a debate amongst architects as to its origins. A view has been expressed that it pre-dates the Doric, but there is no evidence to support that view. However, it was recorded in Italy, in the 16th century, that while the Tuscan design bore great similarity to the fluted form of the Doric, its shaft was plain and it had a slightly more ornate top plate. Because of its strength, it was favoured and used in large multilevel buildings such as concert halls, where strong pillars are required at the ground level to support two or three tiers of balconies above.

So why were these five orders of architecture, and particularly the three mentioned in Vitruvius, included in Masonic ceremonies that may have originated 300 years ago?

From around the ninth century CE, a style of architecture known as Romanesque, came to the fore. It is believed to have started in the Frankish kingdom, possibly in Aachen, which today is in West Germany, not far from the border with the Netherlands, in an area that embraces France, Germany and the Low Countries. Its structural concept was strong, enabling substantial and relatively large buildings to be constructed, but to its detriment it looked heavy and the interior of buildings were quite dark.

In the early 12th century, just after the start of the religious conflicts known as the Crusades, contact with Islamic forces brought an awareness of a range of geometry that had been almost lost in the Western world of Europe. This was the geometry of Pythagoras and Euclid, along with the works of various philosophers of Ancient Greece. When these works were translated from Arabic into Latin, the possibility of a new style of architecture was revealed which became known as the French Style, or what today is called *Gothic*. The main characteristic of this concept is the pointed arch, a style first used in a redevelopment of part of the Cathedral of St Denis, in the Northern suburbs of Paris, just south of Charles de Gaulle airport. Not only did this arch prove to be as strong as the Romanesque, but it had the advantage of a higher level of light penetration, thereby enabling the vast interiors of large structures like cathedrals, to enjoy the benefit of beams of light that appeared to cut in shafts through the gloom. Its additional advantage was that less stone was required in the construction, and hence less cost. Within a few years of the start of construction at St. Denis, the French Style, or Gothic, had become the dominant building technique across Europe.

At Rochester, the foundations of the second oldest cathedral in England were established only a few years after the arrival of St Augustine in Canterbury, showing a clear dividing line between the two styles. The pointed arch enabled the installation of large windows, and the interiors were thereby transformed from *darkness into light*.

*Rochester Cathedral, founded 604 CE. The dividing line between the Romanesque and Gothic styles also illustrates the strength of the arch, while removing all the work associated with creating the Romanesque second tier.*

## From Renaissance classical to Baroque

The rise and spread of Protestantism in the 16th century resulted in the Catholic Church seeking a new architectural style to underpin its status. The result, from around 1600, was a composite design that embraced elements of both *Renaissance* and *Classical* architecture. This new style became known as *Baroque*.

Both the Gothic and the Renaissance architectural styles had resulted in buildings that were quite plain in appearance, except where decoration was added around a doorway. Baroque, however, was a new, very extravagant style that took the basic concept of Renaissance and embellished the outward appearance, with some of the French and Italian works being particularly ornate. However, when it was introduced into Britain, primarily by Sir Christopher Wren after the Great Fire of London, the opulence was more restrained.

*St. Paul's Cathedral, London in the restrained Baroque style.*

Towards the end of the 18th century, a further architectural style evolved which was even more ornate than Baroque. It was used more for interiors and ornamentation, and was more of an extravagant art form than a building style. It was known as Rococo.

*For image, see colour section plate 14.*

In the following timeline chart, while it's not intended to be purist or definitive we can see the main styles and the periods over which they were particularly prominent. What is also evident is that regular Freemasonry was formed during an era when three major styles were current: Renaissance, Baroque and Neoclassical, all of which were influenced by the design approach of the Roman engineer Vitruvius, who is often referred to as the *father of architecture*. While his artistic approach was similar to that of the ancient Greeks, it was additionally based on geometrical knowledge, and by combining these two strands, plus the additional influence of the beauty of the natural world and the human form, it became embodied in the architecture of the Roman Empire. When the empire in the West collapsed in the fifth century, Vitruvius' work was largely ignored, but interest in it was rekindled in the 15th century, at the time of the Renaissance.

With Freemasonry seriously developing at a time when three architectural styles were current, and being associated by name with the process of building in stone, it is not surprising to find references in the ceremonies of the organisation. Perhaps, however, what is more important is the knowledge behind the façade.

## Masonic Memory Review 4

What we can see through the contents of this chapter is how a number of historical events led to the knowledge of the ancient philosophers and mathematicians, like Plato, Euclid and Pythagoras, being largely ignored in Western Europe from the time that Rome collapsed in the fifth century, until it was rediscovered during the Crusades around 1100 CE. The re-emergence of this knowledge led to the development of the Gothic arch around 1135 CE, based upon the geometric image known as the Mandorla, a device that features in Masonic ceremonies and symbols.

Poggio Bracciolini discovered a copy of the manuscript of Vitruvius in 1415 CE, a find that was to inspire the evolution of Renaissance architecture. With it came Neoclassical innovations by men such as Brunelleschi and Palladio, and through their efforts a new design philosophy was developed in the late Middle Ages that was subsequently reflected in public buildings, edifices of state and the country estates of the aristocracy across Britain.

Freemasonry was formalised in 1717, at a time when the three main architectural styles of Renaissance, Baroque and Neoclassical were commonly used in major structures, the Gothic period having ended.

These ancient classical designs feature in the First Degree lecture of Freemasonry, albeit in allegorical representation, and a study of the key components devised by Vitruvius shows that, if the results are to be kept in proportion to the natural world and the human form, the use of two vital implements are required, namely the square and compasses.

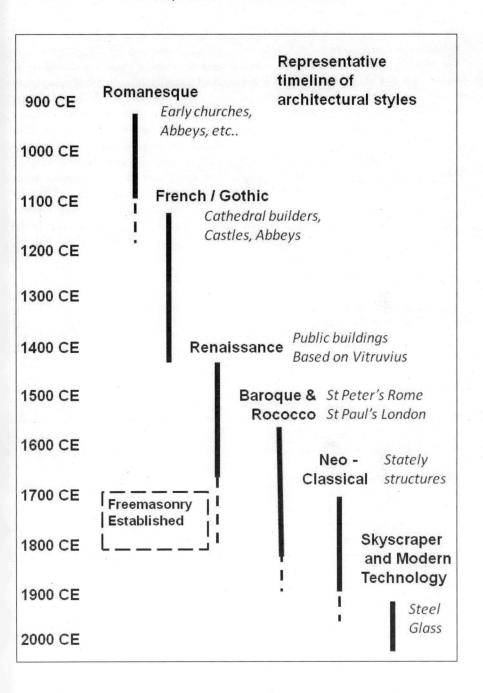

*Chapter 8*

# Decoding tracing allegory

THE TRACERY IN THE windows of some of the great cathedrals and churches of Europe provided the robust structure that supported the weight of the stained glass. Crafted in intricate shapes, the glass of the windows often comprising an array of bright colours when set against the light of the sun is always a source of great admiration to observers, while the tracery itself is often presented in patterns which reflect the geometric expertise of the Master Masons who built them.

The word *tracery* comes from the *tracing floors* used by the Medieval masons, to delineate their plans, in what have become known as the *mason's loft*. Today, only two major such floors exist in Britain, one in York Minster and the other at Wells.

When a member of a Lodge has made sufficient progress in his understanding of the Masonic institution and demonstrated a firm grasp of the knowledge expected of an Apprentice, he is permitted to pass to the next level, that of the Fellow Craft. In the days of the guilds, an apprenticeship lasted for seven years, and a novice being trained was required to live in with his master and his family for the entire period. When the trainee had completed his apprenticeship, he would literally be cast from the home of the master to fend for himself. The superior would thus have completed his obligations to the apprentice – the contracted period being at an end. While the apprentice had been trained in the *secrets and mysteries* of his trade, he lacked a breadth of experience and it was therefore necessary for him to seek new employment, sometimes travelling from town to town to gain work. The term used to describe his status during this period of gaining experience was *journeyman*. Only after a further seven years of expanding his knowledge and experience could he officially be regarded as a qualified tradesman and apply to become a member of a guild. In Freemasonry, the *journeyman* is termed a Fellow Craft who having completed his basic training is required to

*A wonderful stained glass window in Chichester cathedral, at the eastern end of the great church, shows intricate tracery and geometric patterns. (K. L. Gest)*

seek further experience, and with which knowledge he can hope to pass to the next level of Master Mason.

The process of passing from an Apprentice to a Fellow Craft is undertaken ceremonially, and his additional period as a *journeyman* commences with a lecture that brings together further trade *secrets and mysteries* he will need to know. This knowledge is presented to him in the form of a drawing called a Tracing Board, the contents of which are then explained to him.

As repeatedly mentioned, the first Grand Lodge in England was formed in 1717, and the regulations of the fraternity were first published in *The Constitutions of the Free-Masons,* compiled by Dr James Anderson in 1723. The first *Constitutions* make no reference to the Second Degree Tracing Board, in text or image. The earliest positive mention is in *The Ceremonies of Initiation, Passing and Raising: with copious notes as regards the duties of the master, wardens, deacons etc...* compiled and published by George Claret in 1838. The presentation of this work as a small, pocket-sized, blue-covered book seems to be the prototype on which nearly all subsequent printed editions of the ceremonies, were based. We learn that the text of the Second Degree Tracing Board, as used in Lodges today, is approximately 200 years old. If it is older than that, then its origins probably fall into the gap of one hundred years, viz the 18th century, wherein detailed Masonic information is less than clear. If the text of the Tracing Board was only 200 years old something very much older may have been in use prior to that time.

The print was barely dry on Doctor Anderson's *Constitutions,* before there appeared a range of so-called 'disclosures' about Masonic ceremonies, describing what happened at meetings and who was alleged to have been present. These disclosures were often in the form of small low-cost pamphlets, which in some cases were clearly distributed to make money for the writer and were obvious works of fiction. There were others written by individuals who were probably members of a Lodge, who were either being mischievous and trying to make money for themselves, or attempting to throw readers off the scent. Other disclosures were of real substance, although not particularly enlightening except to those who were aware of the ceremonial background. However, some do mention the practice of drawing with chalk by the use of a cord upon the floor or a sheet, lighted candles arranged in the shape of a triangle and the symbolic representation of a builder's square, hanging from a ribbon or chain around a Master's neck. There is a distinct difference between such markings and symbols and the illustrations and imagery associated with the text of the Second Degree Tracing Board, as recorded in the 1838 Claret edition of the ceremonies.

## Origins – circumstantial

One of the earliest records of someone becoming a Freemason is that of Elias Ashmole at Warrington, Lancashire, in the year 1646, details of which are recorded in abundance elsewhere. Around the same time there was also Sir Robert Moray, a close companion of Charles II, and an influential founder of the Royal Society. In 1686, in a book entitled *The Natural History of Staffordshire,* Dr Robert Plot noted that there existed a *Society of Free-Masons* and that it was:

> ...spread more or less all over the nation; for here I found persons of most eminent quality, that did not distain to be of this fellowship.

To have '…spread' over the nation suggests a common root that was inspirational and stimulated widespread appeal. This was in an era when communication methods across Britain had developed little since Roman times; one walked between places, rode a horse if one had the good fortune to own one, or was conveyed in a carriage or trap if one was of sufficient wealth. Just travelling between two major towns 60 miles/100 km apart was an arduous process. So for circumstances to result in any form of organisation spreading 'more or less all over the nation', suggests that some exceptional motivation had inspired it. There is perhaps an answer.

The peoples of earlier periods were not as backward as sometimes conjectured from our lofty position in the 21st century. There is evidence that even 2000 years ago, people living close to Stonehenge held special rites associated with death in their community. Even before the era of Alfred the Great, King of Wessex, it appears that community responsibilities existed over standard funeral rites. These seem to have developed into *religious guilds* which were a form of mutual club, evolving after the upheavals of the Norman conquest, into which members made a regular financial contribution so that when they were unable to work, aged or sick, they would then be cared for by other members of the guild, even providing monies which were graded for married couples or those that were alone. *The Catholic Encyclopaedia* notes:

> The Church encouraged these associations, but it was the members of the guild who personally administered its affairs, such as almsgiving, assistance to those setting out on pilgrimages, repairing churches and the establishment of free schools.

These *religious guilds* were financially supported by leading clergy, city aldermen, merchants and landowners, as well as free men who invested in them. Almost every major town in the country had at least one such guild and in some towns there were several.[39]

When Henry VIII broke from the Catholic Church and papal authority to establish the Church of England, the religious guilds were abolished because they represented groups of individuals over which the state had no control, and which might well have provided a secretive base for revolution. Although these guilds were abolished, the money they had accumulated was not usually confiscated, as it seems that a high number merely ceased to call themselves guilds and changed their designation to *societies or fraternities*. It is highly probable that, as the merchant guilds developed and regular trade extended across Europe, so some of the money held in the guilds and fraternities would have been invested in various merchant schemes to increase the value of the funds, such as financing shipments of wool to Flanders where English wool was regarded as amongst the finest.

When the Protestant Church of England was created, an entirely new administration structure had to be developed. Some members of the clergy under the Catholic Church would have transferred to the new regime, while some were new appointees who would have been aware of the existence of the religious guilds. Indeed, when the guilds were abolished the merchant guilds in London were exempt and became the great livery companies we know of today, one of which was the London Company of Masons. In his book, *The Hole Craft and Fellowship of Masons* published in 1894, Edward

Condor, a former Master of the London Company of Masons, notes that in his opinion, while the London Company had a responsibility for the skills and conduct of the trade, there were members of the Company who were also members of a separate organisation or *society of Free-masons*. Every major town and city in the country had a guild of masons, and attached to almost every guild were religious guilds which were, predominantly, local charities. It is therefore not difficult to imagine that as the new Church of England became established, bishops encouraged the continuation of these *societies and fraternities* because of the community-based charitable function they provided. They cemented the new religious order, providing money for repairs and maintenance to ecclesiastical buildings, pensions and assistance to their poor members as a social service; and, perhaps more importantly, they paid the clergy for funerals. The bishops were builders of a new Church structure, and the main operative builders of the 16th century were the masons. This would explain how the society came to be 'spread more or less all over the nation', and seems to have existed unchallenged, despite the political turmoil taking place. It would also underline the key feature of Freemasonry from the time it was formalised – that of Charity.

Returning to Elias Ashmole, we note that he was made a Freemason in 1646, and records show that he was initiated into a group of men who were landowning gentry, the type of individual who was likely to have invested money in a religious guild or fraternity. There seem to be no records of Ashmole attending meetings or having any other association with the society until March 1682, when he noted in his diary that:

About 5H.PM. I rec'd a Summons to appear at a Lodge to be held the next day at Masons Hall, London.

It is curious that somebody, presumably at the London Company, knew of his being a Freemason, and consequently invited him to a meeting. He attended Lodge, and wrote in his diary:

...I was the senior fellow amongst them (it being 35 years since I was admitted)...

In this single sentence he implies that he had enjoyed some form of continuous membership over the previous 35 years. Ashmole then goes on to name a total of 16 individuals, including himself, who were at the meeting, from which we can deduce that at least six were being admitted as new members at that meeting. Four of those candidates were members of the London Company, which infers that two were not: therefore being a member of the London Company was not a qualification for attending this particular Lodge gathering. At the end of the meeting, all sixteen men retired to have dinner together, of which 14 were, by this time, known to have been Freemasons[40].

It seems clear that this social gathering, with a Lodge of which several members were involved with the London Company and several others were not, may well have been an anomaly as well as a difficulty for the company itself. Hence, they would have wanted to distance themselves from it, as its meetings were not directly associated with the affairs of building and shaping stone for actual work, as dictated by the charter which the Company had received just five years previously. The Charter was awarded in the same year in which the foundations for the new St. Paul's Cathedral were laid.[41] This raises the tantalising possibility that this meeting was the first step in the process of establishing a totally separate organisation, noting that, according to Samuel Pritchard in *Masonry Dissected,* 'there was no organisation or quarterly communications in place prior to 1691', whilst at the same time implying that there was a society in place and holding meetings, but not with a single structure of authority.

As is the case in almost all writings that mention Masonic origins prior to 1717, only so much is presented in the written word. If we tabulate some of the key events that affected Freemasonry and England through the 1600s, we can see that mention of Freemasonry, or the events that may have shaped it, were not spasmodic *(see Table of Events leading to 1717)* There were also a series of events that were major steps in the development of the British nation. The Royal Society was founded shortly after Charles II returned from exile, commencing authorised study and reporting on subjects that were associated with *nature* and *science.* The Royal Observatory at Greenwich specifically studied astronomy and, no doubt, quickly confirmed that Copernican theory had credibility, just a few years after Galileo had been tortured and sentenced to life imprisonment by house arrest and poor Giordano Bruno had been burnt alive by Catholic authorities for believing much the same.

From 1701–1714 there had been the wars of the Spanish Succession, which resulted in the establishment of a *balance of power* across Western Europe. Had Britain and its allies which formed the Grand Alliance failed in that conflict, then the British would, almost inevitably

have been forced to succumb to Papal authority and the whims of a French king. And one cannot fail to note that the Great Fire resulted in the construction of one of the largest and most impressive buildings that London was to see for the next few centuries: St. Paul's Cathedral, in the construction of which *an immense number of masons were employed.* Some of these events were so momentous that they are worth recording in Masonic memory.

## The Tracing Board appears

According to eminent researchers, in the 18th century the shape of the Lodge, a rectangle which was embellished with various other designs, was drawn on the floor of the meeting room by the Tyler, using chalk or charcoal, and erased after the meeting. It was the rectangle that was said to be the Lodge, not the room in which they met. The members would then gather around the drawing. Just as the term *tracery* in stained glass windows is derived from the *tracing floor* in the mason's loft, so too is derived the more recent term of *Tracing Board.*

The *Tracing Board* is believed to represent those that the Master Masons of the medieval period used for sketching out plans. The generally accepted view is that tracing boards of the medieval operative masons were shallow trays filled with a soft plaster into which they would scratch images to illustrate a completed building for the approval of the client, or components of the structure before committing them to a much bigger plan, which would be etched into a *tracing floor* to create drawings that the mason would work from, or from which carpenters could build templates.

*For images, see colour section plates 8 & 9*

Table of Events leading to 1717        Item* The History of English Freemasonry – John Hamill

| Year Affect on FM | Year Event affecting Britain | Notes |
|---|---|---|
| 1599 | | Apprentice Act signed Elizabeth I – crafts trades apprenticeships 7 years minimum |
| | 1600 | East India Company formed |
| | 1603 | Elizabeth I died. James I/IV ascends the throne of England |
| 1603 | 1603 | Thomas Lodge publishes first translation - Works of Josephus |
| 1621 | | London Co Masons admit *speculative masons* |
| 1646 | | *Elias Ashmole made a free-mason at Warrington* |
| | 1660 | Restoration of the monarchy – Charles II |
| 1660 | 1660 | Royal Society founded. Elias Ashmole and Sir Robert Moray amongst the founding members – *both recorded as freemasons* |
| | 1665 | The Great Plague |
| | 1666 | The Great Fire of London – Old St Paul's destroyed |
| | 1669 | Christopher Wren given task of designing new St Paul's |
| | 1670 | Site of old St Paul's cleared for new building |
| | 1670 | Royal Charter issued to the Governor and Company of England trading into Hudson Bay - the Hudson Bay Company |
| | 1675 | Royal Observatory established at Greenwich – astronomy. |
| | 1675 | Foundation stone for new St Paul's is laid with great ceremony on 21st June – Summer Solstice. Building oriented to sunrise on that day. |
| 1676 | | Mention of Masons in *Poor Robins Intelligence*. * |
| 1677 | 1677 | Charter of Incorporation of the London Company of Masons |
| 1682 | | Ashmole attended *Lodge meeting at Masons Hall* |
| | 1685 | Death Charles II. James II ascends to the throne |
| 1686 | | Dr Robert Plot mentions freemasons favourably in *Natural History of Staffordshire*. |
| | 1688 | Son of James II born to Mary of Modena. Fear of Catholic rights to throne. |
| | 1688 | Glorious revolution. Mary II + William III joint monarchs. |
| 1688 | | Randle Holme 3rd wrote – *"I cannot but honour the Fellowship of the Masons because of its antiquity: and the more as being [myself] a member of that Society called Freemasons."* |
| 1692 | 1692 | Elias Ashmole died. |
| | 1695 | Rise of Jacobites – Cheshire Gentlemen |
| 1696 | | Organisation and quarterly communications of freemasons *(Pritchard – Masonry Dissected)* |
| | 1702 | William III died – riding accident. Queen Anne becomes monarch |
| | 1707 | Act of Union between England and Scotland |
| | 1704 | Duke of Marlborough secures victory at Battle of Blenhiem. Estimated that some 42,000 men were casualties of which over 35,000 were enemy troops. |
| | 1708 | The last stone laid in St Paul's cathedral – on lantern at top. |
| | 1711 | The South Sea Company formed – South Sea bubble |
| | 1711 | St Paul's building completed. Declared officially complete by parliament 25 December – Christmas day. |
| | 1713/4 | End of war of Spanish Succession. |
| | 1715 | Jacobite uprising in Scotland |
| 1716 | | Meeting to consider one Masonic body of authority |
| 1717 | | First Grand Lodge – premier Grand Lodge of England |
| 1723 | | Andersons *Constitutions* published |
| | 1723 | Sir Christopher Wren died |
| | 1727 | Sir Isaac Newton Died |
| 1730 | | Samuel Pritchard publishes *Masonry Dissected* |
| 1732 | 1732 | William Whiston publishes translation Works of Josephus |
| 1738 | | Dr Anderson publishes *revised Constitutions*. |

The images *(see plates 8 & 9)* are of a drawing on display in Reims Cathedral, illustrating various processes and trades associated with the construction of that cathedral. One can clearly see the Master and Architect for the project at his tracing board, on which rests a right-angle square with a measuring rod leaning against it.

In the top left-hand corner of the enlarged image (right) is an effigy from the tomb of Hugues d'Libergier, who in the year 1231 was the Master Mason who built the cathedral. In his hands he holds a measuring rod and model of the cathedral, while in the lower left corner is a right-angle square and in the lower right corner is a pair of compasses – the primary tools of a Master Mason.

*Tracing floors* were usually a large area of plaster into which the actual size of components to be constructed were measured and etched. Some such floors still exist in the lofts of the great cathedrals of York and Wells, where vestiges of the original etched plans can still be seen.

In the 1760 pamphlet *Three Distinct Knocks*, an image of a typical floor drawing is shown. Its context has been the subject of much debate amongst Freemasons for decades.

Yet again, by looking outside of the organisation we may find an answer.

The 17th century was the period when many of the great houses of the aristocracy were built in the architectural styles of the Renaissance and classical Greek influences, following the development of the ideas introduced by Inigo Jones through the construction of the Queen's House at Greenwich and the Banqueting House in Whitehall. If indeed the present Masonic organisation was derived from the operative masons, then in the 17th Century they were probably aware of at least the tracing floor at York, or knowledge of it was symbolised and passed down to them in a ceremonial manner. A visit to York Minster reveals a mason's loft, the design of which closely resembles the drawing in *Three Distinct Knocks*, even down to the perspective of standing at one end and looking across the floor to the far wall.

*The inside of the mason's loft at York.*

It would be logical that, when the Master Mason in charge of construction had etched his drawing on the tracing floor, he would call together those skilled masons who were to execute the design and explain what was wanted. They would clearly have to gather around the drawing that had been etched. Thus, by drawing the shape of the York tracing floor, and standing around it, the members were enacting exactly the process that would have been used hundreds of years previously for the Master to communicate what was required. Hence, the *loft* became the *Lodge*.

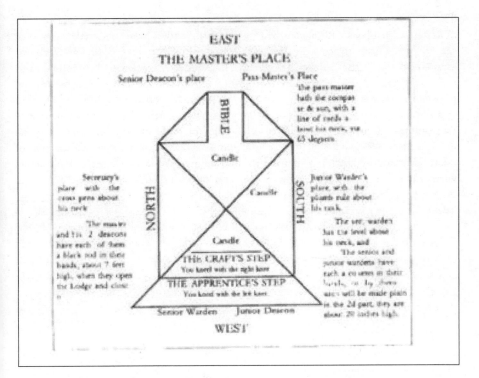

The drawing as illustrated in Three Distinct Knocks.

In the drawing illustrated in *Three Distinct Knocks*, the foreground is presented as three steps or levels, the breadth of which is determined by the square with the diagonal cross. In the photograph of the York loft, there is a staircase that goes at an angle towards the ceiling. Using that angle and the line of the wall to the left (prior to the walkway being added to protect the floor) gives the perspective of the width of the levels. It would appear that the second diagonal was added merely to provide the balance. The three levels are noted as being the Apprentice Step, the Crafts Step and, finally, the Master's Step. It would perhaps be logical that if the Master was to explain the rationale behind a design, he might gather together the relevant individuals with the skills of the trade he expected to be involved, hence the more skilled sculptor masons would be to the front, the journeymen (Fellow Craft) would be behind them, and the apprentices, if invited, would be at the back. It was a way of illustrating the hierarchy.

This development of the floor cloths and drawings seems to have been in place from the very earliest days of the Premier Grand Lodge. An outline of such a drawing is also shown in *Masonry Dissected* of 1730, after which there are frequent references to their use in a range of surviving Lodge documents.

It is believed that the process of drawing the Lodge on the floor became somewhat cumbersome, and that as an alternative the images were painted onto cloths that could be unrolled, and, equally importantly, rolled up again and placed in safe storage. Thus the suggestion is that the concept of the tracing boards was developed from some of the illustrations drawn on such cloths, and over time they ceased to be placed on the floor but were draped over tables or chairs, beyond which the next stage was for them to be tacked to wooden frames in order to be easily transported and stored. For the benefit of the candidate, they could then be displayed in the vertical plane, and today the Tracing Board illustration is usually placed in view whilst the lecture is in progress. Some evidence suggests that early Tracing Boards were placed on a trestle in the centre of the Lodge room floor, while today most Lodges place the candidate in the centre of the floor and the trestle at a location where all members can see it.

*For images, see colour section plate 13.*

The illustration *(see plate)* is from the early 1800s, when the United Grand Lodge of England was being formed. It shows a small group of members of a Lodge gathered around a floor cloth whilst a ceremony is in progress. In the cluster at the rear of the illustration, the Masters are in the front row whilst the Apprentices, we assume, are pushed to the back.

Beyond the 1760s there was a different form of *development*. This was attributable to William Preston, who in 1772 published his book *Illustrations of Masonry* and went on to develop what he defined as a system of lectures. He even established classes and gave lessons about the lectures with the view that the recipients of the information would spread his philosophy, which led to others following his lead.

Some of those responsible for early Tracing Board developments were John Cole, John Browne, Josiah Bowring, John Harris and Arthur Thiselton. Cole, Browne and Bowring seem to have been active between 1800–1820, whilst Harris and Thiselton arrived on the scene after the United Grand Lodge of England was formed.[42]

John Browne was a printer who developed a range of lectures of his own and supplied various Masonic materials, like certificates and summons, as well as some of the earliest coloured Tracing Boards designed to illustrate the subject matter contained in a lecture. Around the turn of the 18th-19th centuries, Browne is believed to have been a resident of Bride Street, London, an address just off Fleet Street and not far from St. Paul's Cathedral, a building he would have seen in all its glory almost every day. He was a member of at least one London Lodge, and wrote the details of Masonic ceremonies in a code which was called the *Master Key*.[43]

To recap, by the 1800s there were two main Grand Lodges: the Premier Grand Lodge, alias the *Moderns*, and the Grand Lodge of the *Antients,* each with their own ceremonies and customs. There was also a third calling itself *The Grand Lodge of All England,* based at York, but this institution, although appearing to have a reasonable following at various times, disappeared from the scene in 1792. Thus, by the time of the formation of the United Grand Lodge of England, the Lodges of Promulgation and Reconciliation had been temporarily created to aid the union process, and the two Grand Lodges were sources of ceremonial input. There was also a substantial development in a range of lectures that may have evolved after the 1760s and then been enhanced by the appearance of the Tracing Boards.

*For images, see colour section plate 5 & 6.*

Returning to Samuel Pritchard's *Masonry Dissected* of 1730, and Anderson's

*Constitutions* of 1723, there appears to be no reference in either to the contents of this second lecture, thereby suggesting it was a later addition. It is well recorded by other researchers that the ceremonies of Freemasonry went through changes in the middle of the 18th century. The term normally used to define these changes was that the *ceremonies were being developed.* Thus the implications are that there were ceremonial aspects that existed prior to 1700 which may have changed after 1723, when the first *Constitutions* was published along with statements concerning *Old Charges.* It is to be further noted that from the 1730s, it seems that there was an influx of people to London who were Freemasons, having originated from Ireland or Scotland and sought to join London Lodges. Some of them were refused, perhaps because of minor variances in proceedings, noting that both these countries had their own Grand Lodge systems. This led to the formation of the *Antients* Grand Lodge, which is then believed to have resulted in further developments in ceremonial content around 1750s–60s. From then until the end of the 18th century, little of the ceremonial content changed, by which time several so-called disclosures had appeared. These revelations were mainly short pamphlets that the authors alleged revealed to the public what occurred in Masonic gatherings. There was clearly some public appetite for this information because several were reprinted many times. The contents of most of these disclosures are of little relevance and are grossly misleading, as one gains the impression that they were fictitious works penned for the purpose of earning the writer some extra income. There was however, one disclosure other than Pritchard's *Masonry Dissected* that has some relevance: *Three Distinct Knocks (1760).* This pamphlet

reveals a ceremonial structure similar to that in use today, but there is no mention of the Second Degree tracing board, which infers that the requisite text was probably developed in the late 18th century at the earliest.

From the foregoing information, it would seem highly possible that the text used for the second lecture was developed between about 1770 and 1800. That being so, the second lecture may well be an allegorical representation of events perceived to have been worthy of recording because of their positive benefit to the British nation, which had taken place in more recent times in comparison with the basic knowledge contained in the ceremonies which may have originated well before 1717.

There are two such events that meet this criteria – the building of St. Paul's cathedral and the War of Spanish Succession.

## Decoding the allegory of the Second Degree lecture

During the ceremony in which an Apprentice becomes a Fellow Craft, the candidate is enlightened with a lecture. It refers to aspects of the building of King Solomon's Temple in Jerusalem, and is based on events and physical attributes recorded by Josephus and the Old Testament, Books of Kings and Chronicles. It is one of the most wonderful ceremonial pieces one might have the honour to present, and is a detailed story filled with drama which, if examined closely, is plainly two stories rolled into one, containing several layers of information. It tells of the building and completion of the temple and the wonderful sight it presented to the children of Israel, while it also highlights the deliverance of the Israelites from their Egyptian slavery as described in the Book of Exodus. It then deals with a war that took place on the banks of the River Jordan between two tribes of Hebrew descendants who were hostile to each other, and the subsequent death of many members of one tribe; finally it reverts to the building, the use of geometry in design and the significance of classical architecture.

What inspired this wonderful piece of ceremony? Who put it together? Is it, like so much of Freemasonry, an allegory that records something else?

The detail of the lecture can be broken into several descriptive parts:

1. The lecture points out that the finished temple was so magnificent that it won the admiration of all who saw it, including people from other nations, implying that it was different from anything else the inhabitants had previously experienced.

2. There were two large pillars at the front of the temple, at the portico, which could be viewed by the worshippers as they approached the temple for services and could be observed from several directions.

3. The pillars were a reminder to all the citizens of Jerusalem of their deliverance from a prolonged period of adversity. During the Exodus, the Israelites were close to the Red Sea and were being chased by a great army of Egyptians who wanted to ensnare them. The Israelites were delivered from their trials by two astonishing events: a pillar of fire provided light and thereby the means of escape using a pathway through the waters of the sea, whilst a dark cloud inhibited the progress of

the pharaoh and his army, such that they were ultimately annihilated by drowning when they too tried to use the same pathway. The Israelites had been delivered from their Egyptian adversaries but they faced a new problem. They were homeless, until they secured an area of land and built a capital city which they called Jerusalem, and thereby started their lives anew, with the founding of a great nation.

4. This was followed by a time when groups of Israelites formed themselves into 12 tribes and settled in an area that bordered the eastern end of the Mediterranean Sea. Amongst these tribal groups, there were two kingdoms in close proximity to each other: they included the descendants of the tribe of Ephraim to the west who bordered the sea, and the other was the tribe of Gilead (Gad) in the east, which bordered the River Jordan. The Gileadites were led by a warrior named Jephthah. On the eastern border of Gad, the opposite side from the Ephraimites, was a kingdom known as Ammon. The King of Ammon had accused the Gileadites of inhabiting land that belonged to them. Jephthah, for the Gileadites, refuted this. A battle between the tribes of Ammon and Gilead broke out and the Gileadites secured victory. The Ephraimites were outraged that their Hebrew cousins had not asked them to join the battle against the Ammonites, and thereby to share in any of the plunder that might have fallen into their hands. Instead, they invaded Gad by crossing the River Jordan and threatened to kill Jephthah.

5. A battle broke out between the tribes of Gilead and Ephraim. The tribe

of Gilead were winning the battle so convincingly that those of the tribe of Ephraim tried to escape back across the River Jordan, but their retreat was cut off and many were killed, having been identified by the tribal accent with which they spoke.

6.    The lecture then returns to the story of the building of Solomon's Temple, and reference to the five orders of architecture: Doric, Ionic, Corinthian, Composite and Tuscan.

7.    This is followed by urging the listener to a study of the orders of architecture, their connection with the natural world and the proportions contained within it. Thereby from this knowledge, and that which can be gained through a study of the seven liberal arts, one has all the ability necessary to design and build wonderful structures.

8.    The lecture also notes that during the building of Solomon's Temple, the skilled stonemasons working on the project, aided by some apprentices, received payment for their work in a room above the main temple, in an area known as the middle chamber, accessed by a winding staircase through a door on the south side of the structure.

9.    Whilst in the middle of the temple, the stonemasons could see representations of several Hebrew figures that were admired for their praise of the deity.

Nearly all the background detail that informs this lecture is contained in the Biblical books of Exodus, Judges, Kings and Chronicles, plus Josephus.

Noting the possibility that the ceremonies and symbols of Freemasonry are allegorical representations of something else, as far as the Second Tracing Board is concerned the question is – what might that something else be? Other than as a nice piece of theatrical rhetoric, what purpose does the inclusion of this description of Solomon's Temple have, other than pointing out that in its day it was a splendid building, and a memorial to the deliverance of an oppressed people; also that a lot of resources were used in building it, and the area inside the temple was where the stonemasons involved in construction went to be paid? Interestingly, a reasonable proportion of the ceremonial text either does not appear in biblical chapters or has been *graphically upgraded*. For example, the place where the craftsmen went to get paid – the middle chamber – is not specifically noted as being the place where the Masons went for their wages, but is merely mentioned in biblical text as being a level of rooms along the side of the temple which was accessed from a porchway on the south side. This is mentioned in 1 Kings 6:8, as follows:

> The entrance to the lowest floor was on the south side of the temple; a stairway led up to the middle level and from there to the third.
> *International Version – Holy Bible.*

As one can also see from this text, there is no mention of a *winding staircase* either, it is just a stairway that led up to the middle level.

The confrontation between the two tribes of Gilead and Ephraim over an earlier battle with the Ammonites has no direct relationship to Solomon's Temple, because the event took place roughly 125 years before the temple was built. It seems totally out of context with the story, other than providing a passage that Freemasonry could make use of. Thus we are looking for other dramatic events that occurred and, for whatever reason, were felt to be worthy of recording in Masonic memory, with the biblical text being used for allegorical presentation.

Referring back to the list of the nine sections of interest mentioned on an earlier page, we can categorise them together with details about St. Paul's Cathedral and the War of Spanish Succession, and other influences, as follows:

| | |
|---|---|
| Items 1-3 | could relate to St Paul's cathedral. |
| Items 4 and 5 | to the wars of Spanish Succession. |
| Items 6 and 7 | to the works of Vitruvius. |
| Item 8 | to the London Company of Masons, who were involved with the rebuilding of St. Paul's after the great fire. |
| Item 9 | artistic decoration in the completed interior of St. Paul's Cathedral. |

St. Paul's Cathedral has been a most awe-inspiring structure since its completion. If we take the biblically related text used in the Fellow Craft ceremony and the Second Lecture, and restate it in the terms of the building of the cathedral and the Battle at Blenheim, we might arrive at the following:

| St. Paul's Cathedral, and the Wars of Spanish Succession restated in the form of the Second lecture | Second lecture text (paraphrased) Based on Josephus and Biblical text |
|---|---|
| **Items 1-3 – St. Paul's Cathedral** | |
| *When the great church in London had been completed by Sir Christopher Wren, the expense of the building and the splendour of the finished structure were admired by all who saw it, including many from other countries, and very quickly its fame, and that of the builder, spread throughout Europe and other accessible areas of the known world.* | When the temple in Jerusalem had been completed by King Solomon, its costliness and splendour became objects of admiration amongst surrounding nations and its fame spread to the furthermost parts of the known world. |
| *On approaching the main door, one's attention was immediately struck by the two great pillars that were set up at the porchway or entrance. Just as the pillars that had adorned the entrance to Solomon's Temple were a reminder of the deliverance of the Israelites from disaster, so these two pillars symbolised the deliverance of the people of London from the ravages of the plague known as the Black Death, from which so many people had died and which had hung like a dark cloud over the city for a full year. The following year the Great Fire had lit up the sky over the city for days. Just as, no doubt, the Temple of Solomon would have been viewed from almost anywhere in Jerusalem and the surrounding countryside, so the new place of worship and thanksgiving rose above all other structures in the City of London and could be seen from many miles around.* | The most remarkable features of the building, which immediately caught the attention, were the two great pillars that were installed at the porchway or entrance. They were set up so that the children of Israel might have the happy deliverance of their forefathers continuously before their eyes whilst going to and from divine worship. During their escape from their Egyptian bondage, two remarkable events occurred – a pillar of fire and cloud. The fire lit the way for the Israelites whilst the cloud made it dark for the Pharaoh and his followers who were trying to overtake them, and who all perished. |

| St. Paul's Cathedral, and the Wars of Spanish Succession restated in the form of the Second lecture | Second lecture text (paraphrased) Based on Josephus and Biblical text |
|---|---|
| **Item 4 & 5 – War Spanish Succession** | |
| *During the construction of this magnificent building, the nation was subjected to the potential of attack by foreign armies from across the sea. Circumstances had arisen in the Holy Roman Empire that on the death of the King of Spain, all his territories, titles and possessions would have been inherited by the King of France, giving him immense power and a vast kingdom across Europe, and lands in North and South America that had provided Spain with immense wealth from gold which they had captured and mined there. Britain allied with other countries to form a Grand Alliance, and fought against the hostile armies. The objective was to ensure a better balance of power in Europe and thereby remove real or implied threats of being dominated.* | Associated with the structure was a memory of an ancient battle. |
| *A great victory was achieved by the Grand Alliance near a small town called Blenheim, on the banks of the River Danube. The French-Bavarian armies had crossed the Danube in a hostile action with the intention of capturing Vienna, a city of great wealth, and thereby preventing the Austrians and the Holy Roman Empire from supporting the Alliance. This would probably have resulted in parts of Vienna being reduced to ashes by fire from actions of the French-Bavarian army.* | An army of Ephraimites had crossed the River Jordan in a hostile action against Jephthah, the renowned Gileadite general. They threatened to destroy him and his house by fire. Jephthah tried all lenient means to appease them. |
| *The Duke of Marlborough, finding no way to appease the French King, drew together his army and went to the aid of Vienna, prepared to give battle. He defeated them, causing many of the insurgents to flee along the banks of the River Danube and other local rivers in an attempt to regain their homelands. Fearing for their lives, many of the enemy troops discarded their uniforms and claimed themselves innocent, but their distinctive accents gave away their true origins.* | When this failed Jephthah drew out his army and gave the Ephraimites battle, defeated them and caused them to flee. To ensure he was not subjected to similar aggression again in the future he gave orders to secure the banks of the River Jordan, knowing that the insurgents had to cross it to regain their homeland. Jephthah gave additional orders that if any fugitives tried to cross the river and were caught, and claimed they were innocent, they should be encouraged to talk and, if they had an Ephraimite accent, they were to be killed. |
| *And it is recorded that there fell on that day as French casualties, or were captured, both on the battlefields and along the River Danube and other adjoining rivers , more than forty and two thousand men.* | The scriptures record that there fell on that day on the battlefield and the banks of the Jordan, forty and two thousand Ephraimites. |
| *And as Blenheim had been the place of this great victory, Queen Anne encouraged Marlborough's reward, and built him an estate with the name of Blenheim.* | After the battle, Jephthah was held in high esteem, and greatly rewarded. |

| St. Paul's Cathedral, and the Wars of Spanish Succession restated in the form of the Second lecture | Second lecture text (paraphrased) Based on Josephus and Biblical text |
|---|---|
| **Items 6 & 7 Works of Vitruvius** | |
| *Meanwhile, the building of the great cathedral continued. When the foundations were put down, the whole structure was aligned with the point on the horizon where the sun rose; the style of architecture was to incorporate the ancient and noble orders of the classical world, especially the Corinthian columns set up at the porchway or entrance, because the ancients used the dimensions of nature in their designs* | The temple of Solomon was aligned on an east-west axis, just as the Tent of the Meeting had been set up by Moses to receive the first rays of the sun each day. The pillars were decorated with emblems of circles connected in a chain, pomegranates, flowers and other attributes associated with the natural world, just as the ancient Greeks would later do in the development of classical architecture, such as the Corinthian Column symbolising nature, the Doric symbolising man and the Ionic as woman, as recorded by Vitruvius, |

| St. Paul's Cathedral, and the Wars of Spanish Succession restated in the form of the Second lecture | Second lecture text (paraphrased) Based on Josephus and Biblical text |
|---|---|
| **Items 8 London Masons Company** | |
| *In the building of this new temple, an immense number of masons were employed. They were mostly skilled journeymen, but also a few masters with their apprentices. As the building progressed the journeymen and masters received their wages in a small room used as the surveyor's office where the problems of the great scheme were sorted out by the architect. The journeymen were paid, as they were justly entitled to be under the charter that governed their craft, in coins of the realm, sometimes called specie. The apprentices, who were indentured to their masters with their names recorded in the great books of the guild, received no pay in coins, but only the food, drink and clothing to which they were justly entitled. To receive their wages, the journeymen entered a small door on the south side of the building where a spiral staircase, a new idea but conforming to the dimensions of the natural world, wound its way upwards.* | In the building of Solomon's Temple, an immense number of masons were employed. They were a mixture of Apprentices and Fellow Crafts. They all received their wages knowing they were justly entitled to them and the reliance they placed on their employers in those days. The apprentices were paid with corn, wine and oil, but the Fellow Crafts were paid with specie which they received in a room on the south side of the temple, after they had ascended a winding staircase. |

| St. Paul's Cathedral, and the Wars of Spanish Succession restated in the form of the Second lecture | Second lecture text (paraphrased) Based on Josephus and Biblical text |
|---|---|
| **Items 9 Decoration in St, Paul's Cathedral** | |
| *Having received their wages, and to avoid congestion on the winding stairs, they came down another set of spiral stairs that linked the space above with the central area of the cathedral, a vast open chamber in the middle of the temple, the place where the altar was to be. Here they noted the wonderful decoration showing some of the Hebrew characters mentioned in the Old Testament who were in praise of their God – Ezekiel, Jeremiah, Isaiah and Daniel. They knew that others would be added later.* | Once in the middle of the temple, and having received their wages, their attention was quite forcibly drawn to several Hebrew figures that were presented to their gaze, and were in praise of their God. |
| *Just as Solomon's Temple took seven years and upwards to complete the temple in Jerusalem, so it took seven years from the time of the great battle at Blenheim for the work on St. Paul's to be finished. The skill of these wonderful masons is reflected in the admiration of the people who gaze on this magnificent structure.* | King Solomon was seven years and upwards in building, completing and dedicating the temple in Jerusalem to God's service. |

*Note: In the Second degree lecture, the apprentice reward is stated as corn, wine and oil. This would be corn = Bread - a lot of cooked food would have been eaten with the aid of bread; wine = drink, probably thin beer or home-made wines, rather than polluted water; and oil = probably tallow oil to make candles for use at night.*

*For image of St. Paul's Cathedral by Canaletto, see colour section plate 7.*

The above, is of course, a hypothetical and circumstantial reconstruction of the events taking place at the time St. Paul's Cathedral was built, but shows how a series of events worth recording and passing down through later generations can be reconstructed as an allegorical lecture. What at first view seems an innocuous story based on biblical text, compiled in an era when religion was a defining aspect of one's life now becomes a real historical record, based on fact.

To put this revised text of the legend into context, it is worth recording a few of the facts about the building of St. Paul's Cathedral between 1675–1710, and the War of Spanish Succession which lasted from 1701–1714, both of which occurred immediately prior to the creation of the first Grand Lodge in 1717.

## St. Paul's Cathedral

There have been four previous cathedrals or large churches on the site that the current St. Paul's occupies. The last cathedral burnt down in the Great Fire of London of 1666 and is usually referred to as Old St. Paul's. The older St. Paul's had been built over a 200 year period and was consecrated in the mid-1200s. When finished it was regarded as the tallest cathedral in Europe, or indeed in the known world, achieved via a magnificent spire.

Like many of the great builders of the era, Sir Christopher Wren was not an architect as we know the term today. He had a passion for astronomy and had held a professorial appointment in the subject at Oxford University. Along with Elias Ashmole and Sir Robert Moray, both Freemasons, he was one of the founders of the Royal Society in 1660, and when Charles II agreed to the establishment of the Royal Observatory at Greenwich in 1685, it was Wren who received the commission to design it. He was thus more of a scientist and engineer with an artistic ability.

Drawing a scheme on paper is one thing, turning a structure as large and complex as the cathedral into a reality is another matter. During the construction process, Wren faced many structural problems that needed to be resolved. To assist him in finding practical and reliable solutions, he turned to Robert Hooke, a fellow associate of the Royal Society.

Wren and Hooke had been at Oxford University together and established a life-long friendship. After the Great Fire, Hooke, who was Surveyor General of London, and Wren had the task of rebuilding the City, both possessing complementary skills. Hooke had a great mastery of geometry, an essential skill as a surveyor, and was also recognised as an architect. He was the Curator of Experiments at the Royal Society, and as such was skilled in devising all manner of equipment necessary to prove various theories. Mention St. Paul's Cathedral and thoughts usually turn to Wren, but Hooke was equally important in the construction and is, sadly, often overlooked. The Hooke Society and other biographers note that

Hooke and Sir Isaac Newton, who was President of the Royal Society at the time, were not particularly friendly towards each other, amid claims and counter-claims for the credit of certain discoveries, and it is alleged that this resulted in Hooke being side-lined in terms of recognition status, apparently the main reason why he was not ultimately acknowledged. In addition, Hooke also designed and built some impressive buildings that rivalled Wren's achievements, but few have survived the ravages of demolition and therefore far fewer buildings remain as examples of his ability to match Wren.

Within the structure of St. Paul's, above the main area devoted to the church seating areas, is a room to the front of the building known as the Surveyor's Office. It is situated near the two pillars at either side of the portico, and is where Hooke and Wren resolved construction problems with John Stonehouse, the Master Mason appointed by the London Masons Company.

During the construction phase, it is highly probable that the only access to this upper level and the Surveyor's office, other than ladders and scaffolding, would have been via the spiral winding staircase that is just inside the entrance on the south side, known as the Dean's Door. The stairway is an open-core, self-supporting cantilevered construction, almost identical to that designed by Inigo Jones for the Queen's House in Greenwich and follows the geometric construction associated with the golden ratio. There is a second route to the Surveyor's office via the staircase, which connects the ground floor to the Whispering Gallery. This too is a spiral, but is built around a central shaft but does not appear to have the same geometric proportions as the former. Access to this latter staircase is via a simple

*Left:* (Plate 1) *The lectern in St. Patrick's Cathedral, Dublin.*

*Right:* (Plate 2) *The stalls for the Knights of St. Patrick.*

**Above:** *(Plate 3) Dr. Samuel Hemming DD (1767 – 1828)*
*Born: England – British*
*Initiated: London.*

**Above:** *(Plate 4) Hipólito José da Costa (1774 – 1823)*
*Born: Brazil – Portuguese*
*Initiated: Philadelphia, USA.*

*Second Degree Tracing Boards, circa 1819.*
**Above:** *(Plate 5) The original design is attributed to John Browne, but the coloured version is attributed to Josiah Bowring.*
**Above right:** *(Plate 6) The illustration is attributed to John Harris, circa 1825.*

*(Plate 7) The River Thames from Richmond House, London, by Canaletto - 1747.*

*It clearly illustrates how St. Paul's Cathedral rose majestically above the skyline, such that it could be seen from any vantage point. The two pillars at the porch-way are clearly visible.*

*Reproduced by the kind permission and assistance of the Goodwood Estate Company Ltd.*

*Left: (Plate 8) Panel as displayed in Reims Cathedral, showing the trades used in the construction.*

*Below: (Plate 9) The effigy from the tomb of Huges d'Libergier, Master Mason - 1231 CE, who built the cathedral in Reims.*

***Above and right:*** *(Plates 10 & 11) Stained Glass Window in the Hall of Remembrance at Freemasons' Hall, London, with its Mandorla images clearly visible.*

*Left:* *(Plate 12) The Abbey Church of St. Galls at the site where Poggio discovered the works of Vitruvius.*

*Right:* *(Plate 13) An illustration from the early 1800s, when the United Grand Lodge of England was being formed. It shows a small group of members of a Lodge gathered around a floor cloth, imitating a tracing floor, whilst a ceremony is in progress. In the cluster at the rear of the illustration, the Masters are in the front row whilst the Apprentices, we assume, are pushed to the back.*

*Left and below:*
*(Plates 14 & 15)*
*The stunning interior*
*and, outside, a*
*representation of*
*the type of small cell*
*believed to have been*
*built by St. Gallus*
*at Lake Constance,*
*to commemorate the*
*1,400 years since*
*his arrival in the*
*area from Ireland,*
*612-2012 CE.*
***All photographs –***
***K.L. Gest.***

*Left:* (Plate 16) A section of the plate from the Book of Kells, showing an image of man, and highlighting the two rosettes. (The above image is from the folio 129v Book of Kells - top left corner slice).

*Right:* (Plate 17) The image of man, ox, lion and eagle, as displayed in the impressive 'Book of Kells'.

*Reproduced by the kind permission of Trinity College, Dublin.*

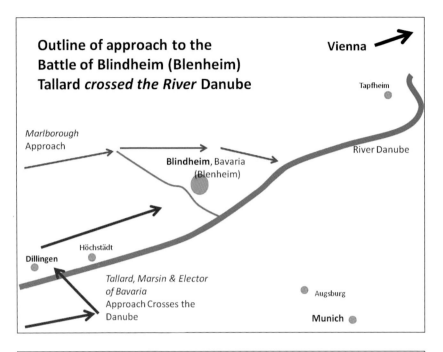

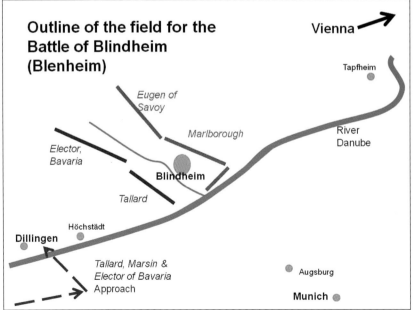

***Top:*** *(Plate 18) The Battle of Blenheim in 1704, showing the River Danube and the approaches, with the French crossing prior to the battle.*

***Above:*** *(Plate 19) The opposing forces at the start of the battle.*

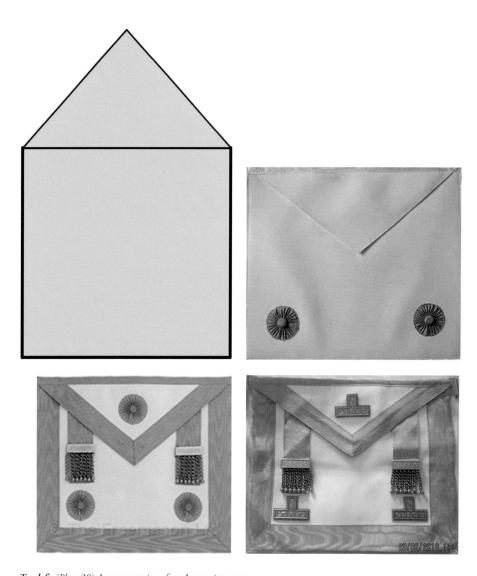

**Top left:** *(Plate 20) A representation of an Apprentice apron.*

**Top right:** *(Plate 21) The progression to the Fellow Craft apron.*

**Above left:** *(Plate 22) The progression to the Master Mason apron.*

**Above right:** *(Plate 23) Apron for Master of the Lodge.*

***Above:*** *(Plate 24) A beautifully handmade early Masonic apron - pre 1800. Note the curved flap.*

***Far left:*** *(Plate 25)*
*Royal Arch sash.*

***Left:*** *(Plate 26)*
*Royal Arch jewel.*

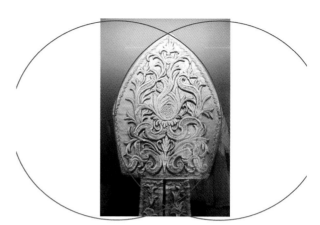

**Right and below:**
*(Plates 27 & 28) Bishop's Mitre transformed into a Vesica, based on the two halves created by the horizontal centreline through the overlapping circles.*

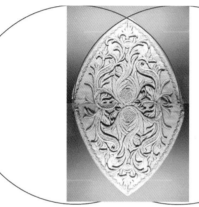

**Above and above right:** *(Plate 29 & 30) Octagram and eight-pointed star in the floor beneath the dome of the replica of the United States House of Representatives, Havana. The diverse use of the symbol illustrates its universality in human development.*

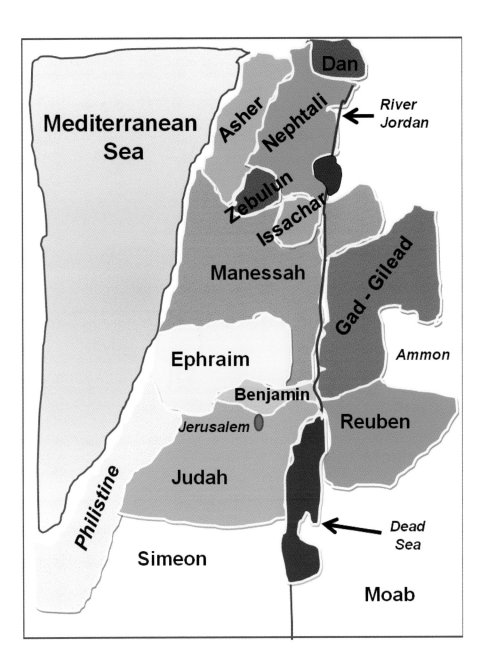

*(Plate 31) Map based on the Holy Land as recorded in Bibles of the late Victorian era, and in The Jewish Encyclopaedia.*

# Outline Development - United Kingdom of Great Britain and Ireland to formation of U.G.L.E - 1813

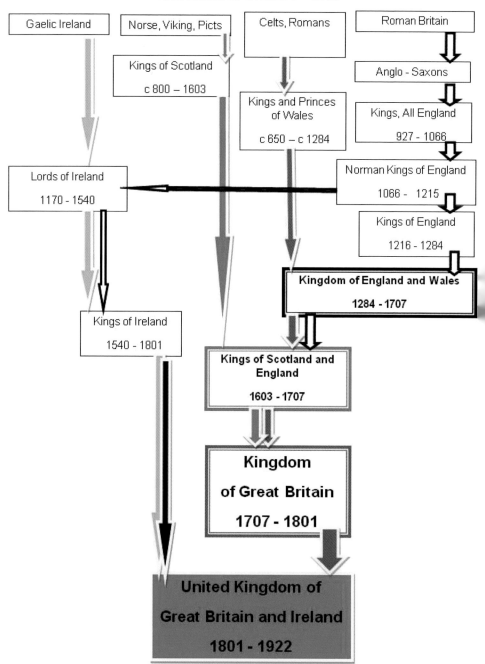

*(Plate 32)*

# Outline Development - religion in British Isles to U.G.L.E 1813

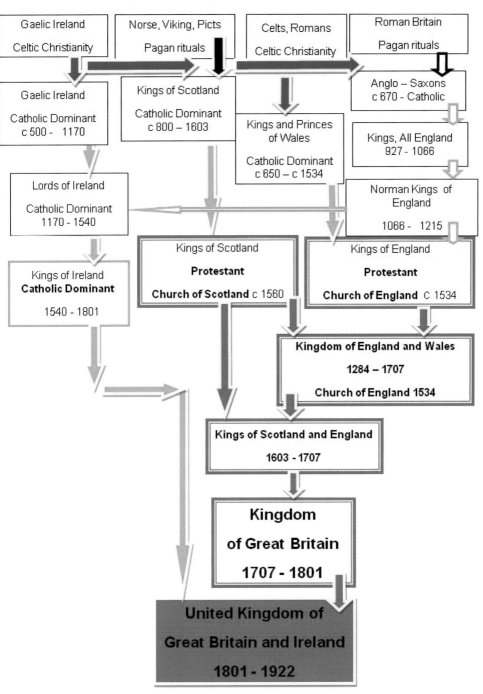

*(Plate 33)*

## Possible outline development of Masonic Ceremony content to 1717-1813

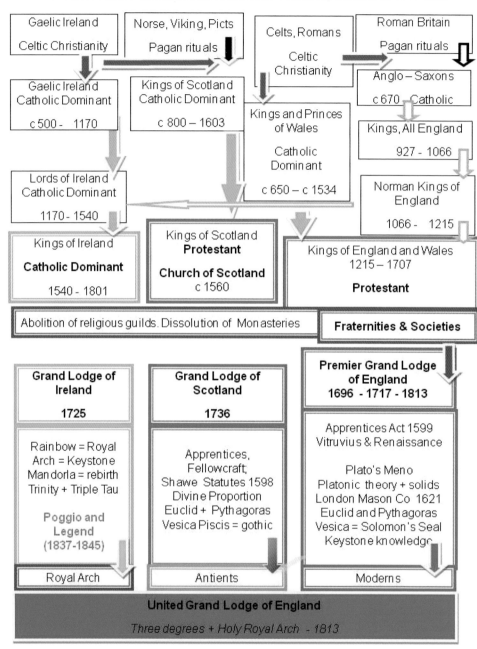

*(Plate 34)*

doorway inside the cathedral, whereas the text of legend refers to a *'porchway or entrance on the south side'*. With important documents and instruments restricted to the surveyor and Wren, access to the staircase on the ground floor and landing areas would doubtless have been guarded to prevent unauthorised ascent. The guards would certainly have been briefed to permit only specific authorised personnel to the upper areas.

This was an era when, due to the amount of construction work needed after the Great Fire, London was inundated with itinerant workers, many of whom were unskilled, but claimed a range of qualifications in order to obtain work. The London Company of Masons, monopolised the supply of skilled masons and associated trades, as defined by their charter. There would have been many unskilled workers who claimed to be masons, in the hope of obtaining employment on favourable terms for some duration, and so therefore deterring such opportunists would have been essential.

The cathedral was also built during a religious era when puritan dogma was still strong, and the interiors were left substantially without decoration. However, in the Victorian era the cathedral received most of the rich decoration that is now to be seen, which was mainly paid for by the various London Livery Companies. Indeed, one such ceiling panel, to the south of the altar, carries the symbol of the Square and Compasses.

As one emerges into the nave at ground level from the stairwell leading to the Whispering Gallery, the four walls that encompass the area are decorated with images of four Old Testament biblical figures: *Ezekiel, Jeremiah, Isaiah* and *Daniel,* Hebrew characters who hold a significant place in various Masonic ceremonies.

While the cathedral as a whole is defined as being of the English Baroque style, the portico reflects the classical architectural period with its two great pillars, *having been set up there as the most conspicuous situation by which the Londoners might have their happy deliverance from the great pestilences of plague and fire, continuously before their eyes whilst going to, and coming from, divine worship.*

**Top:** *The west-facing front portico and the two pillars set up at the entrance.*

**Above:** *The porchway or entrance on the south side – the Dean's Door.*

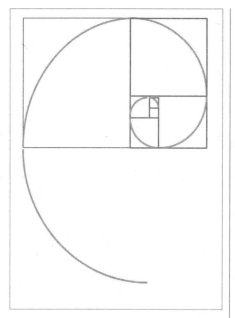

*The Golden Ratio spiral as seen from the ground floor, built into the spiral staircase inside the entrance on the south side.*

The cathedral is 365 feet high, analogous with the number of days in a solar year; it is oriented east to west along the line of the meridian, associated with the day on which the foundations were laid by Wren, the architect and astronomer.

## The influence of the Wars of Spanish Succession, the Golden Fleece and Roman Eagle, on Freemasonry in 1717

These wars hinged around the death of a Spanish king of the Habsburg dynasty who had no male successor, which would have resulted in his titles and lands being passed to his cousin, the King of France.

In the 11th century, a family then living in Germany became particularly wealthy and built a small castle on a hill at a place called Habsburg, a region which eventually became part of Switzerland. Today, this castle still exists, although a major highway now passes in tunnels beneath the hill. In the course of time, members of the family styled themselves *von Habsburg,* meaning *from Habsburg.* This family prospered and by marrying wisely, they not only relocated their power base to Austria by the middle of the 13th century, but acquired the title 'King of the Romans' (Holy Roman Emperor) for the most senior member of the family, including Otto the Great and his son Otto II, also gaining other titles in a line of dynastic succession that continued for several centuries thereafter.

The title of King of the Romans had been conferred on Charlemagne nearly 400 years after the fall of Rome, when he was crowned in the year 800 CE by the Pope. Thereafter, this honorific remained the inherited title until the recipient was officially crowned by the ruling Pope, when he assumed the status of Emperor of the Holy Roman Empire. For several hundred years the House of Habsburg ruled large areas of Europe, and at one stage their titles became associated with the King of England and Ireland, when the Tudor Queen, Mary I, married Philip II of Spain, a direct descendent of the House of Habsburg. Mary I and Philip ruled jointly, just as Mary II and William of Orange would do several generations later. Mary Tudor died childless, and in consequence the crown of England transferred to Elizabeth I, and the rule of Philip over England ended.

In 1430, Philip the Good, Duke of Burgundy, founded in the city of Bruge (part of modern Belgium) the Most Illustrious Order of the Golden Fleece, one of the most renowned Orders of Chivalry. Philip was from an equally important dynastic family, and through selective marriages by his forebears, he inherited an impressive list of titles and lands that extended across most of north-eastern Europe, producing a substantial income. He had a son, Charles the Bold, who was ambitious to gain a crown for himself, and this resulted in several battles against the French King Louis XI, culminating in Charles' death at a battle in Nancy. On his death, Charles the Bold's daughter, Mary, inherited everything and as such was probably the wealthiest person of those times. Indeed, she is often referred to in documents as *Mary the Rich*. She was just 19 years of age and unmarried when she inherited, and thus became a target for male suitors who saw the potential to gain considerable prestige. The person she chose was a member of the Habsburg dynasty, Archduke Maximilian I of Austria, son of the Holy Roman Emperor. As part of the marriage arrangement, Maximilian agreed to protect the wealth and titles Mary had inherited, although through the marriage they became associated with the Habsburg line. Shortly after, Louis XI of France saw the prospect of enlarging his kingdom by seizing some of the prosperous territories that Mary had inherited. Maximilian honoured his commitment to defend the territories and defeated Louis' army retaining the control and protection over her lands. Thus branches of the House of Habsburg controlled much of both eastern and western Europe by the 16th century.

Maximilian von Habsburg and Mary of Burgundy had a son, whom they named Philip. The young Mary of Burgundy died after a riding accident when Philip was still a very small boy and so, at a very young age, he inherited all his mother's titles including that of the Duke of Burgundy.

In due time, the young Philip married Juana, the daughter of Ferdinand of Aragon and Isabella of Castile. Ferdinand and Isabella had effectively created the country of Spain through their marriage, and by evicting the Moors from the southern areas of the Iberian Peninsula. They had a son, Charles, who on the death of Philip his father, inherited the titles of the House of Burgundy and those of his grandfather, Maximilian von Habsburg, thereby becoming King Charles I of Spain and King Karl (Charles) V of Austria, Emperor of the Holy Roman Empire. He thereby held all the titles and territories of the Houses of Burgundy, Castile, Aragon and the Austrian Habsburg line that were associated with his ancestors.

Ferdinand and Isabella of Spain had financed the voyage of Columbus to the Americas, which ultimately led to the vast import of gold, jewels and other precious objects secured in South America and shipped back to Europe. This not only provided great wealth for Charles I/ Karl V, but also meant that the Spanish Habsburg line now controlled territories in both North and South America and the Caribbean. At the same time, the Most Illustrious Order of the Golden Fleece moved with the inheritances and became the primary Order of Chivalry in the Low Countries of Europe, Spain and the Austro-Hungarian Empire.

Due to ill health in later life, Charles V abdicated and divided his territorial control between his two sons. Philip II (later to marry Mary I of England) acquired Spain, the Netherlands and Italy, while his second son acquired the Austro-Hungarian territories by which he became Emperor Ferdinand I of the Holy Roman Empire. This division resulted in the Order of the Golden Fleece also being divided into Spanish and Austrian Orders.

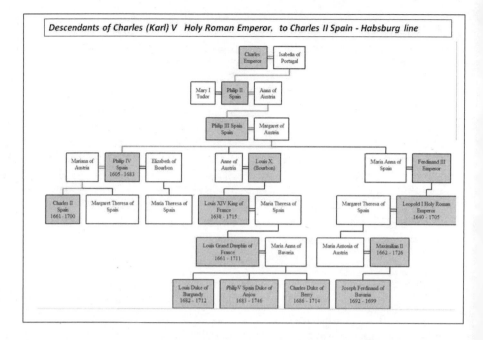

The Habsburgs and Burgundians were not the only major lines of family descent in Europe to seek dynastic power, as the Houses of Valois and Bourbon were both familial groups which had descended from earlier dynasties.

The House of Valois traced its origins to the 14th century and was intermingled with the House of Burgundy. Until Mary, daughter of Charles the Bold, married Maximilan von Habsburg, the lordships of Burgundy were titles held by the lines of the House of Valois, who in addition provided the line of succession for the Kings of France until the male line became extinct in the mid-16th century.

Catherine de Medici had married a king from the House of Valois and had several children, the first of whom, Francis II, who was to marry Mary Queen of Scots, but died young. Her two other sons who also died young, included one styled as Henry III of France. At one stage of his reign there was a possibility that Henry could have married Queen Elizabeth I of England, but he was assassinated by a disaffected monk before final arrangements were completed. Thus the male line of descendants of the House of Valois came to an end and the throne of France was transferred to the House of Bourbon.

The House of Bourbon also traced its origins back to the 14th century; it was a family of nobles who, like the Habsburgs, married well and over time increased their power and influence. The two houses vied for power several times over the centuries and, by the year 1700, the Kings of France were of the House of Bourbon while those of Austria and Spain remained associated with the House of Habsburg.

The Spanish Habsburg line of succession ended in 1700, when Charles II of Spain died in early middle age without any surviving offspring but nominated a member of the House of Bourbon as his successor. At first this seems bizarre, as there were other

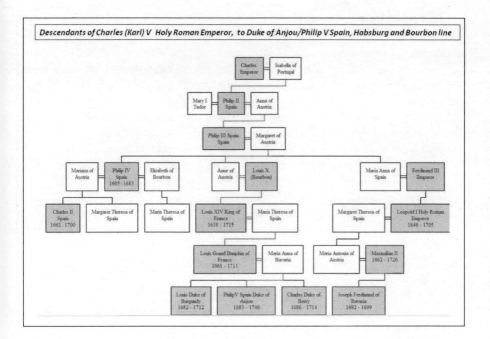

**Descendants of Charles (Karl) V Holy Roman Emperor, to Duke of Anjou/Philip V Spain, Habsburg and Bourbon line**

descendants of the Habsburg line that had an equal claim to the throne of Spain. One such individual was Leopold I, Holy Roman Emperor a direct descendant in the Habsburg line from Charles I of Spain/Charles V of Austria. However, there had been two separate Habsburg marriages within the House of Bourbon, including that of Philip IV of Spain who had married Elizabeth of Bourbon. Thus the lines of descent were set more in favour of the Duke of Anjou, and through the House of Bourbon he became King Philip V of Spain. On the death of the King of France, Philip Duke of Anjou, would have been in the position to claim the thrones of France and Spain, and thereby have controlled most of Western Europe and the territories overseas associated with each crown. The political and military threat this posed for Britain, the Netherlands, Portugal and Prussia was immense, while the remaining strongholds of Habsburg territory in Eastern Europe would have also been insecure. Thus the Grand Alliance was

formed, in which Britain joined forces with the threatened nations to force an agreement whereby this threat could not occur. This was the War of Spanish Succession.

The Battle of Blenheim in 1704 occurred because the Franco-Spanish faction believed that, if they could defeat the army of the Holy Roman Emperor and secure Vienna, then the Austro-Hungarian Habsburgs would not be able to participate in the Grand Alliance. With Austro-Hungary and the Holy Roman Empire reduced to virtual spectators, the prospect of a victory by the House of Bourbon and its descendants could be turned on the remaining combatants. If the Netherlands went down, then Britain, Prussia and Portugal would each have been isolated and potentially defeated one at a time. Thus stopping the Bourbons reaching Vienna became crucial in the early stages of the war.

*For images of the battlefield layout, see colour section plate 18 & 19.*

The Franco-Spanish army had crossed the River Danube, seeking to advance on Vienna. For the defenders, the battle of Blenheim was led by the Duke of Marlborough who secured a great victory on behalf of the Grand Alliance. This prevented the Bourbons from reaching their objective and undermined the possibility of the Habsburg-based Austro-Hungarian Empire being removed from the alliance. The Bourbon army grossly outnumbered that of the Grand Alliance, yet the tactics and logistics employed by Marlborough ensured a decisive victory and the Bourbon supporters were forced to flee back over the Danube towards their homes. Historians assess the total casualties, as follows:

| Combat force – Battle of Blenheim | Casualties (estimated) |
|---|---|
| Grand Alliance under Marlborough | 7,000 total |
| Franco-Spanish Armies | 42,000 total |

In Masonic text, the Franco-Spanish casualties are quoted as '..forty and two thousand…'

With Vienna saved and the Austro-Hungarians still in the Alliance, Marlborough was richly rewarded and decorated by Queen Anne, the British monarch.

The Bourbons went on to many victories during the 12 years of battle and ultimately a peace settlement was reached in 1714, yet it did not last.

In the agreement, Philip V was acknowledged as the King of Spain and was able to retain some of his overseas territories, but was excluded from the line of descent to the French crown. This was a time when the French were actively supporting the Jacobite cause to reinstate the House of Stuart to the thrones of Scotland and England, and the arrangement thereby removed what might otherwise have been a serious military threat to the British nation. Ironically, Queen Anne, as a daughter of James II, was of the House of Stuart and the last British monarch in the direct Roman Catholic line, but thereafter France ceased such support for the Jacobite cause and acknowledged Anne as Queen of Britain. Spain was forced to relinquish some of its territories and ceded Gibraltar to Britain, while the French also conceded some of their American colonies to Britain. At the same time, Spain also abandoned its sole rights to the slave trade it had developed in the Caribbean, which in turn were assumed by Britain.

Among the intriguing consequences of the settlement of the Wars of Spanish Succession was its effect on British trading interests. To capitalise on business prospects, a new company was established by the Society of Merchant Adventurers, which operated alongside the existing East India Company, and the Hudson Bay Company. This new enterprise was the South Sea Company, whose shares became very popular as the prospect of increased wealth from the new territories that Britain had gained appealed to investors. Amid great euphoria, the shares rapidly increased in speculative value, yet the company collapsed in 1720 – the 'South Sea Bubble' had burst, and many wealthy investors lost their money, with some ruined.

Thus the War of Spanish Succession and its aftermath were very significant for British overseas territorial development and political stability at home, at the time that Freemasonry was being formalised in 1717 and thereafter. It also provided a stimulus for the development of the Royal Navy and its ultimate base in Gibraltar. The Navy had been sadly neglected through the English Civil Wars with little or no investment until around 1675; and the memory of these events, and the outcome in favour of the nation, would have been worthy of recording and appear to have been preserved in Masonic Memory.

**Top:** *The Imperial emblem of the Holy Roman Empire. (K. L. Gest)*

**Above:** *The tomb of Mary the rich (Burgundy), Bruges, Belgium (K. L. Gest)*

*Author's note:*

*When the Premier Grand Lodge was formed, the first Grand Master in 1717 was one Anthony Sayer. Very little is known about this person or how he came to be selected for this highly prestigious role. At the time of his appointment, he must have had some considerable social influence and bearing to be elected. Later records suggest that, by the mid-1720s, he was holding a very junior Masonic office by comparison with his heady start, and that he died in 1741 a very poor man, having several times in between sought charitable support from the Grand Lodge. His funeral was attended by quite a crowd of gentry, and despite his unfortunate decline he received a decent burial, which suggests it was paid for by others and underlines the high regard with which he was viewed. This raises the possibility that he may have been a financial casualty of the South Sea Bubble crash. This led him, no doubt like many others, to withdraw from most of the social ventures that his former wealth, however modest, may have enabled him to enjoy. Thus the explanation may be that in 1717 he was considered a prosperous individual with good connections in the City of London, such that it resulted in his election to the key position; he endured the financial crash of 1720 and lost a considerable amount of money, and dying poor some years later. This incident would also have had a profound effect on many of those early brethren; hence, in Masonic memory we refer to some individuals of being of rank and opulence, and the possibility of being reduced to the lowest ebbs of fortune's wheel by some calamity. Hence the charitable aspects of Freemasonry are ongoing, and have been in evidence since its formation.*

## The Holy Roman Empire's abolition

The Holy Roman Empire and the position of Emperor were abolished by Napoleon Bonaparte in 1807, at a time when discussions were being held about unifying the two Grand Lodges. The political and economic benefits to Britain that resulted from the War of Spanish Succession and its subsequent settlement, would have been obvious to many of the aristocratic descendants associated with Freemasonry, and especially those who benefited from an education at the University of Oxford or Cambridge. This was also the era in which the Second Degree Tracing Board, and the associated lecture, was probably developed.[44]

## Three, Five and Seven or more steps

There is one further aspect of the Second Lecture that is often presented without any thought for the meaning behind the words, yet it is connected with Vitruvius and architecture.

Its focus is the winding spiral staircase, which is noted as consisting of three, five and seven or more steps. These steps are used rhetorically to infer that three persons control the management of the Lodge – the Master and his two Wardens – being properly organised when two Fellow Crafts are also present, making five in all, and perfect in its formation when two apprentices are also included, making a total of seven. The steps reflect, in many respects, the process of climbing to a respected position as enjoyed by the Master, in comparison with the lowly status of an Apprentice. There is also, however, an allegorical interpretation associated with the knowledge of a stonemason or builder.

A set of stairs or steps needs some regularity of tread depth and height, so that those using them will not stumble and fall, especially where to do so would lead to acute embarrassment. Thus Vitruvius used an ingenious method of defining the regularity of steps, using the three, four, five triangle of Pythagoras.

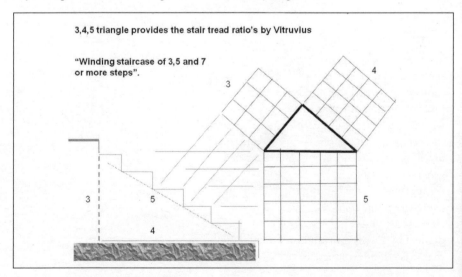

3,4,5 triangle provides the stair tread ratio's by Vitruvius

"Winding staircase of 3,5 and 7 or more steps".

This method, not only sets the regularity of one set of 7 steps, but once measured, can be replicated in multiples steps – *3, 5* and *7* or more. The three, four, five triangle is a key emblem of the Master of the Lodge. As Master, he is expected to be highly skilled and knowledgeable about his craft, so although he receives due recognition in Freemasonry when he becomes the Master, he is, in Masonic terms, taught this knowledge as a Fellow Craft – the journeyman who is adding to his skills by experience.

## Masonic Memory Review 5

It would seem that the development of the Second Degree Tracing Board lecture used in Masonic ceremonial, may not have been developed until the latter years of the 18th century, perhaps a decade or so prior to the creation of the United Grand Lodge of England. John Browne may well have been the originator of this lecture, primarily to provide a market for his coloured tracing boards, although it may equally have been based on an earlier ceremonial devised in the mid-1700s when the Wars of Spanish Succession, the collapse of the South Sea Company, the completion of St. Paul's cathedral and the death of Sir Christopher Wren were still in living memory.

At the time the United Grand Lodge of England was created in 1813, Napoleon was still two years from being defeated at Waterloo, when the final abolition of the Holy Roman Empire would see the position of Emperor ended. The French King, executed in the revolution, was of Bourbon descent, and the defunct Emperorship was of the Habsburg line, which would have brought together the preceding knowledge involving the French and Spanish thrones.

The religious text involving the war between the Ammonites and the Gileadites, and the resultant battle with the Ephraimites, has direct parallels with the Battle of Blenheim, even down to the number of estimated casualties. Yet at the time that the Wars of Spanish Succession were taking place, St. Paul's cathedral in London was still in construction.

Around 100 years prior to 1813, those truly momentous events would have doubtless enhanced the security and pride of the British nation, while the beneficial effects of those activities would have had an obvious effect upon those involved in developing the ceremonial content up to the promulgation process, and would thus be worthy of recording. It would appear that someone with a very interesting turn of mind created one of the most fascinating of all the ceremonial lectures within Freemasonry, and in repeating it the memory of those important events was retained and passed on from generation to generation.

It seems that what appears on the surface to be an insignificant statement using the numbers three, five and seven, is in fact a reflection of an important element of designing steps or a staircase, ensuring regularity of the tread, as defined by Vitruvius, and implemented by a builder. This is yet further evidence that everything in Freemasonry is there to serve a purpose.

## Chapter 9

# Of Noah and Adam

IN THE OPENING PAGES of Andersons *Constitutions* of 1723, the following text appears:

To be read at the admission of a *NEW BROTHER,* when the MASTER or WARDEN shall begin, or order some other brother to read as follows:

Adam, our first parent, created after the Image of God, *the great Architect of the Universe*, must have had the Liberal Sciences, particularly *Geometry*, written on his Heart; for even since the Fall, we find the Principles of it in the Hearts of his Offspring, and which, in process of time, have been drawn forth into a convenient Method of *Propositions*, by observing the Laws of *Proportion* taken from *Mechanism*: So that as the *Mechanical Arts* gave Occasion to the Learned to reduce the Elements of *Geometry* into Method, this noble Science thus reduc'd, is the Foundation of those Arts, (particularly of *Masonry* and *Architecture*) and the Rule by which they are conducted and perform'd. No doubt *Adam* taught his Sons *Geometry*, and the use of it, in the several *Arts* and *Crafts* convenient, at least for those early Times; for CAIN, we find, built a City, which he call'd CONSECRATED, or DEDICATED, after the Name of his eldest Son ENOCH; and becoming the Prince of the one Half of Mankind, his Posterity would imitate his royal Example in improving both the noble Science and the useful Art.

Nor can we suppose that SETH was less instructed, who being the Prince of the other Half of mankind, and also the prime Cultivator of *Astronomy*, would take equal care to teach *Geometry* and *Masonry* to his Offspring, who had also the mighty Advantage of *Adam's* living among them. But without regarding uncertain Accounts, we may safely conclude the *old World*, that lasted 1656 Years, could not be ignorant of *Masonry*; and that both the Families of *Seth* and *Cain* erected many curious Works, until at length NOAH, the ninth from Seth, was commanded and directed of God to build the *great Ark*, which, tho' of Wood, was certainly fabricated by *Geometry*, and according to the Rules of *Masonry*.

NOAH, and his three Sons, JAPHET, SHEM, and HAM, all *Masons true*, brought with them over the *Flood* the Traditions and Arts of the *Ante-deluvians,* and amply communicated them to their growing Offspring; for about 101 Years after the *Flood* we find a vast Number of 'em, if not the whole Race of *Noah*, in the Vale of *Shinar*, employ'd in building a *City* and large *Tower*, in order to make to themselves a Name, and to prevent their Dispersion. And tho' they carry'd on the Work to a monstrous Height, and by their Vanity provok'd God to confound their Devices, by confounding their Speech, which occasion'd their Dispersion; yet their Skill in *Masonry* is not the less to be celebrated, having Spent above 53 Years in that prodigious Work, and upon their Dispersion carry'd the mighty Knowledge with them into distant Parts, where they found the good Use of it in the Settlement of their *Kingdoms, Commonwealths,* and *Dynasties.* And tho' afterwards it was lost in most Parts of the Earth, it was especially preserv'd in *Shinar* and *Assyria,* where NIMROD, the Founder of that Monarchy, after the Dispersion, built many splendid Cities, as *Ereck, Accad,* and *Calneh,* in SHINAR; from whence afterwards he went forth into ASSYRIA, and built *Nineveh, Rehoboth, Caleh,* and *Rhesin.*

Anderson's 1723 edition of the *Constitutions* is the first time that any written text relating to the ceremonies and constitutions of Freemasonry, appears after the initial formation of the Premier Grand Lodge in 1717. It is not difficult to estimate that as Anderson was a Presbyterian Minister, and thereby deeply committed to his religious beliefs, that he should begin his constitutions with a biblical quotation, just as the Old Testament has a similar beginning relating to the arrival of man, and the intelligence he possessed. After this initial appearance of the quotation, numerous other Masonic writers followed his lead, with the result that there was soon a plethora of texts appearing, having the same quotation, wherein Adam and Noah are credited with an important connection to Freemasonry.

Reference to Adam and Noah appears in the translation of Josephus' *Antiquity of the Jews* published by the Presbyterian Minister William Whiston in 1734, as well as an earlier version translated around 1603 by another Presbyterian Minister, Thomas Lodge. Anderson would also have been well versed in the elements of biblical text, such as the construction of the Tower of Babel being built with stone. Scientifically based archaeology would not be organised for another one hundred and fifty years, so it would naturally have led him to consider that the skills and tools required to build the tower would be similar to those of the era in which he lived. Thus, it is logical that Anderson should start with the first people on Earth, as recorded in the Old Testament, and relate them to the development of knowledge and its links with the Liberal Arts and Sciences, as Adam even reappears in legends associated with the Royal Arch.

Although the connection with religion is evident, there may be an allegorical reason that is less obvious, for their inclusion in earlier Masonic texts. In the Old Testament we are told that Noah was instructed to build an ark of very specific dimensions, and then to fill it with one male and one female of all the known animals of the world, that they might reproduce their kind and restore the species to the world after the flood. The details of the ark are contained in Genesis, Chapter 6. The King James' Authorised version records it as follows:

Make thee an ark of gopher wood; rooms shalt thou make in the ark, and shalt pitch it within and without with pitch.

And this is the fashion which thou shalt make it of: The length of the ark shall be three hundred cubits, the breadth of it fifty cubits, and the height of it thirty cubits.

A window shalt thou make to the ark, and in a cubit shalt thou finish it above; and the door of the ark shalt thou set in the side thereof; with lower, second, and third stories shalt thou make it.

In the twenty-first century world, we are all probably conversant with images of the *ark* that have appeared in films, cartoons and children's books, and the fact it was a manageable craft. There are many people who will claim to have read the Old and New Testaments of the Bible from the start to the finish, but many will read the words without necessarily digesting and understanding what it represented. A second look at what was being asked of Noah, and the associated logistics, reveals things on a very different scale from the picture-book images.

A cubit was the measure of the distance between the elbow and the tip of the middle finger, measuring to approximately eighteen inches, or half a metre. The Ark would have been around 450 feet/137 metres long, 75 feet/23 metres wide x 45 feet/14 metres high. This is the length of around one and half football pitches, nearly as wide as the Titanic and as high as a four or five storey building, and certainly no small boat.

We can be reasonably confident that the era for the flood and the construction of the ark was well before 5,000 BCE, for the pyramids of Giza were supposedly built around 2,500 BCE, and the ancient Egyptian kingdoms extended back to around 3,500 BCE; there were moderately advanced groups living on the Islands of Malta and Gozo around 4,500 BCE; the ancient City State of Sumer is believed to have been founded around 4,500 BCE and the inhabitants are also believed to have built the Tower of Babel. On this basis, any mass extinction would have necessarily taken place around 5,500 BCE at the latest, and the construction of a boat of the size indicated, was an impressive commitment, and required an enormous amount of skill. The boat was made of wood, in a period of time several thousand years before the construction of Solomon's Temple, and the building of the Great Pyramid. Metal nails to hold the wood together did not exist, and examples of boats used on the River Nile circa 2,500 BCE, displayed in the small museum to the rear of the Great Pyramid of Giza, show that a technique of assembling the boats by tying the elements together with thin rope was employed. Biblical scholars have assessed that based on the text of Genesis, some 45,000 animals of all shapes and sizes would have had to be housed on the Ark, together with enough food for the entire contingent for about twelve months. This was therefore a very heavy boat and unlikely to have been held together with thin rope, and to house this kind of weight would require the vessel to be of a proper rib and keel construction, just to hold it together. Furthermore, if the ark was made from planks of wood one cubit wide and ten feet long, around three hundred thousand planks would have been necessary. Assuming that the ark was built somewhere close to where Sumer was later founded, then trees may not have been particularly large in diameter, and if one obtained six good planks per tree, this would require the cutting of fifty thousand trees, with the logistics of moving trunks to a place where they could be transformed into planks. Considering the locality and the type of tree possibly available, modern specialists suggest that the wood quoted in the text of Genesis as being gopher wood, was probably cypress pine. There are other suggestions that gopher wood is now an extinct species.

Subject to the size of the wood needed, it would have meant taking trees from an extensive area, and with no modern cutting equipment, any form of saw was likely to have been very primitive and not very sharp, although it is possible that the trees were felled using a team of oxen. Notwithstanding this, if two men could fell two trees per day, it would take seventy five years to collate the trees necessary. Having cut or pulled the trees down, they were then required to be dragged, possibly by teams of oxen, over many miles and rough terrain to the place where they could be rendered into planks. Assuming they were sufficiently organised with men and equipment to produce two good planks per day, then it would take two men about seventy five years to fulfil this task. The use of wooden pegs hammered through the planks and into the ribs of the boat like rivets, would probably have been insufficient even if they had existed. Additionally, specialist tools would have been needed to make the holes in the planks and the ribs of the craft, necessitating some tens of thousands of holes and their relevant pegs, all of a regular size. Then there was the waterproofing of the finished craft with pitch, both inside and out, and the only likely place for supplies of such material was around the Dead Sea, the location of the later biblical cities of Sodom and Gomorrah, two communities that are believed to have quarried and traded in pitch.

A vessel the size of the Ark would have required a very significant quantity of that material which would have to be transported to the site where the Ark was being assembled. From some very basic assumptions about the construction complications, it is not difficult to estimate that the labour required to build this vessel would have amounted to around three hundred man years at the least.

This was definitely not a minor undertaking, especially if one considers the relatively primitive tools and ability, which are believed to have been at their disposal, and the construction of such a vessel would represent a massive management exercise even by standards today. It involved a knowledge of sophisticated ship design thousands of years prior to Archimedes discovering the principles of displacement that enabled things to float; of materials sourcing; the transport and logistics of moving materials from their source to the site the boat was assembled; manpower; the development of expertise that would enable tree trunks to be produced into planks of wood; and so on. Even if there were several teams of workers involved in the project, it would have taken many years to complete, irrespective of the highly dangerous task of rounding up and capturing of all the animals, and associated transport prior to loading. Therefore, the credibility of this biblical story is somewhat questionable, with the knowledge available today.

Towards the end of the 20th century, new theories were advanced to explain the flood, and it has been agreed that although the ancient civilisations of Europe and Asia Minor knew little about the rest of the world, nearly every major civilisation on Earth possesses a myth or tribal story involving a great deluge thousands of years ago. William Whiston suggested that a comet may have crashed into the sea; others have intimated that a period of intense rainfall occurred around 7,500 BCE which lasted for about 100 years, thereby erasing great fertile grasslands which we now see as the Sahara desert; and the melting of large areas of ice around Greenland at the end of the Ice Age, with the melted water causing sea levels to rise dramatically and bridging a land sill near Istanbul, that resulted in sudden flooding of the Black Sea.[45]

In the world of three hundred years ago, there were no such explanations for the flood, so the story of the Ark as told in Genesis, would have been viewed and interpreted in a very different light. After the flood, the Old Testament tells us, that Noah's sons, JAPHET, SHEM, and HAM, together with their wives, departed in three different directions and thereby created the human populations that developed around the world.

In the Medieval period, when the great cathedral structures of Europe were being built and the stonemason was in particular demand, maps of the known world were scarce. One of the most famous from that period is the *Mappa Mundi* which recent research indicates was probably drawn around the year 1300, and is retained in Hereford Cathedral, and places the centre of the known world as Jerusalem. This was of course a single map, and not readily copied and available to the masses, being a departure from earlier styles of maps that are known as T-O maps.

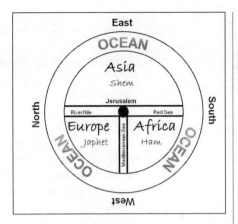

*Above:* A T-O map schematic.

*Left:* A medieval T-O map image.

In that early period, the known world comprised of three continents. Most of Europe was known, as was North Africa, the Middle East, and a corridor of territory which extended from Persia through Northern India into China. All of this land was deemed to have been surrounded by sea. Thus the T-O maps divided the world into three continents, Europe, Africa and Asia, with Jerusalem at the centre.

In the Medieval period, the three sections of the known world depicted in the T-O maps, were associated, for religious purposes, with the three sons of Noah and their descendants, and their habitation around the world after the flood. Shem was assigned to Asia, Ham to Africa, and Japhet to Europe, and it was assumed that the distinguishing features of the races associated with the three continents derived from this separation of the three brothers.

Thus, when Anderson, and later Preston, referred to the *old charges* and made comments in them with respect to Noah and his sons, they were probably making reference to the known world as it was then considered to be, represented by the T-O maps in the Middle Ages. Even at the time Preston was developing his system of lectures, the first British settlements in Australia were just commencing, with the first fleet arriving in Sydney Harbour in 1789. Large areas of the Pacific Ocean, and the full extent of the land mass known as North America, had still to be explored, and there was almost nothing known of the Polar regions or central Africa. Thus the above representation of the world in the mid-late 18th century would probably still have held some credibility, especially in a religious context.

## Masonic Memory Review 6

References in early Masonic texts and ceremonies to Noah and Adam, clearly have a few credibility problems when one contemplates the biblical account in some detail. Yet, if one considers that they are referring to the T-O map concept, then we again have an element of ancient knowledge that is being preserved in the Masonic format.

Unless one had a special interest in ancient maps or mapping concepts, then the knowledge of these special forms of recorded detail about the world, would have been unknown to earlier Masonic writers and researchers, so the mythology was thereby perpetuated. Yet, to the early monastic communities that developed them, they were a way of perceiving the world in a religious context, and in the ceremonies of Freemasonry, they underpin those religious references, whilst through their geometric design, they enable the *wonderful works of the deity* to be estimated.

## Chapter 10

# Allegory – decoding Masonic regalia

AROUND THE TURN OF the 18th and 19th centuries, Freemasonry was exposed to pressure caused by the French Revolution. There was a necessity to comply with the Unlawful Societies Act and the Unlawful Oaths Act, as well as risks of accusations of blasphemy being levelled at any organisation by the ecclesiastical establishment. This exacerbated the merging of the Grand Lodges of the *Antients* and the *Moderns* to create the resultant structure of the United Grand Lodge of England. There also needed to be a system of checks and scrutiny in the management of its affairs to ensure that the institution fully complied with legislation wherever it operated nationally, or in its dominions overseas where Lodges had been formed. It was at this time that Freemasonry seemed to cease being an organisation in which the primary content of its ceremonies and symbols were ancient wisdom and knowledge, becoming a hierarchal institution with a strong charitable, social and moral tone which it retains to this day. Despite this change, considerable knowledge is still retained, albeit in allegorical form. The ability one requires and the tools needed to decipher the allegory are not evident, because there is no obvious standard code structure and each element of Masonic ceremonial needs to be considered separately.

The most striking evidence of this change of emphasis is in the regalia worn by the Lodge and Chapter members, for in the period up to 1800 aprons were all individual. They were handmade, some embroidered and some painted, perhaps by the member concerned or one of his family, and probably added to over time as their knowledge increased. There seems to have been some consistency in that knowledge because various themes and images appear across a range of old aprons.

*For images, see cover illustration and plate 24.*

So, why do we have the regalia designs that now exist, and do they mean anything? It must be noted at this point that in the following analysis only the regalia in use by Lodges operating under the United Grand Lodge of England are considered. Scottish and Irish regalia have a somewhat different imagery.

Details which define exactly how the regalia's design was derived seem, like much of the detail about early Freemasonry, to be missing. According to archivists, it seems that designs were created and presented to the Grand Master in the early 1800s by the officials responsible for the promulgation and union processes; and in some cases changes were requested and made, but this seems to be the extent of existing information. Minutes of meetings at which such decisions were made are very sketchy on detail, so to try and understand the design rationale involves a process of reverse engineering.

In the same era that Masonic regalia was being standardised, a decree was issued in 1814 relating to British civil dress codes. The momentum for this seems to have originated because, whenever French ambassadors were presented at Court, they were immaculately dressed in smart uniforms with gold braiding, whereas no such organised presentation existed in England. As British influence around the globe gathered momentum and its prestige was enhanced with the defeat of Napoleon Bonaparte on land and sea from Spain to India, although the Battle of Waterloo was still to take place, it was resolved that Britain should also adopt an appropriate dress code. Such a code still exists and is issued by the Lord Chamberlain's Office, often referred to as the *ambassadorial dress code*. It was against the background of the preparation of this decree that Masonic regalia was designed, and incorporated in the *Book of Constitutions* of 1815.

The origin of the aprons as a symbol of Masonic regalia is unknown, though a range of claims, some quite imaginative, have been made by various researchers over the past century. For example, a triangular image on ancient Egypt statues has been cited as an indication of an apron and from this is was deduced that the person to whom the statue is dedicated must have been a Freemason in ancient times. Egyptologists dismiss this idea, pointing out that the triangle was a place on a statue to write an inscription relating to the person being honoured, by virtue of their stature and acclaim warranting the creation of a statue. Another common claim is that the Medieval stonemasons wore thick lambskin aprons that covered the front of the body, to protect their clothing from damage when a stone was being sculpted into the intricate patterns displayed in churches and cathedrals. This suggestion is also open to question. Anyone who has ever undertaken any craft activity which involved wearing a protective leather apron covering the front of the body will know it is difficult to bend and turn, the ability to do so being a key feature of the stonemason's craft not for just a short time, but for many hours of the working day. If a quarryman of old was cutting a stone from a rock face, he was unlikely to have worn an apron of any description, and if he was shaping a square or rectangular stone to a designated size, to be shipped to a site for building or carving, he was again most unlikely to have worn such an apron. If the ashlars were to be used in a wall of a building, then these blocks would be installed by the builder or masons, who would probably not have had such an apron either. On the other hand, an expert Mason undertaking a delicate carving may have had need of a range of chisels with different end profiles, close at hand. These tools of trade were the basis of his livelihood and he would always keep them secure. It was therefore appropriate to have a small sheepskin bag with a pocket and flap, in which he kept his range of tools, the flap preventing the inside of the bag filling with any sharp chippings from the sculpting process. Furthermore, as these tools were nominally his only means of livelihood he would have taken them with him at all times. Therefore a lamb-skin bag, whilst tied around his middle when working, may well have hung to the side at other times. Furthermore, his clothes were probably the last thing he was concerned about, as working at close quarters when carving a stone was more likely to result in dust and fragments of stone hitting his eyes. Having made these observations, it is interesting to note that the image on show in Reims cathedral (in an earlier chapter) depicts the craftsman at work wearing a covering over the front of his clothes.

However, it has the appearance of a light covering made of cloth and not heavy lamb skin. The Reims cathedral image was, it seems, created in the second half of the 20th century, which raises the question as to whether it is a true depiction of the craft as it would have been in the 13th century, or if the Masonic tradition which was active in France, influenced the drawing by illustrating the apron.

Notwithstanding any of the above observations, an Egyptian connection is worth revisiting. The Masonic apron is regarded as a badge of honour, and the symbols on it indicate the significance of the person within the Masonic structure. After the introduction of the Renaissance style of architecture into England by Inigo Jones – and the desire on the part of the aristocracy to have homes built or modified to reflect the new style, and/or incorporate those championed by Andre Palladio – interest in the ancient philosophies grew. During the 18th century and well into the 19th, it was usual for the members of well-to-do families to visit the so-called ancient world on the *grand tour*, especially of Greece and Italy, and later to venture to Egypt where statues with the apron-like image may have been seen. As members of several aristocratic families were also members of Masonic Lodges, it would not have been unreasonable for them to reflect on the Egyptian imagery when the new apron design was being considered prior to 1815 – it marked a visual statement of honour, and any symbols or other markings placed on it reflected the stature of the person wearing it.

The individual aprons from the era prior to 1815 may well have been a reflection of the tool bag of the skilled mason, with imagery relating to the secrets and mysteries of the stonemason's craft embroidered or painted on the front face as a motif of ownership.

## Decoding the Entered Apprentice apron

Yet again, we should remember that we are dealing with aspects of an organisation that was presumably influenced by the building craft of stonemasons from the medieval period and the knowledge needed to fulfil their tasks in a practical, simple, and easy to remember manner. Therefore, if the aprons, as currently used, contain symbolic representation of knowledge, whether handed down by generations or developed in the era prior to 1813, it would be logical for it to appear in the dimensions, style, markings or other forms of presentation of Masonic regalia.

In the 1815 *Constitutions*, the apprentice apron is described as:

> A white lamb skin, from 14 to16 inches wide, 12 to 14 inches deep, square at the bottom, and without ornament, white strings.[46]

What the above description does not mention is that the apron also has a triangular flap that extends from the top edge of the apron to the centre. Also, from the dimensions shown above it is clear that the aprons could be made exactly square, which is the appearance most often conveyed. The aprons are plain and without decoration.

This design seems to be a reflection of the process of training an apprentice in the guild system that developed and flourished in the medieval period. The guilds rigorously protected the skills which referred to the *secrets and mysteries* of the trade. Such knowledge was the basis of one's livelihood and skill, so apprentices were only made privy to it once they demonstrated to their master that they were proficient in what had been previously imparted to them. The apprenticeship was for seven years and the training process was progressive throughout that period, and once the training period was completed the apprentice was usually turned out of his lodgings and job by his master on the day that his full seven years ended. The apprentice had lived and worked with his assigned master for the required period and it had expired the master had no further obligation to him. It was usual and expected that he would become a journeyman, going from job to job for another seven years at least to gain a broad experience by working on a range of projects, before he could be accepted as a free man and eventually become a Master Mason within the guild. The main point, however, is that that when he started, usually at the age of 13 or14 years, the indentured apprentice knew nothing of the trade so the plain apron reflects that condition. Likewise in Freemasonry, when a new member enters a Lodge for the first time, he knows nothing of its *secret and mysteries*.

When an Apprentice joins a Lodge he is regarded as having been *admitted on the square*, for in *Masonry Dissected* by Samuel Pritchard, when the new member is asked what is the shape of the Lodge he responds that it is a *long square*. The initial reaction is to think of the long square as a rectangle, but that might not be what is actually meant as it could equally refer to an enlarged square.

The Entered Apprentice apron is essentially square with a triangular flap. In one of the works of the ancient Greek philosopher, Plato, a verbal exchange takes place between Socrates and Meno on the subject of virtue. Socrates states that he has been told by priests that the soul of every living person has always existed, even long before the person was born, and that the soul knows everything

there is to know but mortals are unaware of how to recall it. He is pointing out that some intelligence is already built into every being and to prove this theory he takes Meno's slave, who is assumed to have been uneducated, and demonstrates through a question and answer process that the boy has the ability to reason on subjects in which he may not have been instructed. Socrates demonstrates this by using a simple exercise in geometry. The following is a paraphrased version of part of the exchange:

Socrates draws a square in the dust on the ground and states that the side lengths are each of two feet, asking the slave boy how long the sides of the square must be to double the size. The slave initially suggests that the length of the side be increased to four feet, but it is pointed out that two x two = four square feet, so by using the slave's suggestion we have four x four = 16 square feet, the result is four times the area, when he really needs eight square feet. The slave is puzzled but, noting that eight is half of 16 he suggests that the sides should be three feet, because it is in the middle of two and four. This is also obviously wrong because three x three = nine square feet, still larger than that required. The slave is now totally confused. Socrates draws a horizontal and vertical line through the square, dividing it into four squares to demonstrate that when something is doubled it increases in both height and width, and that the word double may have two meanings in this context because there is perimeter and there is area. Thus doubling the perimeter results in four times the area, so it is important to know which of the two you wish to double. Socrates also noted that the slave's first answer was correct for perimeter, but not for area.

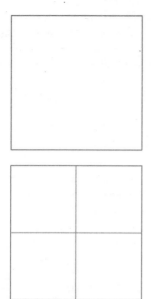

*Top and above:* Socrates and the slave, the original square and the one with smaller squares illustrating that doubling the perimeter results in its expansion in length and width.

Socrates then draws a new square in the dust and asks if it is about the same size as the previous square, and the slave boy acknowledges that it is. He then draws a diagonal line through it, from corner to corner, and asks the slave if each part of the square amounts to half. The slave responds that it appears to be, so Socrates does exactly the same thing as previously drawing a diagonal line across the square from the opposite corners, thereby creating four small triangles in the large square. Socrates points out that if drawing the diagonal line one way created two halves, then obviously doing the same thing from the other corners replicates this action exactly. As the outer square has not changed in size, it must mean that each of the triangles that the two diagonal lines have created must be exactly one quarter of the area of the original square. The slave boy agrees. Thus, says Socrates, if

we now construct the four triangles outside of the square by effectively folding them back, we have a square that is exactly double the area of the original, because the four quarters are exactly equal to the area of the original square.

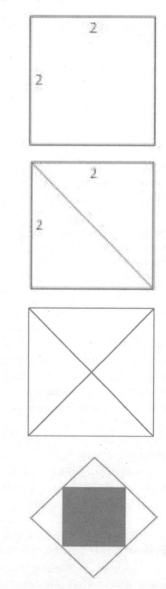

*Top to bottom: The square, divided into triangles, folded out to double the area of the original.*

148

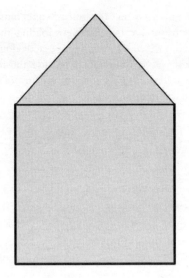

*The shape of the apprentice apron with flap that is ceremonially folded out.*

and, as a journeyman, was expected to travel and undertake a range of different works to gain experience. This was usually for a period of at least seven years, during which time the guild would monitor his progress and, if satisfactory, he could attain the status of a Master Mason. With the starting age of an apprenticeship usually being at 14 years, it follows that the majority of journeymen commenced their next level of training and experience at the age of 21, the age of transit from boy to manhood in those times. The regalia apron comprises the following:

*A plain white lamb skin, similar to the entered apprentice, with the addition only of two sky-blue rosettes at the bottom.*[47]

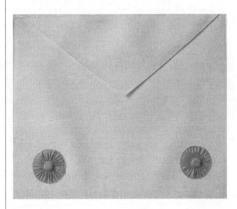

*Fellow Craft apron*

The strings on the Apprentice apron are sufficiently long to enable them to pass round the body and tie at the front, holding the flap up. This is believed to have been the origin of the expression *keeping your end up*.

From this it would seem that the Apprentice apron is a reflection of a basic element of geometry and of knowledge contained in the works of the ancient philosophers, in particular, that relating to the proportions of perimeter and area as described in the lesson on virtue contained in Plato's *Meno*.

This would seem to be an important early lesson in geometry for the Apprentice stonemason to learn. The Apprentice has thereby been initiated into the knowledge *on the square*.

## The Fellow Craft (journeyman)

The name really refers to that period under the old guild system, when the apprentice had finished his training

The symbolic addition of the rosettes is a mystery in itself. The obvious suggestion is that they indicate that the wearer has completed his time as an apprentice and moved up to the second degree. Rosettes, however, contain other symbolism.

The image of the rosette has been used for thousands of years in different cultures to symbolise a range of mythologies. It has represented, among other things, the sun, moon, kingship, power, fidelity, a badge of honour, and there are some writers who claim it to be a symbol of the Virgin Mary. Taking the latter first, it is most unlikely that it symbolises the Holy Virgin, although the colour blue is associated with her in the list of liturgical colours used at various times in the Church year. Any Masonic references to religion in Craft lodges are related to Old Testament text not directly connected with the later virgin birth, although some would argue that it was foretold by the prophets. The Virgin Mary is an icon of the Catholic faith, and at the time the regalia was being designed Catholicism held no status, as we have seen in earlier chapters.

*The Book of Kells* is a seventh to ninth century compilation of Christian iconography and Celtic art, produced at monastic centres in Ireland, and is currently held at Trinity College, Dublin. One of the items, recorded as *folio 129v* portrays images representing the four evangelists, three of them represented by animals or birds that have links to biblical text. The first image in the sequence shows a representation of a human form symbolising *a man*. The human form holds in its hands two rods which extend just below the image, and at the end of each rod is a symbol of a blue rose. Noting earlier observations about the involvement of the Reverend Samuel Hemming in defining the ceremonies after the creation of the United Grand Lodge of England, it is difficult to imagine he was not aware of this Celtic image linking two blue roses with the image of man. It is possible that he used that imagery to add a layer of allegory to symbolise a connection with the guild system when a journeyman was at the second major stage of his

development as a master stonemason, and in his early years of manhood.

*For image, see colour plates 16, 17 & 21.*

The symbol of the rose is the national flower of England, and has been since the conclusion of the civil wars known as the *Wars of the Roses,* when the House of Lancaster, symbolised by a red rose, the House of York, symbolised by a white rose, merged to settle a dispute about the line of kingship. The rose was further identified with England as a symbol during the Tudor period when England separated from the Holy Roman Empire, and has continued to be used as a national symbol, so it is not surprising to find it being used at the time when the United Grand Lodge of England was formed. Around 1813, the colour blue was also regarded as the colour of light, as evidenced by the blue sky above and blue of the ocean, and without light we cannot see the glories of nature around us. In the description of the rosettes they are defined as *sky-blue,* and in ceremonies, one is urged to study the hidden mysteries of nature and science.

The sun and the moon also hold similar significance. In Pritchard's *Masonry Dissected*, there is a part of the ceremony which states:

*Q. What form is the lodge?*
*A. A long square.*
*Q. How long?*
*A. From East to West.*
*Q. How broad?*
*A. From North to South?*
*Q. How is it situated?*
*A. Due East and West.*
*Q. Why so?*
*A. Because all churches and chapels are or ought to be so.*

It then adds:

*Q. Have you lights in your Lodge?*
*A. Yes. Three.*
*Q. What do they represent?*
*A. The sun, moon and Master Mason.*
*Q. How are they situated?*
*A. East, South and West.*
*Q. Why are there no lights in the North?*
*A. Because the sun darts no rays from*
*there.*

The use of the shadow of the sun and the position at which it appeared over the horizon each day was important in the alignment of churches, because they were oriented to the meridian at which the sun rose on the feast day of the saint to which the church was dedicated. The moon would have been significant because the cycles of the solar calendar tend to govern civil matters, while for several millennia, the cycles of the moon have governed religious affairs. Indeed, they still do especially for the setting of the date of Easter: the first Sunday after the first full moon after the spring equinox.

The Fellow Craft is also encouraged to understand some of the hidden attributes of nature and science, and to learn how to align the central axis of a church is one such aspect. It involves understanding that the earth rotates on its axis and as it orbits around the sun, the position where the sun rises over the horizon varies every day because the axis is leaning and has a wobble. This is not the kind of knowledge one would expect the majority of the population to have known or understood in the early 18th century. Even today, most people accept the fact that the sun rises in the east and sets in the west daily, but are unaware that it is a *hidden mystery* or illusion of nature created by the sun remaining stationary and the earth

rotating in an anti-clockwise direction. This is just one item of *hidden knowledge.*

The two other possible reasons for the rosettes being included are as a badge of honour and fidelity. Having joined a Lodge and shown himself to be a person of integrity, the Apprentice is thereby permitted to make the second real step in his Masonic career, the apron with two rosettes reflecting a degree of honour and indicating that he had successfully completed that step. A Freemason also makes a pledge of fidelity not to disclose the *secrets and mysteries* of the Craft, in exactly the same manner as apprentices in the Medieval period made a vow to protect the trade into which they had been admitted.

Hence, as there is a reference to *honour and fidelity* in ceremonies, it would seem logical to link this with the emblem of England and the colour of light, *sky-blue*, which illuminates the beauty of the world, and would be a valid reason for the rosettes inclusion.

Yet it is most possible that the rosettes provide a further link with Plato's *Meno.* In analysing the Apprentice degree, we noted how the design of the apron appears to reflect the aspect of geometry that enables a square of unknown size to be doubled in area. Through *Meno,* we are also rewarded with a second lesson.

Continuing the paraphrased story, Socrates returns to his original square, and reminds the slave that a square increases in size by perimeter and in extending both length and width, thereby resulting in essentially four squares of the same size. He reminds the boy that by drawing a diagonal line, corner to corner, across one of the smaller squares, cutting that square into two equal parts, and proceeding to do the same through each square, he creates a diamond shape in the centre.

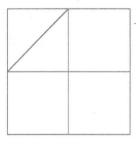

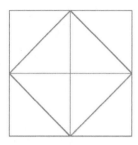

thereby becoming exactly half the area of the original square.

The Fellow Craft apron has its flap folded down but, when coupled with that of the Apprentice, it results in an image of the diamond shape representing half the area of the outside square created by the apron.

This would have been an important second lesson for a trainee Mason to learn, for in the absence of any definite intention on the part of the designers in the Union's early days, this is perhaps a plausible explanation of the symbolic representation of the Fellow Craft apron: a second lesson in basic geometry, a second step *on the square* as indicated by the two rosettes.

## Master Mason regalia

The *Master Mason* apron is something rather different. It is described as follows:

> The same,[as the Fellow Craft] with sky-blue lining and edging, 1½ inch deep, and an additional rosette on the fall or flap. No other colour or ornament shall be allowed, except to officers and past officers of lodges, who may have the emblems of their offices in silver or white in the centre of the apron.[48]

Thus Socrates points out that by drawing a diagonal line across each of the smaller squares to create the diamond-shaped pattern, and reducing each square to two halves, it follows that the resultant diamond shape/square at the centre will equal the area of four of those halves,

This apron is awarded after one has satisfied the assembled brethren that the member concerned understands the knowledge communicated in the previous degree, a considerable part of which is based upon legend relating to the building of Solomon's Temple and the two pillars described in the books of 'Kings' and 'Chronicles' in the Old Testament.

There has been mention of the two groups of tassels in the official description of the apron, leading some to speculate that it is a reflection of an old stonemason's apron with the strings that held it being tied at the front and hanging below the flap around the waist. It is this author's contention, however, that if the apron is a reflection of knowledge, then the physical attributes of strings in a hanging position is an unlikely answer.

The most noticeable characteristic is the flap. First, the blue edging allied with the tassels appearing to form the letter 'M', could only signify *Master Mason*. Second, it is in the form of an isosceles triangle, which is defined by two angles and two sides being the same. What is not so obvious, however, is the position of the rosettes as they form an equilateral triangle.

*Note how the sides of the triangle set the position for the tassels.*

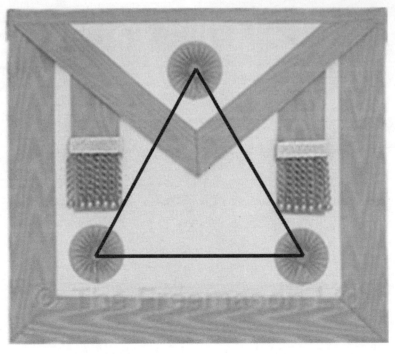

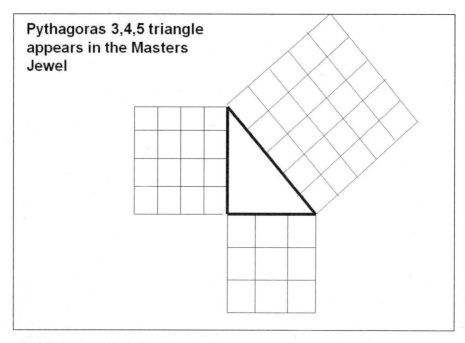

**Pythagoras 3,4,5 triangle appears in the Masters Jewel**

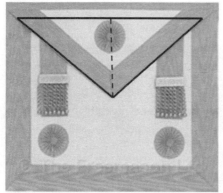

*Above and left:* Pythagoras' theorem in the Master Mason apron and reflected in the Master's jewel.

There is one further attribute. If the base line of the isosceles triangle moves down to the top edge of the rosette, it will form a continuous line with the lower edge of the waistband, which in turn enables the large isosceles triangle to be divided into two parts, each being of the ratio three, four, five as a reflection of Pythagoras' theorem that the *square on the hypotenuse of a right-angled triangle equals the sum of the squares of the other two sides.*

If the flap of the apron is lifted and folded outwards, then the overall representation would be akin to that of an ancient temple of Greece or Rome. In the absence of any other drawings or images depicting how Solomon's Temple may have looked, it would not have been unreasonable for individuals educated in the 1700s, and then associated with the design of the regalia, to have considered the same Greek and Roman concept of temple configuration for that of Jerusalem, and reflected it in the apron of the Master Mason. If that was the case, then the two hanging, tasselled ribbons could represent the two pillars as described in 'Kings' and 'Chronicles', and the foundations on which each pillar was mounted. These, being beneath the surface, comprise of different soil structures depending on the location and the underground layers at their base. The tassels, therefore, perhaps emphasise the need for firm foundations to support the structure and for good foundations as expressed to the Apprentice at his initiation. The silver clips above the tassels would represent the base or plinth on which the column would sit, especially as invoked by the Ionic and Corinthian styles outlined by Vitruvius.

Inigo Jones took great interest, we are told, in the works of the Italian designer Andre Palladio, who made great use of the triangular pediment. As the influence of Renaissance architecture was incorporated into the stately homes of the aristocracy and landed gentry, so the triangular pediment became a regular feature of such structures as shown below, in a wing at Hampton Court Palace designed by Sir Christopher Wren.

*The pediment as incorporated at Hampton Court Palace, complete with pillars.*

Returning to the symbolism of the tassels, the number seven has long been regarded as a sacred number, with the days of the week being one example. In the Book of Genesis it states that the deity made the world in six days and rested on the seventh, and in the past other writers have speculated that it is a reference to the old ceremonies as outlined in *Masonry Dissected,* wherein the exchange between the Master and the member is:

Q. What Makes a Just and Perfect Lodge?
A. Seven or more.
Q. What do they consist of?
A. One Master, Two Wardens. Two Fellow Craft and two Entered Apprentices.

There are, however, two sets of tassels, making 14 in all, so only one set of seven seems unlikely to be the answer.

In Masonic ceremonial, King Solomon is *seven years and upwards in the building, completing and dedicating the temple…* but that does not produce an exact number. On the other hand, an apprenticeship was defined as being for seven years and the period of being a journeyman was seven years or more, both functions reflected in the two previous degrees, the Entered Apprentice and the Fellow Craft. Thus it is highly likely that the two sets of tassels reflect those time periods, which would be a minimum total of 14 years from the start of an apprenticeship to being accepted as a fully qualified and experienced craftsman, with the possibility of eventual recognition as a Master Mason within a Guild. There was one other important piece of information that was regarded as the ultimate secret of a Master Mason in the Guild system, and it again reflects in Plato's *Meno*.

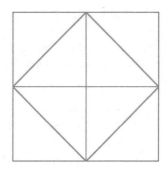

We have noted that Socrates has taught the slave boy about doubling the perimeter and area of a square of unknown dimension, and also to reduce the area of an unknown square by half. Socrates notes that we have a square with a diamond at the centre which is half the area of the outer square. To this he now adds the diagonal lines, corner to corner, that were used in doubling the area.

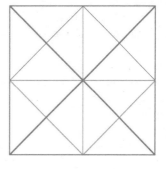

By drawing lines at the points of intersection with the diagonal lines, the resultant square at the centre is exactly half the size in perimeter of the outer square.

These processes for sizing a square of unknown dimension were regarded as the most important secrets of the master stonemasons in the Medieval period.

The description of the apron dimension states that it should be 14-16 inches wide and 12-14 inches deep, with edging of 1½ inches. If the apron is actually made at 15 inches wide and three inches removed to

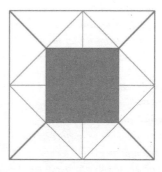

allow for the two edges, then the square in the centre is 12 inches wide. Likewise, there is no edging along the top edge of the apron beneath the flap. Thus, if we make the apron 14 inches deep and use the point where the side of the flap corresponds with the outer edge of the white area, as a marker, we are left with a square in the centre of the apron with side measurements of 12 inches, thereby replicating the square created by following Socrates' instructions. This knowledge, obtained from the *Meno*, represents the *third step on the square.*

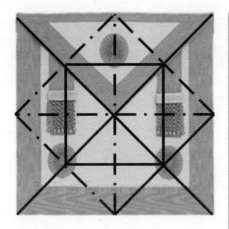

However, if the Master Mason apron was of square dimensions, as allowed for above, the solution of Plato's *Meno* would become all too obvious and was probably the original intention of the designers. If one then notes that the letter 'M', created by the flap and tassels, is within the white area of the apron, it could be an allegorical statement of *masonry being on the square* and give credibility to the observation in *Masonry Dissected* relating to a *long square*.

*Author's Note:*
*The dimensions of many aprons produced today do not appear to comply with those originally set down just after the Union of the two Grand Lodges. A minor variance in the positioning of the rosettes, the vertical centre alignment of the tassels, and the cutting and stitching of the flap to the main body of the apron will result in the geometric significance being undermined. Whereas the original description requires a border of 1½ inches, some more recently produced aprons have edging that is over two inches wide. It is highly probable that over the past two centuries, this geometric significance has been lost by the regalia manufacturers, especially as new manufacturers have entered the market, and the apron has become a 'commodity of a style of uniform' with a visual representation of the original requirement rather than the geometric ornament that seems to have been intended. If the central area of the apron is made exactly 12 inches square with a border of 1½ inches, the geometry is perfect, especially when the base line for the equilateral triangle is the lower edge of the white square created by the blue border. Sadly, a 'corporate design manual' that sets out the exact dimensions and positioning of components, that could be used for manufacturing purposes does not seem to exist.*

## Master Mason University

Given the observations noted above, and that Renaissance architecture had been introduced in England in the early 1600s, and also that *speculative/ accepted masons* are believed to have been admitted to the London Company of Masons around the year 1620, it would not be unreasonable to suggest that the Master Mason apron is a reflection of the Palladian style of architecture that was particularly popular with the aristocracy in the era 1620-1800, and of the time periods of training and experience that a young man must first have undertaken in order to become a Master Mason of the London Company and thereby be considered to have sufficient competence to execute such constructions.

The edging of the apron is the next item to consider. In the circumstance where the flap is folded back to create the image of a temple, the two side edges would represent the outer pillars holding up the portico. The dimension is also such that, if the apron is 15 inches wide, then there can be 10 such edging widths across the face of the apron. The number 10 has long been regarded as the most perfect number, reflecting 10 fingers and 10 toes.

If one leaves the outer positions and then removes alternate spacing, we end with approximately the correct spacing of the pillars, with an appropriate wider entrance area, that seems to conform to the pillar spacing used in ancient temples.

During the course of the Master Mason degree ceremonial, members are urged to make a study of the liberal arts and sciences, which was the basis of a Master of Arts degree in the era when the regalia was being designed. This encouragement to undertake a course of study may well be reflected in the colour of the edging of the aprons: if we accept that the apron actually contains knowledge, then the place where knowledge and understanding is taught, is a university. During the lifetime of those responsible for the design of the aprons there were only two universities in England, that of Oxford and Cambridge. Oxford was founded *circa* 1167, although it claims teaching in the city started at an earlier date, while Cambridge claims its foundations from *circa* 1209 and was started when a group of academics from Oxford left and set up a rival institution following the execution of two Oxford teachers. The traditional colours of the two universities are Oxford – garter blue (dark blue) and Cambridge – light blue. The Union with Scotland in 1707 that created Great Britain also provided access to St. Andrew's University, which had been founded by papal decree *circa* 1410.

The University of Durham is usually cited as the next to be formed in England, with a date of 1832, but Kings College, London, claims a foundation date of 1826, although it was not ratified by charter as a university at that time. However, both bodies were founded well after the design of the aprons was agreed and promulgated from 1814.

From the foundation dates, it could be argued that Oxford was therefore the senior of the two oldest universities in England. In Freemasonry, the higher administrative levels of the Provinces and Grand Lodge have dark blue aprons and a Lodge cannot be established without their agreement, thus from the one others are formed. This then seems to be a reflection of the foundation of the two key universities, the two main centres of learning and knowledge in England around the start of the 19th century.

There are two further aspects of the apron that require scrutiny and are probably never considered by modern Freemasons. The Apprentice and Fellow Craft aprons are usually furnished with cords tied around the body to hold the apron in place, while the apron of a Master Mason has a strap, usually about the same width as the edging, secured in place around the body by a hook and eye. When the strap is surrounding the body, it is symbolising the circle, a geometric character that has no beginning or end. To draw a circle requires that the starting point is in the centre and it can only be a perfect circle if *every part of the circumference is equi-distant* from it. When worn correctly, the centre-front of the band sits over the navel, the centre from which one derives life before birth and is geometrically the centre of the body. The circle symbolises many things, including some aspects of religion, but mostly the regularity of the cycles of the *hidden mysteries of nature and science,* reflected in the sun rising in the east; the effect of the moon on the tides; the seasons especially the Spring being a period of rebirth, after the winter months when all is dormant. The hook and eye on the ends of the straps show the hook to be plain on the inside and patterned on the outside. Close inspection of this pattern will reveal that it is the symbol of a snake, and the head of the snake fits through the eye of the other half of the strap. The symbol of a snake, swallowing its own tail creates a circle that has long symbolised eternity. When the hook is therefore in the eye of the second strap, it is completing that circle and thereby representing the symbolism attached to it. There is also the element of ancient iconography which sometimes features the image of a snake or serpent. Once a year, a snake will shed its skin, in a process of renewal. Thus, such iconography sometimes features the snake to symbolise rebirth or resurrection, a process that is similar to the cycle of the seasons, as is implied in the ceremonial of the Master Mason.

## The Provincial Officer's apron

For some years prior to the formation of the United Grand Lodge of England, a regional structure of management had been in place. The counties immediately surrounding London have long since been referred to as *the Provinces*, meaning that they were away from the jurisdiction of the City of London. As the Masonic movement expanded, so the regional administration was based, like much of the judicial and local government authorities, within county boundaries. In consequence, the regional management and local structure of English Freemasonry became known as a *Provincial Grand Lodge*. One must assume that, for compatibility purposes, the officers and duties of the *Provincial team* were a replication of those of the *Craft* Lodge, but with a higher degree of responsibility while exercising control on behalf of United Grand Lodge. Indeed, every Provincial Grand Master is appointed

to office by the Grand Master, hence membership of a Provincial Grand Lodge is perceived to be superior to the ordinary Craft Lodges. It is universally accepted that it takes some years for a Brother to advance on an annual basis through the relevant ceremonial offices in his Lodge, as well as assuming a role in the Lodge administration or charity functions, thus proving himself to be a worthy member for many years before being admitted to a Provincial Grand Lodge.

As a senior and distinct level of authority, Provincial Lodge members are recognised by a change in the colour of the regalia; for while the ordinary Lodges have regalia of light blue texture, those of the Provincial Grand Lodge are of dark blue, sometimes described as *royal blue* or *garter blue,* being the colour associated with the insignia of the *Most Noble Order of the Garter.* This supreme Order is the preserve of the British Royal Family, and is only conferred on foreign royalty or other notable dignitaries at the behest of the Sovereign.

There is also a broadly-held opinion that the colour of the Provincial regalia is a reflection of the dark blue adopted by Oxford University. In terms of longevity, as noted in an earlier paragraph, Oxford claims a higher ranking than Cambridge in much the same way that the Provincial Lodge has a higher ranking than a Lodge.

We have seen that aprons of each of the three degrees reveal unique characteristics, including a subliminal knowledge that would have been important for the stonemason and master mason builder, of former centuries, and presented in allegorical form. A similar situation appears to apply to the Provincial Lodge apron and regalia.

*For images of Craft regalia, see colour section Plate 20, 21, 22, 23, 24.*

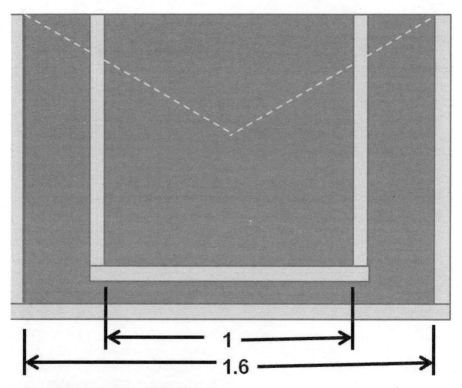

Beneath the flap on the apron can be seen a square, defined in gold braiding. This square, and the overall size of the apron seem to be a reflection of another important geometrical element of ancient knowledge used in stonemasonry, known as, *divine proportion* or the *golden ratio*.

This incorporates two numerical values: 1.618 and 0.618, often rounded to 1.6 or 0.6. Geometrically, these proportional symbols can be achieved by starting with a square. At a point halfway along the base of the square, a pair of compasses are extended to one of the top corners, and an arc that represents a semi-circle extends to the baseline of the square. The additional element to the side of the square represents 0.618 of the width of the square, thus it follows that the width of the square plus the length of the additional segment with be 1.618 of the sides of the square. This is shown in the following illustrations.

The resultant rectangle is in the proportion of width to height that the ancient civilisations, particularly of Greece and Rome, regarded as the perfect ratio for the construction of temples, hence the term *divine proportion*.

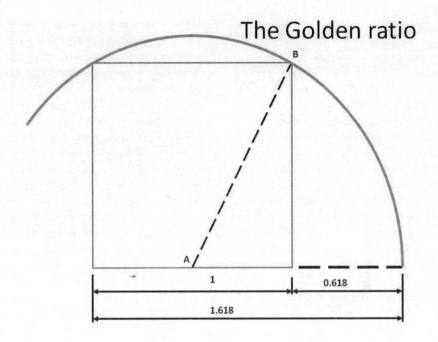

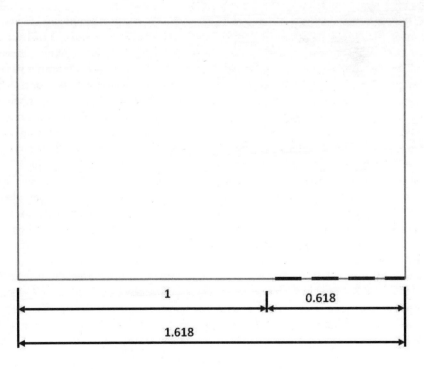

Noting that this is the basic design for the regional Grand Lodge regalia, it is fitting in so far that anyone in a position of responsibility within a region is expected to operate in a moderate, measured way by keeping every action proportionate to the circumstances that evolve. Furthermore, as the knowledge contained in Freemasonry is progressive, one would expect it to be derived from a level within a Craft Lodge, prior to the officer being promoted to a Provincial rank. This seems to be the case, as we will see in due course.

In this one simple design, the superiority of authority and time over the Craft Lodges and their membership are illustrated in the background colour, whilst the size, and the outlined square in the centre, seem to imply reference to proportion.

## Allegory in the dimensions

However, none of this answers two outstanding questions: what inspired the design of the aprons, as recorded in the 1815 *Book of Constitutions*, to have the rather strange dimensions of 14 to 16 inches wide and 12 to 14 inches deep?

Let us again remember that nothing in Freemasonry is created by chance, all of its symbols and ceremonies, are there for a purpose. Could it be that the dimensions actually refer to dates – 1212, 1213 and 1214, and 1414, 1415 and 1416 – and if so, what do they represent?

In an earlier chapter about the allegory of the Second Degree tracing board, it was pointed out that the text seemed to have a clear reference to the rebuilding of St. Paul's Cathedral, Old St. Paul's having been destroyed in the Great Fire of London in 1666 that devastated the city. According to chroniclers there was a previous catastrophe in the year 1212,

when the whole of London was burnt to the ground, including a church that stood on the site later occupied by old St. Paul's and the later building attributed to Sir Christopher Wren.

In 1213, the French King was planning to attack and invade England, but King John heard of these plans and put together a small fleet of ships, as well as calling upon a troop of knights, to stop the attack before it had a chance to leave port. Under William Longspee, Earl of Salisbury, this small English fleet sailed to Damm, in Flanders, and there found over 1,500 ships prepared for the invasion but very lightly defended. The English ships sailed into battle, seizing over three hundred enemy vessels and destroying, sinking or burning the remainder, while managing to escape before French reinforcements arrived at the scene. Had this attack not been successful, it is highly probable that England would have again been invaded by the French and the course of British history would have changed. This is recorded as the first victory of the newly developing Royal Navy, a fleet which, in 1813-15 would be the cornerstone of communications, trade and protection of the growing British Empire.

The year 1214 was when Oxford University received its charter recognising it as an institution with its own rules and governance, and dark or garter blue is the colour of Oxford University and the Provincial and Grand Lodge structures. The charter was issued on 20th June, the eve of the Summer Solstice.[49] It should, however, be noted that the Order of the Garter, to which 'garter blue' refers, was not formed until 125 years later (1348), by Edward III.

It is also worth noting that in 1214 there was a growing rift between the barons and King John. This rift culminated the following year 1215 with the signing of the document *Magna Carta*.

In 1414, the Council of Constance (Lake Constance) commenced. It was to this council that Poggio Bracciolini had attended as a member of the papal entourage, and later enabled him to visit several monastic communities nearby, which in turn led him to discover a number of manuscripts of the works of the ancient philosophers.

1415 was the year of the Battle of Agincourt, led by Henry V. It was also the year in which John Wycliffe was placed on trial and sentenced to death by burning at the Council of Constance, and when Poggio discovered the works of Vitruvius, the father of architecture.

And 1416 is the year that the rediscovered works of Vitruvius were translated into Italian, which started the era which became known as the Renaissance.

To summarise, it seems that the design of the apron of the degree of a Master Mason is:

- A refection of the two universities in England, with Cambridge being highlighted in the colours of the Craft Lodges; hence the Master Mason apron refers to a centre where the liberal arts and sciences could be studied and a Master of Arts degree awarded.
- A representation of Solomon's Temple as envisaged in the early 19th century, complete with pillars, foundations and plinths.
- Triangular geometry – isosceles and equilateral.
- A circle symbolising eternity.
- The two periods of seven years of an apprenticeship and journeyman prior to becoming a Master Mason in the Medieval period.
- The completion of an education in basic geometry created by the descriptions in Plato's *Meno*.

- The establishment of the Royal Navy and its importance to Britain.
- The preparation of the signing of Magna Carta.
- The rediscovery of Vitruvius and the start of the Renaissance.

## Allegory of the collar

There is one other item of Craft regalia to mention, the collar and jewel.

As with any social organisation having a regular form of governance, Lodges have a Treasurer and Secretary, and a chain of other offices associated with ceremonial and charitable undertakings. Each officer of the Lodge is usually a Master Mason, with each office having its own symbol attached to the collar, worn around the neck. The collar is described as: *'light-blue riband, four inches broad'.*[50]

The design is such that when worn, the front from the shoulder to the navel, represents an isosceles triangle, while that around the neck is a semi-circle.

In the Fellow Craft degree, the candidate is apprised in a lecture concerning the building of Solomon's Temple, based on the text of Josephus, plus the biblical books of 'Kings' and 'Chronicles'. In describing the pillars they are said to be clad in brass or bronze, possibly to signal the start of the Bronze age. The cladding is defined as being: *'four inches, or a hand's breadth in thickness'.*

As mentioned in an earlier chapter, as the human body is perceived as representing a structural pillar, the collar represents that shell of bronze that encased the pillars of Solomon's Temple, while the semi-circular element around the neck represents the column itself.

*Author's note 1:*
*Although the dimensions of the designs were issued by Grand Lodge, as Freemasonry grew so regalia suppliers started manufacturing and selling the aprons and collars. In recent years there have even been manufacturers from overseas countries such as China that have sought to enter this market. Also in recent years, some of the dimensions and positioning of the decorations of the aprons has drifted slightly. In researching this chapter, I noted that the older aprons seem to provide the dimensional accuracy for the creation of the equilateral triangle.*

*Author's Note 2:*
*The next level in Craft Freemasonry is the Master of the Lodge. It might seem appropriate, therefore, to deal with that regalia in this chapter. I am deferring it to the next. In the opening chapters I noted that the role of the Master is not considered as a degree, and has all but been side-lined within the prevailing structure. It will be more coherent, therefore, to deal with this item in one chapter for overall completeness.*

## Masonic Memory Review 7

What appears at first to be rather uninteresting regalia, though it displays the level of seniority within the Masonic hierarchy, actually also infers that there is a range of historical knowledge, references and ancient geometrical wisdom in the fabric. Furthermore, it seems to be there by deliberate design, conveying information in an allegorical form rather than by mere coincidence. Our attention is again drawn to an earlier statement that Freemasonry is *'a peculiar system of morality, veiled in allegory and illustrated by symbols'*. In this case the symbols are the regalia.

All of these attributes form a continuous connection with the various strands of Freemasonry and the information considered most important to record, in the century prior to the creation of the United Grand Lodge of England.

As yet we have not looked in any detail at the Master Degree, but as we will see, it is a degree that adds to the knowledge pool.

*Chapter 11*

# The Master of the Lodge and the rank of Past Master

IN THE EARLY PAGES of this book, it was noted that the role of the Master of a Lodge appears to have been side-lined within the hierarchy of the organisation. Yet it is to that position that members elect one of their number, perceived to be the highest honour that any Lodge can confer on any of its members. Additionally, a study of the knowledge associated with this office suggests that it is a precursor to understanding the structure, symbolism and ceremonial present in the Holy Royal Arch of Jerusalem; the pinnacle of regular Freemasonry.

Has the role of the Master been therefore relegated? And if so, why? The failure to regard the office of Worshipful Master as a degree, is not the consequence of some recent political change, but based on decisions taken some 200 years ago. When the United Grand Lodge was formed in 1813, a statement was issued to the effect that there were only three degrees in English Freemasonry – namely Entered Apprentice, Fellow Craft and Master Mason including the Supreme Order of the Royal Arch. It is odd that the Master of the Lodge was omitted as a degree when one appreciates that the ceremonial process for the installation of the Master, is as detailed as any. The ceremony of the Installation embodies the imparting of esoteric knowledge, and while the Master is elected by all members of the Lodge, only those who have previously been installed as a Master

– i.e. Past Masters are present during the ceremony.

The role of the Worshipful Master is certainly not an extension of the Master Mason degree, otherwise it would be described as such, and neither is it part of the Provincial Lodge structure. Furthermore, the Holy Royal Arch was obliquely referred to in the Master Mason degree, implying that it was considered to be a part, or extension of that ceremony.

To further confuse matters, senior officers of the Provincial Lodge are present throughout the Installation of the Master, a practice which has long been established. During such meetings they witness the work of key participants, which is mentally noted, and the results may well determine the particular Provincial rank with which the Brother may be invested in the future. This underlines the perceived importance of the office of the Master, and the significance of the entire ceremonial.

Despite all this, the role of the Master is effectively an isolated island in Freemasonry. But it wasn't always so.

## The Guild Connection

The Grand Lodge of *Moderns* and that of the *Antients* had a number of individual Lodges under their control before the union in 1813, each electing a Master at its head from earliest times.

For many years, the Lodge had been seen as a reflection of the place where the stonemasons worked. On very large projects, such as cathedrals, the structure is likely to have gone through several different influences and designs over a prolonged period of time, perhaps even several centuries. In most cases, the cathedral would not have been close to the site where the stone was actually quarried, and which would therefore need to be transported to the place where the building was being erected. As it was not possible to fashion irregular shaped rocks at the quarry, they were transported to a designated *stone-yard*. Here the stones were hewn into the size required and *boasted for carving*, and the initial marking took place prior to conveyance to the building site. The process known as *boasted for carving* is a stonemasonry terminology. In some buildings – cathedrals, churches and monuments being good examples – a pattern or illustration may be quite large and extend over the face of several stones both vertically and horizontally. To accommodate this, the face to be carved will be left rough and slightly protruding, enabling the required image to be carved insitu as a continuous operation, at an appropriate time in the construction process.

On a large project there was a continuous stream of horse-or oxen-drawn carts arriving at the building site with the prepared stone. Blocks needed for walls and flying buttresses were likely to have been of one particular size, whereas those needed to create sections of a large pillar to take the weight of the roof would have been of different dimensions. Thus, stockpiling the stone for use was a necessary requirement, otherwise the building process would have been extremely erratic. It appears that the *hewers* were lesser skilled, yet they possessed special knowledge concerning the characteristics of different types of stone, and were able to assess where and how they could be employed to achieve the necessary results, before passing them on to more skilled hands for completion. It should also be remembered that the work, for the most part, was initially undertaken in the open with very little protection from the vagaries of the weather.

The role of the builder mason was very different however, lifting the blocks into position, and ensuring they were straight and vertical, in order to conform with the overall plan. Some buildings had been assembled with such skill, that courses of blocks (ashlars) seem to have no mortar between the layers. This was achieved by hollowing the top, bottom and ends of the block slightly and filling them with mortar, so that when they were butted together a thin layer of mortar would squeeze out and seal the gap, making them weathertight, whilst the hollow provided a key that locked them all together. It is evident that the builder masons were constantly working in the open and thus exposed to the extremes of weather.

The skilled masons who were able to reproduce intricate designs and patterns could be regarded as sculptors and would have worked on the same block for several days, consequently requiring a modest shelter in order to perform their allotted task. The stone and chip dust were likely to have been in small amounts by comparison with the *hewers*, and the range of tools, especially chisels, would have been more extensive than those of some of the mason's counterparts, and had to be close at hand.

The word *Lodge* means a shelter, which may have been little more than four poles holding up a basic roof strewn with straw, and it is likely that several such Lodges may have been erected on a construction site.

The Master Mason would usually have been someone who was highly skilled in all aspects of the work to be undertaken, a good organiser and project manager, the person who would oversee all the work. Before the advent of the architect as known today, the Master Mason was also the designer, and the main individual who dealt with the client.

These are very different images to the ones we normally associate with masons and the lodge in the Medieval period. In the case of a very large construction project, such as a castle or cathedral, meetings between the master mason and the workers would be held onsite. However, it was also usual for the men of the local guild to elect one of the members to represent their views at wider guild functions, where several trades might meet together as a local council to arrange fairs and markets.

The guild structure was not only required to have a master elected by the members, but also two wardens. The master was responsible for the overall interests of his respective trade, while the wardens acted as his assistants. The role of a warden was to ensure that the members only undertook work as free men that they could afford; that the prices charged were those set by the trade, or embodied in legislation, and not devised to undercut a fellow tradesman; that apprentices were receiving proper instruction and making suitable progress. The wardens were the inspectors, policemen and enforcers of the trade.

Considering the above points, it might easily be concluded that the master was not a role directly associated with the working of the stone, but was more about elected guild management responsibility, and the reason why the role of the master was set aside from the degrees of masonry. There may even be another answer.

According to material held at Freemasons' Hall in London, the Royal Arch was a degree that was practiced as far back as the 1730s. One highly credible writer notes:

> ...Vibert suggested that the Royal Arch originally formed part of a ceremony for the Installation of a Master of a Craft Lodge, but there is no evidence for this ceremony, at the time at which the Royal Arch was developing, being anything other than a ceremonial placing of the Master in the chair without any esoteric content...[51].

The word 'esoteric' is one which is often misunderstood or misrepresented. It means:[52]

- *A doctrine that is intended to be known by a few initiates.*
- *Something that is meant for a few individuals who have a special interest or knowledge.*
- *Special knowledge that is restricted to a few individuals – a secret.*

Like all the other degrees, the ceremonial is intended to be known only by a few initiates with special knowledge, and restricted to those individuals – the Past Masters.

The above comment in respect of *Vibert* suggests that the Installation of the Master was an important ceremony, and that it may have included esoteric material which was later removed and established with ceremonial content of its own – namely the Royal Arch. If that indeed happened, then it implies that the ceremony of the Installation of the Master embodied a considerable fund of knowledge of which some special understanding was needed.

When one completes a term as a Master, one is defined as being a Past Master, with no ceremony being attached to that status, although it is usual to assume administrative positions in the Lodge such as Secretary, Treasurer, Almoner, Charity Steward, etc. Yet there are references to the probability that in a previous era when certain knowledge was practised within a degree ceremony. Indeed, it seems that, shortly after 1813, in order to qualify to become a member of a Royal Arch Chapter and to occupy a chair, one had to have been an Installed Master of a Craft Lodge. This situation continued until about the mid-1800s when the Royal Arch Chapters experienced falling numbers and the qualification for joining the Order was effectively downgraded to being a Master Mason.

Therefore, until recent times, the role of Master or Past Master was deemed to be of far greater significance than it is today. The qualification of being a Master Mason to join a Royal Arch Chapter became merely a matter of convenience to increase membership, nothing to do with a level of knowledge or understanding from previous degrees. The fact that this change could have been undertaken with such ease and readiness suggests that those making such a decision had no idea regarding the significance of any esoteric knowledge that was available to a Master, or its impact on a true understanding of the Royal Arch.

The above remark about the placing of the Master in the chair

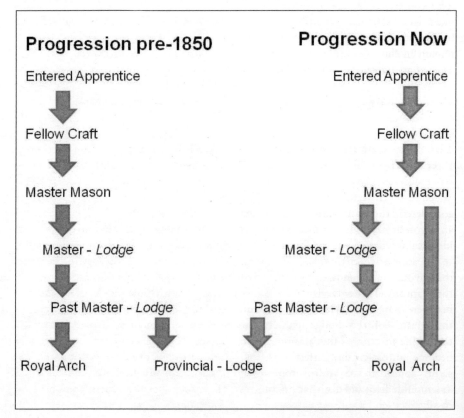

without esoteric knowledge is worth consideration, because the ceremony does indeed embody this knowledge, which raises the question of how it got there and where it came from. In fact, this knowledge is so important that it is virtually impossible to understand the symbols of the Royal Arch without an appreciation of the mystic knowledge of a Master, or a Past Master.

Based on records in the archives at Freemasons Hall, London, it seems that the degree of the Royal Arch was practised by Lodges of the two original Grand bodies. Records confirm that Royal Arch Chapters existed in the 1750s, with evidence of possible existence as early as the 1730s. Indeed, if, as previously suggested, the Royal Arch ceremonial was created out of that of a former Master degree, then it would be logical that some trace of it would remain in the ceremonial of installing a Master, as indeed seems to be the case.

So can we define what that knowledge was?

## The regalia of the Master and Past Master

When the Installation ceremony is completed, the new Master is awarded an apron as his badge of office which is identical to that of a Past Master.

In an earlier chapter we looked at the layout and geometry of the first three aprons. The only visual difference between that of the Master Mason and the Master of the Lodge is that the three blue rosettes of the Master Mason become three symbols that, on first sight, appear to be an inverted letter 'T' moulded in and finished in bronze or silver.

The 1815 *Constitutions* define these symbols as being *parallel lines*. They are described thus:

> The masters and past masters of lodges to wear, in lieu and in the places of the three rosettes on the master masons apron, perpendicular lines upon horizontal line, thereby forming three several sets of two right-angles; the length of the horizontal lines to be two inches and a half each, and the perpendicular lines one inch; these emblems to be of riband, half an inch broad...[53]

One of the definitions of the word *riband* is '..a flat rail attached to posts', which the emblem today certainly seems to represent.

Sadly, we have no records which define exactly what these emblems are meant to represent. Several early writers on Freemasonry described them as being *Taus*, and were a precursor to the *Triple Tau* featured in the Royal Arch – that Royal Arch connection once again. Yet this cannot possibly be.

This argument is difficult to sustain unless the emblems are each rotated so that they represent a Tau, but the proportions are not precise when fitted together to form a representation of the Triple Tau.

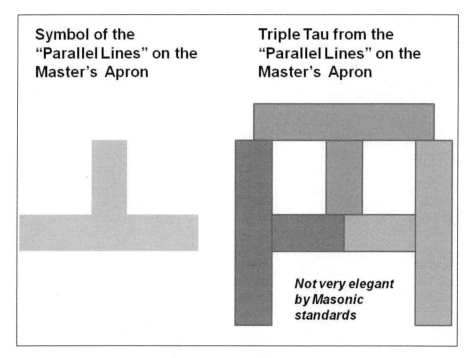

Symbol of the "Parallel Lines" on the Master's Apron

Triple Tau from the "Parallel Lines" on the Master's Apron

*Not very elegant by Masonic standards*

*The emblems turned to symbolise the Triple Tau – which is dimensionally incorrect*

It is worth noting however, that the symbol used on the aprons, is to be found in illuminated Celtic scriptures produced in Ireland some 1,200 years ago, and one image in particular has a distinct connection with the Royal Arch, as we will see later.

There may be another reason as to why this symbol is used. There are eight right-angles to be found in each emblem. In ancient numerology, the number eight is a symbol of eternity, and if one visits any of the great cathedrals of Britain and Continental Europe, one will usually find the symbol of an octagon somewhere close to the altar, or sometimes in the shape of a spire as revealed in the ceiling tracery. However, one has to naturally look upwards, which in a bygone era inferred looking towards heaven and

thereby to eternity. By virtue of the fact that the octagon exists, it is an indication that operative masons of *olde* would have known of this connection.

Next, there are three symbols, so three sets of eight right-angles make 24 in total. There are 24 hours in each day, which means that *the Earth rotates on its axis in its orbit around the sun* by 15 degrees in what is called an hour. In Masonic terms this is defined by a rule (measure) of 24 inches, which is divided into three parts; part to be spent in prayer and service to the deity, part to be spent in labour and part in sleep. Hence the three symbols, each with their three right-angles, have a close resemblance to the three equal divisions of the day as mentioned in our ceremonies.

Other than creating an obvious width to the symbol which enables the eight right-angles to be defined, there seems to be no logic to this dimension. In the earlier ceremonies of the Fellow Craft and the Master Mason, there is mention from the Old Testament of Solomon's Temple which was built to house the Ark of the Covenant. If one takes the length of the short side of the symbol (one inch) and adds the width to which it is attached (half an inch) then the shorter side becomes one and a half inches whilst the length remains two and a half inches. The Ark of the Covenant was a wooden box, protected by a coating of gold, with end dimensions of 1.5 cubits and a length of 2.5 cubits. So the symbol appears to have a link to Solomon's Temple through the Ark. There's more: if we divide the shorter length by the longer length we get 1.5/2.5 = 0.6 or 2.5/1.5 = 1.6 (rounded)

These two numbers are recognised symbols of *divine proportion* or the *golden ratio*. This ratio was extremely important to the ancient masons in defining the proportion of the height of a building to width and length. For example, it is employed extensively in the layout of the Queen's House at Greenwich, the first built in the Renaissance style in England by Inigo Jones. Thus, three symbols on the apron, two in the horizontal plane and one elevated may well symbolise proportion in the three planes of a building length, width and height. (This is illustrated further in an earlier book, *Mandorla and Tau*). As the Master is responsible for the management and good rules, it may also symbolise the need to exercise proportion in all actions within the Lodge.

There is one other possibility with geometric connections – the theory of parallel lines known as *Euclid's parallel postulate*. Other of Euclid's assumptions and theorems are symbolised in several ways throughout Freemasonry, and the description from 1813 uses the term *parallel lines*.

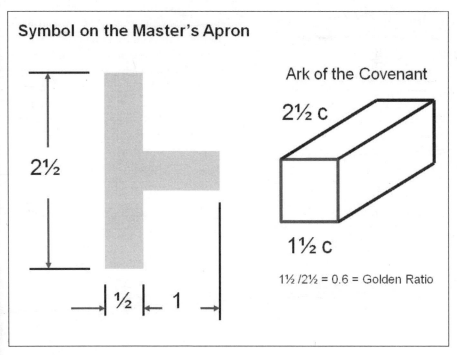

**Symbol on the Master's Apron**

2½

½   1

Ark of the Covenant

2½ C

1½ C

1½ /2½ = 0.6 = Golden Ratio

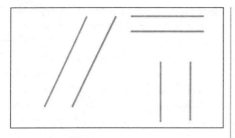

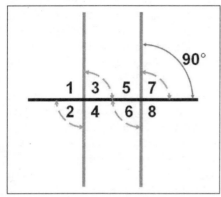

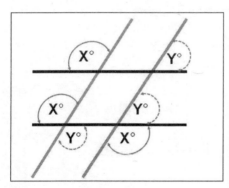

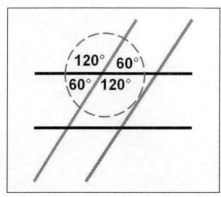

Put simply, the postulate states, that if you have any two lines in any plane such that the distance between them remains exactly the same, they travel in the same direction and no part moves closer or further away from the other, and they never meet, then they are parallel. If two parallel lines are in the vertical plane and are crossed by a third line in the horizontal plane, then all the angles between the bisecting lines will be right-angles of 90 degrees. If two parallel lines are in an angled plane and cut by two parallel lines in the horizontal plane, then the opposite angles will always be equal and the angles at the point where two lines meet, one horizontal and one angled, will always add up to the same as a circle: 360 degrees. It will be noted in the above illustration, that two vertical parallel lines crossed by one single horizontal line will create eight right-angles, the same number as each of the emblems on the apron.

From this, we can gauge that there is already a great deal of esoteric knowledge in the Master's Degree, just reflected in the three symbols of the apron, plus the consolidated knowledge that would have been gained from those of the other degrees relating to dates, the equilateral triangle and Plato's *Meno* that demonstrates the characteristics of being *on the square*, already shown in another chapter.

## Decoding the Master's Installation

The new Master receives his apron, the badge of office, during the Installation ceremony. Like previous Craft ceremonies, the underlying legend continues with elements relating to the building of Solomon's Temple. There are several physical actions undertaken by all the Past Masters present, followed by the new Master being instructed in them. These actions produce a series of geometrical figures in whole or in part, or in the symbolism of them. There appear to be three that have specific significance.

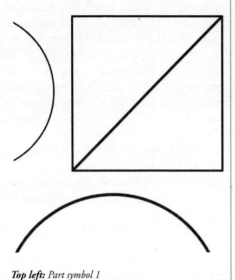

*Top left:* Part symbol 1

*Top right:* Continuation of Symbol 1

*Above:* Part symbol 2

It should be remembered that progression in the hierarchy of Freemasonry normally requires that one will have been the Master of a Lodge prior to becoming a member of a Provincial Lodge, although there are specific exceptions, an example being where a longstanding member may have an illness which inhibits or prevents him holding the position of Master.

It would seem that symbol 1 is, through its two parts, an instruction in the knowledge of *divine proportion* or the *golden ratio,* keeping in mind that in an earlier chapter on the subject of regalia, the geometrical significance appears to be illustrated in the design of a Provincial apron. The Master would be expected to know this knowledge prior to progression. Part 1 symbolises the part of the circle that touches the square, and is in the horizontal plane, while the continuation of symbol 1 is the square illustrating the corner from which the arc is described.

As far as part symbol 2 is concerned, this is created by the Past Masters and, during the ceremony, no specific understanding of any knowledge about it is conveyed in

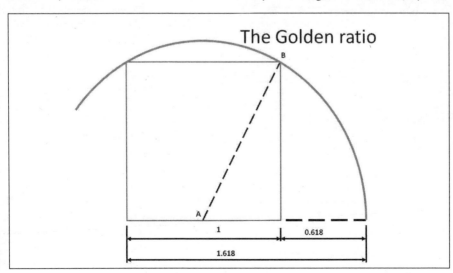

any form of words. Yet, looked at coldly on paper, it is very clearly part of a circle and in the vertical plane.

From the very earliest days of Freemasonry, and in particular from the mid-eighteenth century, there have been specific Lodges known as *Masters Lodges* where the members are by definition *Past Masters,* members who have previously been installed as Masters of a regular Craft Lodge. It has already been noted that an earlier qualification for becoming a member of the Royal Arch was to have been a *Past Master* but that this qualification was removed solely for the expediency of increasing the membership of the Royal Arch, and by so doing, the knowledge contained in the Master and Past Master degrees, was sidestepped. Yet, as stated above, it seems that Past Masters possessed esoteric knowledge that was passed on to the Master after his installation, possibly by being a member of a *Masters Lodge.* That knowledge may have been of *Vesica Piscis,* because without it much of the symbolism of the Holy Royal Arch is unintelligible.

## The esoteric knowledge of the Past Master Degree

*Author's Note:*
*The subject of Vesica Piscis, also known as the Mandorla, has already been explored by me in two earlier books,* The Secrets of Solomon's Temple *and* Mandorla and Tau. *The basic principles are repeated here for consistency of the case being presented.*

Part symbol 2 (above) is a section, or chord of a circle. It is also in the vertical plane. Vesica Piscis is created when two circles, each of the same diameter, are constructed such that the circumference of one touches the centre of the other. This creates a pointed oval in the centre: the Vesica.

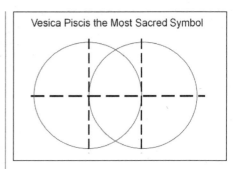

Vesica Piscis the Most Sacred Symbol

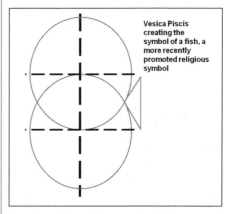

Vesica Piscis creating the symbol of a fish, a more recently promoted religious symbol

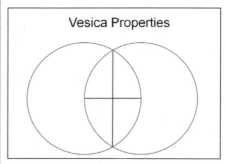

Vesica Properties

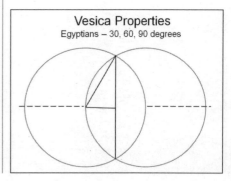

Vesica Properties
Egyptians – 30, 60, 90 degrees

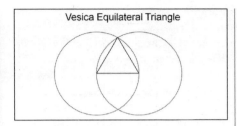

Vesica Equilateral Triangle

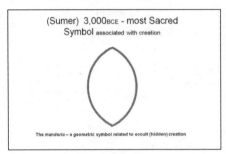

(Sumer) 3,000BCE - most Sacred Symbol associated with creation

The mandoria – a geometric symbol related to occult (hidden) creation

whilst the same line creates an angle of 60 degrees to the horizontal centreline. By replicating the same angles in the second half of the Vesica, one has two sides of an equilateral triangle completed by the third line along the base. It is one of the most important of all the geometric constructions of the knowledge of the operative masons in the Middle Ages, and it is the basis of the geometry used for the style of architecture in all the great cathedrals and abbeys that were built between 1135 CE and approx 1485 CE – the French style that we know as *Gothic*.

Having constructed the two circles, a diagonal line extending from the apex of the Vesica to the centreline of the oval creates an angle of 30 degrees with the vertical centreline through the Vesica,

*The below images show:*

1. Geometry of circles in Vesica Piscis that create the Gothic arch.
2. The presentation of the linked arches in Romsey Abbey, Hampshire.
3. The presentation of the linked arches in the west-face tracery of Lincoln Cathedral.

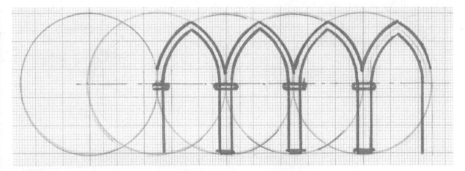

Nearly all the cathedrals and abbeys of England built until around 1485 CE have remnants of the linked arch patterns; Canterbury, Rochester, Durham, Peterborough, Chichester and Ely are good examples not illustrated above. Sometimes the pattern is in external walls that might have been a cloister, and sometimes inside. All of the cathedrals and abbeys built in the era to 1485 CE were of course associated with the religious beliefs and dogma of Roman Catholic worship. Earlier in this book, mention was made of an organisation that has become known as the *Cheshire Gentlemen's Club*, a group of land-owning gentry who were Catholics and who engaged in clandestine activities to encourage the return of the Royal House of Stuart to the thrones of England and Scotland, following the abdication of James II of England in 1689. Members of the Legg family were alleged to have been members of that organisation, and within the house at Lyme Park in Cheshire, which was part of their estate, that same pattern can be found in decorative wood panelling throughout the building.

**Below:** *Linked arch decoration in wood panelling at Lyme Park.*

**Bottom:** *The house at Lyme Park, Cheshire.*

Sarum Chapter Seal "Ad petitiones & ad causas." 13th Century. The bronze gilt matrix was in use up to the year 1936. vide Cat Seals Brit Mus. Vol 1. № 2216.

*Top left: The Mandorla high on the western face of Strasbourg cathedral.*

*Above left: The Mandorla in a 13th-century seal, Salisbury Cathedral.*

*Top: The widespread use of, and reverence for, the Vesica particularly in France where gothic architecture is believed to have originated, is illustrated by the Vesica symbol from which the Virgin Mary and her child are emerging, above the entrance to the tomb associated with Leonardo da Vinci.*

*Above: The Mandorla in ecclesiastical vestments circa 1450 CE, Switzerland.*

In continental Europe, the symbol linked to Gothic architecture was shown in a slightly different way – as the *Mandorla*. Just as the linked arches represent the symbolism in England, so the Mandorla was used in cathedrals and abbeys in France and other territories or situations where Roman Catholic influence was high. Just as the linked arches can be found somewhere in English cathedrals, the same is true of the Mandorla on the Continent.

For several thousand years, the geometric capabilities of the Mandorla/Vesica seem to have been well known by the civilisations of Sumer, Egypt, Greece and Rome, where it was always regarded as an extremely sacred symbol. This was because the shape is somewhat similar to the female vulva of all human and animal life, the source of life and thereby the creation of us all. Thus, as it was a key characteristic in the use of Gothic architecture in important ecclesiastical buildings, so it was adopted in the Roman Church to symbolise rebirth into heaven. The symbol usually has an image of the Christ within it, as shown with that above the tomb of Leonardo da Vinci, to convey that He is the one the Church urges us to follow by adherence to the Christian doctrine.

So what of the bishop's mitre? If the widest point is taken as halfway around a curve and two halves are joined together, we get the image of the mandorla.

*For images, see colour section plate 27 & 28*

One can see that there is a very close resemblance (making allowance for the angle of the original photograph and the manufacture of the mitre) between this item of ecclesiastic attire and the Vesica/Mandorla image previously shown.

There is yet a further possible link with Freemasonry. Prior to the creation of the United Grand Lodge of England, the aprons worn as part of Lodge regalia were not the regimented uniform that exists today, associated with hierarchical development, but were hand-made by the wearer, a friend or member of the family. Most, although by no means all, exhibited a characteristic that may have been associated with a Master/Past Master degree. The flap was curved.

*For image, see colour section plate 24.*

Some aprons from the pre-1800 era do have a triangular flap. It raises the possibility that the junior members of a Lodge, who had not yet passed through the Chair to become Masters, had aprons with triangular flaps, while those that were Past Masters had one that was curved, thereby indicating they knew the ancient knowledge about the Vesica/Mandorla and the creation of equilateral triangles geometrically enabled by the interlinked circles.

## The lost circle – hierarchy versus knowledge

From the foregoing illustrations and observations, there is clearly tantalising evidence of a strain of esoteric knowledge that remains within Freemasonry and is associated with the role of the Master and Past Master. The knowledge seems to demonstrate how to construct an image to comply with the dimensions of *divine proportion,* as a gateway to later promotion to a Provincial Lodge. It would also seem that the Mandorla/Vesica and the link with Gothic architecture, were probably associated with the Past Masters. As we will see in a later chapter, without such knowledge there would be serious shortcomings in understanding some of the symbolism attached to the Royal Arch. So, if it is that important, how did it come to be sidelined?

The inconvenient truth is that this author can find no real evidence to indicate why this happened, but by looking outside of the Masonic organisation, one can understand how it may have occurred.

The first reason relates to religion. At the time the union of the Grand Lodges was being considered, a time-lapse of a little over half a century had passed since there were forces within the country – some associated with the aristocracy and long-standing families of high repute, plus gentleman landowners – that were actively seeking the reintroduction of the Catholic religion and the reinstatement of the House of Stuart to the thrones of England and Scotland. Roman Catholicism was all but outlawed in the land and anyone who was an adherent of that faith was denied access to higher ranks of employment and position in society. The Duke of Sussex was not only a member of the Royal family but a man of strong Christian beliefs who in his younger days, had considered joining the Anglican Church. It is difficult to perceive how, against such a background, knowledge of a geometrical symbol strongly associated with the Roman Catholic faith could have been permitted to sit centre stage and be associated with the most senior position in the Craft Lodge structure, at a time when positive discrimination in favour of Protestants was the order of the day. Thus the position of the Master was retained because of its link with the guild structure of Medieval masons, and the ceremony, while retaining the character of a foregone era, was diminished in favour of being merely a vehicle by which the person elected to the position of Master was installed in the Chair of King Solomon. Having passed through the Chair, each Past Master was deemed useful for the administration of the Lodge prior to promotion to the Provincial Lodge structure.

The second reason was the link between female sexuality and the Vesica/Mandorla. Freemasonry has always been a male-dominated organisation, so to appear to venerate female sexuality would have been absolutely unthinkable. Furthermore, Queen Victoria ascended the throne of the United Kingdom of Great Britain and Ireland in 1837. This was at a time when Freemasonry was going through a period of *fine tuning* after the creation of the UGLE, 20 years previously. As the Victorian age progressed it became an era of moral uprightness and sexual modesty, and any reference to female sexuality in a male organisation would have been intolerable amongst members who considered themselves respectable individuals.

Then there is a third reason. During the 18th century, the Industrial Revolution had begun. Although there was a development of new ideas as the application of science and engineering gathered momentum, it had little effect on the lives of the majority of people until after the end of that century. Freemasonry continued to develop, including the transmission of knowledge at the various levels within the organisations of Grand Lodge as they then existed. By the time the United Grand Lodge of England was formed, the British Empire was expanding with opportunities for trade in a range of commodities. It resulted in the need for plantations and mines in many parts of the world, to provide the raw materials for this growing industrial and commercial era of adventure. As the wealth from these ventures increased, so too did the number of banks and other financial institutions, such as insurance companies, and as they also grew they opened branch offices to extend their reach to even more customers. That expansion, especially in those that handled money, dictated that all actions were scrutinised; managers of branches were required to be of unerring honesty, setting a high standard of behaviour amongst the employees in their charge, but also within their families and among those with whom they associated. Thus within these organisations were created layers of middle management in the form of charge-hands, foremen, supervisors, managers and controllers of various kinds and also hierarchies, with promotion through the ranks dictated by ability, diligence, loyalty and conduct. This was fine during working times, but in the evenings and periods of leisure, the distractions and temptations of life were in plentiful supply. For the supervisor or foreman to be seen in a public house, drunk and disorderly, could be career-limiting in the extreme. Thus big financial institutions or industrial and commercial businesses encouraged their employees to attend church on Sundays, to adopt lives of prudence, temperance, and to be just and upright in all their actions. Wives were expected to stay home and not work, and equally expected to play an active part in charity-related events organised by churches and other such groups.

These were the principles that entirely underpinned the virtues of Freemasonry. Men likely to achieve promotion within their companies, were encouraged to join organisations such as Freemasonry, Odd Fellows, Order of Buffaloes, etc., that provided the moral backbone to society and kept their members away from the wayward temptations of life. Needless to say, with the passing of time, managers became members and those considered to have future potential for promotion within their sphere of influence were also encouraged to join. Those members of Lodges that worked hard and performed their parts well, conducting themselves impeccably in social gatherings and assuming administrative roles within their Lodge with great diligence, would find themselves promoted within their work environment in due time.

As membership grew, the number of Lodges and Chapters increased, and brethren who demonstrated their further interest in Freemasonry by becoming Founders of a new Lodge, with the subsequent commitment it demanded, were certain to acquire a great measure of recognition when they were eventually considered for promotion. Thus the cycle continued until the mid-20th century, and being seen to perform well at Lodge meetings, knowing ceremonies word perfectly and performing actions correctly, in order that a positive note be taken by the representative Provincial Officers present, became more important than anything else. Knowledge actually contained in the symbolism and ceremonial of Freemasonry became less important, to the extent that it gradually died. As the significance of this ancient knowledge diminished, it was replaced with ever more exotic notions, especially in the Victorian era when new ideas or experiences from other cultures were transmitted by the growth of the British Empire, moulding with that which was already in place, reinterpreting it. During one period of the Victorian age, there was a great interest in séances, attempts at communicating with departed loved ones and various other occult ideas, when the writer Helena (Madam) Blavatsky became a high-profile activist in these areas. There were several obviously intelligent and highly regarded Freemasons of the time who were greatly influenced by her ideas and interpreted them with a Masonic meaning, judging from some of the papers that exist in Freemasons' Hall, London.

There is one last set of reasons. During the First and Second World Wars, men from diverse backgrounds were thrown together in military units and groups which were dependant on each other, existing in close proximity for very long periods. They witnessed horrific sights and sounds they would never wish to see again, and endured a great deal of hardship. They did things together as acts of war that they could never contemplate in a peaceful period. At the end of these World Wars, thousands of men all over the world were released from their wartime activity and returned to the real world. Many missed the comradeship and community of the men they had known, so organisations like Freemasonry flourished with new members as they enjoyed the select company of their fellows, and the camaraderie of the officers club and mess halls. Their primary interest was to have an enjoyable gathering with like-minded individuals and forget the past, or relive the parts that best suited them. Who could blame them? But for Freemasonry there would be a negative aspect, for these men were not really interested in geometry and history, they were used to military hierarchy. This probably resulted in very few members having any real connection with, or appreciation of, the allegorical knowledge contained in Masonic ceremonies and its symbols. As a consequence it became even less familiar.

As the wealth of the nation continued to grow and nationwide state-sponsored education came into being, much of this ancient knowledge that had been carried forward in Masonic ceremonies was taught in schools and its relevance to Freemasonry alone was impaired.

Against this background and the legislative responsibilities that arose in the early years of the 19th century, it continued to have an effect for the next century and a half. It is easy to understand how hierarchy and administration became important in a growing organisation during the mid-Victorian period. The position of the Master and the Past Masters became important tools within the structure of local management, but the allegorical knowledge contained in these two degrees in particular was totally lost, becoming mere ceremonial activities associated with the Installation of the new Master.

However, it seems that it was not entirely lost as evidence of the links remain. For there were some that understood its significance, even if it did not feature in a recognised manner in Lodge-based ceremonial.

## Remembrance in the garden

The Great War of 1914-1918, had a devastating effect on the whole of Europe, being a 'war to end all wars', at least until the next – some 21 years later. After the Great War, it was decided that those Freemasons who had fought and made the ultimate sacrifice should be honoured. A rather old building on the edge of the Covent Garden district of London had long served as the headquarters of the United Grand Lodge of England, but it was decided it should be replaced with a new building that would serve primarily as a lasting memorial to those who had lost their lives.

A new Freemasons' Hall was designed and money to assist with the cost of construction was raised by contributions provided by Lodges across England. Contributing Lodges became known as *Hall Stone Lodges*, and behind and above the main entrance at the junctions of two roads is the *Hall of Remembrance*, a most elegant and peaceful place in which are recorded the names of all the English Freemasons that fell on the battlefield in the defence of the British nation, in conflicts around the world from 1914 to the present day. The Hall is illuminated during daylight hours by sunlight that streams through an array of stained glass windows and creates the atmosphere of dignity and respect one would associate with such a place.

In the stained glass windows we find the ancient and most sacred of symbols to be connected to a former Master and Past Master degree, the Mandorla/Vesica.

*For images, see colour section plate 10 & 11.*

As previously stated, the knowledge contained in the Master and Past Master degrees is important if one is to understand the symbolism of the Royal Arch. Before dealing with that subject, we must also understand a little about the transmission of knowledge in the period between the fall of the Roman Empire and the arrival of Renaissance architecture in England, with Inigo Jones, and the building of the Queen's House in Greenwich.

## Masonic Memory Review 8

The detail contained in this and the previous chapter shows that the regalia of Craft Freemasonry appears to be more than decorative dress which has been contrived to suit a hierarchy, but carries within it allegorical messages to be conveyed at every stage.

It also highlights the importance and significance of the Master/Past Master degree, which becomes even more obvious when we look at the Royal Arch. It emphasises the period when this degree was side-lined for the expediency of increasing the membership and thereby the viability, of the Royal Arch degree; those that agreed and orchestrated the change had either lost sight of or failed to see, that the Degree of Past Master contained esoteric knowledge derived from ancient wisdom. It is that knowledge which provides the bridge between the Craft Lodge structure and that of the Royal Arch. Ignoring it had, in effect, resulted in the lost links of Freemasonry.

Was it done deliberately? Was it done by individuals that were already ignorant of the contents but totally wedded to the concept of hierarchical control within the organisation, at a time of Empire and colonial expansion and administration?

There are layers of history and philosophy embedded in this *peculiar system of morality, veiled in allegory and illustrated by symbols.*

*Chapter 12*

# Knowledge in Freemasonry – lost and found

*Author's note:*
*In the first part of this chapter, I am repeating points I have made in earlier works, or in this book. I repeat them here, albeit with some modification, to ensure a complete picture of events, rather than requiring the reader to refer elsewhere.*

FOR MANY GENERATIONS OF the development of man, knowledge and skills, in so many areas of life were passed on verbally from one generation to the next by parents, either telling their offspring how to do things or getting them to participate at an early age, such as hunting or gathering food where survival was their primary concern.

Around 6-8,000 years ago, groups of individuals that had previously been very itinerant began to settle in places like the 'Fertile Crescent', the area of land that is today between the Tigris and Euphrates Rivers. As their peoples began to grow and harvest food in specific locations, rather than following the nomadic lifestyle that could result in unreliable food supplies, so they began to take more notice of the seasons and the appropriate times of the year to collect seeds, how and when to sow them and when to harvest crops. Once food was specifically cultivated, a means of storage became desirable so that during periods when food was less plentiful, stored quantities would supplement their needs. This knowledge about the seasons led to the study of the movement of the patterns of the sun and the moon, and then the planets and groups of stars. These generations of long ago monitored and measured the cycles of life, and some of the earliest known structures to demonstrate this process can be found on the islands of Malta and Gozo in the Mediterranean Sea, where some of the earliest known structures for monitoring the movements of the sun were built. These monitoring devices were not just caves or wells, they were specifically constructed, and in effect became some of the first astronomical instruments ever developed, revealing some of the first scientific discoveries ever made.

Because of their value in the quest for survival, these new scientific instruments became more elaborate in their design, as with the development of obelisks. Ultimately, where these structures were placed became centres of great reverence, evolving into the early temples. In order to monitor what these new scientific instruments revealed, so specific individuals held responsibility within the community to collate and understand what was being observed; in time, these human repositories of knowledge of the universe and how it worked became priests, and their scientific instruments became places of worship. To retain this knowledge, in some communities priesthoods became hereditary lines of descent, and as their knowledge and proven experience grew, so too did their power and influence.

One place where the climatic conditions and natural resources were available for all these things to come together was the ancient state of Sumer, in the southern end of the Tigris-Euphrates basin. From there, it seems, this knowledge gradually rippled out and spread across the neighbouring territories, eventually being absorbed into the fledgling civilisation of Egypt whose priests developed it further. Over several generations, the scientific monitoring expertise in Egypt became more specific and accurate in its development, and the understanding of the natural world transformed into astronomy (the process of observing how the heavens worked), and astrology (the science of predicting where the sun, moon and stars would be at any given time), arithmetic, geometry and philosophy. So far advanced in their time was their understanding and knowledge that adepts from other tribes and evolving civilisations visited Egypt to learn and exchange information and glean knowledge. Some were Hindu priests from India or philosophers such as Pythagoras from the early development of Greek culture, who being adepts themselves had studied and acquired as much new knowledge as they could, adding to the pool of universal knowledge: Pythagoras' theorem is one such example, while the Hindu culture developed an understanding of evaluating numbers and solving mathematical problems that we now know as algebra.

Through the development of the ancient civilisation of Greece, so more practical and philosophical ideas developed, and a range of new problems were solved; Archimedes, Anaxagoras, Socrates, Plato, Euclid, Eratosthenes and Aristotle, to name but a few, all contributed to the growth of knowledge. In their own times, their ideas were not always universally accepted or welcomed by the hierarchy of the day; some were put to death and others exiled, but their knowledge lived on, being retained and built on by others.

Thus was the accumulated knowledge of mankind gradually developed and recorded, first on clay tablets baked in the sun and then on thin animal skins and papyrus to be copied, distributed and stored in priestly centres or facilities like the great library at Alexandria in Egypt. In time, the Greek civilisation fused with its Roman descendant and for several hundred years the Greco-Roman Empire became the dominant civilisation of the Mediterranean, Europe and the Middle East.

The Roman Empire had grown so large during the first two centuries of the Common Era that it was administered as two separate territories – the Empire of the East and the Empire of the West. The year 306 CE found a Roman officer in York, by the name of Constantine, whose father Constantinus ruled the Western Empire and who, prior to his passing in that city, had already nominated his son to be his successor. There were others that vied for power and, over the next six years, Constantine not only travelled back to Rome but had to defeat several armies of challengers on route. His last battle before securing his inheritance took place on the banks of the River Tiber, and has passed into history as the Battle of Milvian Bridge. According to tradition, prior to the battle Constantine received a vision, inspiring him to victory over his enemy by having his troops fight under the sign of the Christians, who up to that time had been the subject of repeated periods of persecution. He adopted the Chi-Ro sign which his soldiers painted on their shields, despite remaining loyal to their own pagan beliefs, and Constantine was victorious. With the defeat of his opposition in the year 312 CE, Constantine was finally able to secure the inheritance his father had nominated as ruler of the Western Empire of Rome. In 313 CE he issued the Edict of Milan, in which he freed the Christians from any further persecution and granted tolerance for all in the empire to follow their own religious beliefs. After an initial period of peace, several difficulties arose across the empire resulting in more bloody battles, with challenges to Constantine's leadership that came from the Empire of the East, until in 325 CE he finally defeated his last remaining challenger and in so doing became the undisputed leader of the entire Roman Empire.

Following the Edict of Milan, the Christian religion grew and became the state religion of the Roman Empire. In 325 CE, Constantine encouraged a gathering of bishops at the Council of Nicaea to consider the merits of Arian Christianity, which denied the Divinity of the Christ. A great dispute ensued between the Bishop of Alexandria and Arius in which neither would give way, and Constantine therefore encouraged the Council of Nicaea to resolve the issue. Arius was defeated and sent into exile, although he was rehabilitated later; yet despite this great deliberation, Arianism continued to flourish in specific pockets of the empire over the subsequent centuries. The resultant doctrine of the prevailing Roman Church became the basis for the Christian faith as it spread throughout the Roman Empire.

In 330 CE, Constantine founded a new city to be the centre of the Roman Empire. He initially called it New Rome and it was centred in an area of the Bosporus which had previously been part of the ancient Greek territory of Byzantium. The new city was quickly renamed as Constantinople in honour of its founder, and the state that grew out of the old Roman Empire

eventually became known by the original Greek designation of Byzantium, which continued for around 500 years.

Around 450 CE, over 100 years after the creation of Constantinople, the Roman Empire of the West, collapsed. The vacuum was filled by war-making individuals seeking to control ever greater areas of Europe, while still paying homage to the Emperor in Byzantium and the Church, still based in Rome. The great accumulation of the original knowledge from the ancient Greek philosophers, and other great thinkers, gradually declined in its use and reference.

Around the year 622 CE, a new religion was created which we know as Islam. Mainly by conquest, it spread very quickly through North Africa and the Middle East, and, by around 800 CE, the Roman/Byzantium Empire had little more territorial control than that of the country we know as Turkey. In an effort to appease the invaders, the Emperor offered to share the works of the great Greco-Roman philosophers with the Arab conquerors, which was accepted. A school was established in Baghdad to collate the relevant information, where teams of scholars spent the next 25 years translating it into Arabic and the school become known as the *House of Wisdom*. For the next few centuries, this fusion of philosophical knowledge together with new developments, ideas and discoveries made by successive generations of Islamic scholars, took the region into a golden period of development as the foremost civilisation in the known world.

Meanwhile, the same philosophical knowledge, was not entirely lost to the West. With Constantinople being established in a Greek-speaking area of the Mediterranean, the language became native to Byzantium, but with the fall of Rome the use of Greek gradually declined, with the parchments and papyrus on which the works of the ancient philosophers were written falling into disuse, and the materials often recycled or destroyed.

The gradual loss and disregard of this knowledge across the Western world resulted in the period being referred to as the *Dark Ages,* yet it was not as bleak as some believe. There was still progress, often inspired by activity in the monasteries; vineyards were developed and other forms of agriculture and storage improved; various mechanical devices such as waterwheels were created. However, the loss of the Greek language subdued the philosophies of the old world and copies of many documents were stored away in the libraries of long-established monasteries, to remain untouched for centuries.

Ireland was one centre where this loss was less obvious, for Irish monks apparently continued to faithfully copy works in Greek, to preserve their meaning, and while that language ceased to be used in the rest of Western Europe it was still widely known in the monasteries of Ireland, which became centres of great philosophical learning. It was from there that many famous monks set out on their missionary expeditions, including men such as St Patrick, who along with Columba another of the patron saints of Ireland, established a monastic community on the island of Iona on the west coast of Scotland. The missionary work of Columba and his successors in Scotland and Northern England is best recognised because of their influence in establishing the Celtic Christian monastic communities which existed prior to the Synod of Whitby. Meetings were held in 664 CE at the Monastery of St Hilda, where Celtic and Catholic leaders met and agreed to adopt a single form of religion for the British Isles, from which time Roman Catholicism became the main religion of all England.

Irish monks were in demand across the Carolingian Frankish Empire, with requests from Charlemagne for them to visit his main capital, the former Roman spa town of Aachen, shortly after his coronation in Rome in 800 CE as King and Emperor of the Holy Roman Empire.

One who embarked on such missionary work was Gallus, an Irish monk who set out with St. Columbanus for Rome. In an area of Switzerland close to Lake Constance, Gallus felt a little unwell and, liking the area to which they had travelled, decided to remain and established a small cell for himself. He died there in 646 CE, and a small church was built on the spot where he was buried. Charles Martel, the first Carolingian king of the Franks, encouraged a monk by the name of Omar to go to Lake Constance and guard the relics of Gallus, in veneration of whose name Omar encouraged the erection of a monastery. The monastery developed under Martel's successor, Pepin the Short, and by the time of Charlemagne, Martel's grandson, it had become a centre where numerous manuscripts were copied and exchanged with other distant monasteries, including those of Ireland. Today, the monastery houses a great library containing many very ancient manuscripts and has been adopted as a World Heritage site.

Among the manuscripts believed to have been retained in Ireland were copies of the works of Plato, the father of philosophy, and Euclid, also deemed the father of geometry, whose theorems appear in Freemasonry, as do some specific works of Plato.

Meanwhile, Islamic forces thrust forward with their conquests and the spread of their religion through North Africa, from where they captured Sicily and the Iberian Peninsula before pushing north into France. Charles Martel halted their progress near the town of Poitiers in central France, and forcing the Muslims back over the Pyrenees. Gradually, most of Spain and Sicily were also recovered.

In 1099, the First Crusade took place in an effort to recover Jerusalem and the Holy Land from the Islamic invaders, because of their importance to Christianity. The arrival of the Christian armies in Jerusalem and surrounding territory, brought the invading knights into direct contact with their Islamic counterparts; shortly thereafter, copies of Arabic translations of the works of the Greek philosophers that had originally been transferred from Byzantium were seized and sent to Rome, where over the next 25 years they were translated into Latin. As the information these documents contained was revealed, so monks travelled to the Holy Land specifically to obtain this Islamic knowledge for themselves, while others went to southern Spain to learn from Muslim communities in the great cities of Toledo and Grenada. The result was a revival and interest in the works of the great philosophers of earlier ages.

One of the most influential men in Europe at that time was Abbot Suger of the abbey dedicated to St. Denis, the patron saint of France. (A community of the same name now exists in a district of the Northern suburbs of Paris.)

An equally famous and influential man of that time was Bernard, later known as St. Bernard, a man who tradition has it was a primary instigator in the cult of the Virgin Mary that has since become, a major aspect of Roman Catholic doctrine. Bernard is also noted for having been a founding motivator of the Knights Templar, and it has long been suggested that prior to their first expedition to Jerusalem they were known as *St. Bernard Knights*.[54]

Abbot Suger, it seems, was impressed by the new knowledge that was coming to light in the translations taking place in Rome, and the upsurge in interest generated across Europe, resulted in some monastic communities rediscovering knowledge they had previously possessed and which had lain idle for many years. At the same time he would have been aware of the efforts of his acquaintance, Bernard, in what amounted to the re-establishment of female worship that had existed in earlier civilisations, and along with it the sacred knowledge of the Mandorla. This new knowledge, the transmission of other developments from the Muslim world, Bernard's quest and the rediscovery of the works of Euclid combined to create the pointed arch of Gothic architecture.

So around the year 1124, when the abbess of an abbey to the north of Paris, indicated their intention to build a cloister, this seemed the ideal opportunity to employ the new pointed arch idea. Thus again according to tradition, the new cloister was built at the Abbey of Morienval, close to the town of Compiegne. This proved sufficiently successful for Abbot Suger to begin to rebuild the abbey church of St. Denis, starting in the new style at the western end, thereby enabling a greater penetration of light into the core of the structure. The abbey church was one of the oldest in France, and having been built on the site of a small sixth-century church; it became the centre for coronation of the Kings of the Franks during the Merovingian period, and today still retains many of their tombs.

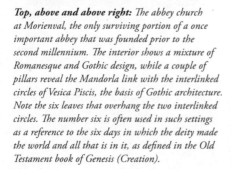

**Top, above and above right:** *The abbey church at Morienval, the only surviving portion of a once important abbey that was founded prior to the second millennium. The interior shows a mixture of Romanesque and Gothic design, while a couple of pillars reveal the Mandorla link with the interlinked circles of Vesica Piscis, the basis of Gothic architecture. Note the six leaves that overhang the two interlinked circles. The number six is often used in such settings as a reference to the six days in which the deity made the world and all that is in it, as defined in the Old Testament book of Genesis (Creation).*

**Above right:** *A temple in Delhi, India, showing the interlinked triangles creating the symbol often referred to as Solomon's Seal, and an arch design similar to the Gothic. Such architectural features* predate the development of Gothic in Europe, although regular cultural contact with India had yet to be established.

Gothic architecture became the standard used in most cathedrals, ecclesiastical buildings and new state-sponsored works across Europe, until towards the end of the 15th century. Many of the major monastic communities of England had been established in the ninth century or earlier, and were in need of redevelopment by the 12th century. Several of the great churches which later became cathedrals were damaged by natural events such as storms and fire, or needed repairs or extensions. Wherever any such building work was undertaken after the 12th century, it invariably, though not exclusively, involved the Gothic arch.

One of the first cathedrals in Britain to enjoy the benefits of this new concept was Canterbury, where work commenced in 1174 – although it is argued in some quarters that Durham was the first, where pioneering work on rib vaulting was undertaken as early as 1133.

*Author's note:*
*As discovered when researching this background, early vaulting seems to have been designed on the ratios of the cube, where each leg is a vertical corner.*

The main Gothic era continued until around the start of the 16th century, but came to a shuddering halt when Henry VIII dissolved the monasteries and separated England from the Holy Roman Empire. Commensurate with the Tudor period in England, the era of the Renaissance was gathering pace, revisiting the architectural styles of ancient Greece and Rome, their connections with nature, and remoulding them into a new architectural vision. The life of Andre Palladio, regarded as one of the greatest Italian architects, ran concurrently with the Tudor period. Shortly after Palladio died, the Englishman Inigo Jones learned the Italian language, and set off to study in Italy. It seems he was enamoured with the work of Palladio and obtained copies of some of his design philosophies, along with those of Vitruvius. He returned to England and won favour with James I, in consequence of which he designed the Queen's House at Greenwich Park, regarded as revolutionary in its time, together with the Banqueting House in Whitehall and many other buildings.

It could be argued that he, more than any other person, was the greatest single influence in the development of the Renaissance style in England, along with the practical use of the previously lost ideas of Vitruvius.

*Chapter 13*

# Rebuilding the Royal Arch – symbolism

---

*If thou canst comprehend these things,*
*thou knowest enough.*
*Nothing is wanting but the key.*

SO STATES ONE OF the observations in Latin on one of the main emblems of the Masonic Order of the Holy Royal Arch. The problem is that at no time is one ceremonially advised what it is that one needs to comprehend, or to know enough about - or indeed where to find the key, or the lock. Indeed, the *exaltee*, as a new member is known, is told at the end of his ceremony of admission that *a perfect understanding of the secrets of the Royal Arch* will be gained once one has passed through the highest office in the Chapter – referred to as *passing through the Chair* –as with the Master of a Craft Lodge. Thus one may be led to believe that - pass through the Chair and all will have been revealed, the key will have been discovered and all will be understood; but sadly this is not so. This author has not yet found anyone in the hierarchy of Freemasonry who can explain what one is expected to comprehend, to know enough about, or indeed where the key fits. Yet again this underlines that knowledge originally associated with the *degree* may have long since been lost – or overlooked.

One of the first things a new exaltee is told is that it is '*a peculiar system of morality, veiled in allegory and illustrated by symbols*'. Thus, if there is knowledge

of some kind contained within the Royal Arch ceremonies, it should still be there. It is a just a case of peeling back the allegory.

The majority of members of a Royal Arch Chapter find it to be the most absorbing of all the ceremonial levels within regular English Freemasonry. Master Masons are encouraged to join on the grounds that it *completes* the Third Degree they have already attained. This implies that there is something that they still need to know, something incomplete or missing that is revealed in the Royal Arch ceremonies. Maybe that was the case at one time but as with so much in Freemasonry, the vast majority of members of the Royal Arch devote many hours to learning the words and actions associated with each ceremony and office, hoping they make a good presentation and perform their tasks well as the hierarchy demands, trusting it may place them in good stead for possible promotion to higher office. Yet, so few spend any time at all attempting to understand what is actually being conveyed, and whether it may result in a revelation of that which is missing or incomplete.

Almost all the knowledge that is embedded in Masonic ritual comes to an end in the Royal Arch. Although regarded as an extension of the Master

Mason degree, most members regard it unofficially as the *Fourth Degree*, which is really not surprising. The Third Degree of Master Mason is referred to ceremonially as the *sublime degree of a Master Mason*, and it is a level to which one progresses. Even the Master or Past Master roles are progressive situations within the Craft structure, so one does not have to join each level because one is already a member of the Lodge. However, the Royal Arch is not a natural progression as a Brother must be formally admitted into it, which is ceremonially referred to as the *Supreme Degree*.

In fact, at various stages within the ceremonies of Royal Arch there is regular reference to it being a *degree*, so continuing to define it as an extension or completion of something else is therefore stretching the bounds of credibility.

In reality, when the Master/Past Master degree is taken into account, the Royal Arch could perhaps be regarded as a *Fifth Degree*. Freemasons are told that there are five points of fellowship, a statement which the vast majority of members do not really understand, so making the Royal Arch the *Fifth Degree* may actually make a logical link.

At the time of the Union of the two Grand Lodges in 1813, the Royal Arch was officially recognised and defined as part of *pure ancient Freemasonry*, but the Supreme Grand Chapter was not formed until 1817. The process of the integration of the Grand Lodges took much longer than had been anticipated, perhaps hindered by the rapid expansion of British trade interests and the Empire, along with requests to instigate new Lodges overseas. As a result, the ceremonial structure of the Royal Arch was not defined until 1834, when it was observed that it was a completion of the Master Mason degree. For the next

150 years, this term of *completion* led to a fairly constant debate as to whether the degree of a Master Mason, or the individual who did not go on to join a Royal Arch Chapter, was in some respect inferior to the status that the Royal Arch conferred, or whether something was missing or incomplete. An attempt was made to resolve this dilemma as late as 2003, when a pronouncement was made that *the Supreme Order of the Holy Royal Arch* [was to be considered] *an extension to, but neither a superior nor a subordinate part of, the Degrees which precede it.* If, however, it is shown that the Royal Arch does contain information and knowledge that can only be truly appreciated if one has grasp of the allegories of all four degrees, including that of Master/Past Master, then it would demonstrate that the Royal Arch is the *Supreme Degree* as defined in 1817 and 1834. Thus the pronouncement of 2003 reinforces the possibility that the knowledge behind the allegory of the Royal Arch, and indeed the former degrees, has been lost or deemed irrelevant at the most senior levels of Freemasonry.

## Background to Royal Arch development

Quite where the Royal Arch *degree* originated has been something of a mystery for over 200 years; even the origin of the title is uncertain. In the past, some writers have suggested that the name was derived from records in Scotland – the Dumfries No. 4 MS of 1710 that uses the phrase: '*No lodge or corum of masons shall give the Royal secret to any suddenly but upon great deliberation*'.[55] It has also been the subject of conjecture that, as the Medieval masons were builders of castles, palaces and defensive systems that provided the home and base, for the administration of the realm by the monarchy of that era, so they appointed a *King's Master Mason* to supervise the work – it was a *Royal Art* – which over time with accent differences in speech, translated to Royal Arch.[56] There were earlier writers, particularly those educated in the mid-late Victorian period of the 19th century, who hypothesised that the *Arch* is a reflection of the great curve across the sky created by a rainbow. With its upmost point of the curve close to heaven, and the lower ends rolling down to earth, the rainbow became a symbol of a *holy arch*. Again, in the late 18th century, the image of a rainbow featured in a range of Masonic items, including Tracing Board illustrations. While there is considerable speculation about the origins of various arch forms, the only one that is actually mentioned in current Royal Arch ceremonial is the *catenarian arch, which has a shallow contour.*

Some researchers have believed in the past that the ceremonies came from France, or even from Ireland, while others considered it to be the remnants of a degree that existed at York; yet others assert that, during the development of the Masonic ceremonies in the 18th century, and the process of union of the Grand Lodges, it was *mutilated* from other ceremonies. This implies that it was a compilation of segments of ceremonies not thought worthy of retention, or in conflict with the preferences of the two main Grand Lodges. Ironically, however, both the *Moderns* and the *Antients* worked Royal Arch ceremonies within Lodges that were under their jurisdiction, so to agree to the Royal Arch being distorted in any way seems somewhat irrational. One of the most highly regarded writers and

researchers on the history of Freemasonry, Bernard E. Jones, whose published works appeared in the 1950s, suggested that the Royal Arch ceremonies were not created or mutilated during the Union process but appeared as a complete package, probably around the 1730s.[57] If this was the case, then somebody or some group must have compiled it and identified it at that instant in time as a worthy ceremonial. Having been accepted as a worthy addition, it was demonstrated to a Premier Grand Lodge gathering where those who saw it were so impressed that it was promulgated through other Lodges. How else could it have spread and grown? Jones also makes a rather interesting statement:

> ...Although Count Goblet d'Alviella suggests a union between the Medieval masons and philosophers, most students (the present writer [Bernard E. Jones] among them) cannot see even the slightest possibility that the Royal Arch has developed from operative masonry...[58]

In this one statement, we are confronted by two issues: the first relates to the connection between the Medieval masons and the philosophers. Throughout this book, there are many instances of connections with the Medieval masons, Plato's *Meno* being just one example, as a means of understanding the simple geometric process of halving and doubling a square. Many of the ancient astronomers were also philosophers, and the masons of *olde* needed their knowledge to align churches, in particular on an east-west axis; knowledge of the Mandorla/Vesica is also related to what was known by the philosophers; and then we have Euclid and Pythagoras represented in the three, four, five triangle, or the connection with Divine Proportion.

The second issue is in respect of the Royal Arch being derived from operative masonry, which must surely depend on the knowledge that was being conveyed, and at a particular time and place. If one considers that the knowledge employed by the operative mason was complete by the year 1350, when Gothic architecture was at its zenith, and remained unchanged until the mid-1700s, then this statement has substance. On the other hand, it ignores any other developments in the few decades prior to the formation of the Premier Grand Lodge in 1717, which had been retained by the operative masons by the year 1691 as a consequence of the arrival of renaissance architecture, and that continued into the following decades. If such was the case, a claim suggesting no link with the operative masons would be of little substance, especially if that knowledge could be identified. Therefore, to dismiss a link between the Royal Arch and operative masonry is irrational, but, perhaps more importantly, it demonstrates that when Bernard Jones compiled his books, the allegorical meaning behind Freemasonry had probably been lost to the majority of members, as in the preceding era the primary motivation had been hierarchical. Neither should it be forgotten that in the first half of the 20th century, the majority of members in influential positions within the organisational structure of Freemasonry were probably university-educated in the classics as promulgated in the late Victorian period, and connected with the institutions associated with running an empire. They would never in their lives have worked a stone with a hammer and chisel.

One good example of this relates to the ancient study of the process of doubling the volume of a cube. This may link to the possible method of operative masons for establishing the size of the square base on which a Corinthian column would be set, at a period when Renaissance architecture was developing in England, following the great Gothic cathedral building boom some 250 years earlier.

It is perhaps also worth contemplating that what now exist as the ceremonies of the Royal Arch may not necessarily be the same as those when they first appeared in the early 18th century, and were likely to have changed during the process of the Union. In addition, there were several other changes that took place in the mid-19th century, not to mention the developments which took place a century earlier.

The main point is that there were already very entrenched opinions which developed in Freemasonry regarding its character and origins, some of which have already been highlighted. The reality is that the origins of the Royal Arch prior to 1813 are shrouded in uncertainty, and therefore we can only rely on the traditions we now possess as a possible vehicle for understanding the merits of the ceremonial contents, structure and symbolism.

With the prospect that there may be knowledge beneath the surface of the ceremonies and symbols of the Royal Arch, our quest to reveal the allegory is yet another search for hidden knowledge.

## Inside the Chapter room

Of all the degrees and levels of regular Freemasonry, the Royal Arch is noticeable as the one with the most obvious religious overtones. This should not be denigrated, for we should remember that

200–300 years ago, when Freemasonry was being formalised, the world was a different place. In every country of the Western world, religion, whether Protestant or Catholic, was a dominating factor in the life of the nation and most of its citizens.

As within the Craft, the room is set out on the cardinal points of the compass, with a specific East-West alignment, reflecting the old traditions of both religion and the operative masonry. But why should this be so? Freemasonry and Royal Arch are not brotherhoods which dictate that the room is a substitute for a church or any other religious structure. Rather it is related to the passage of the sun that, due to the great illusion of nature, rises in the East and sets in the West.

As with all Masonic ceremonial, any connection with religion draws on the books of the Old Testament –the same familiar source in all the Abraham-based Christianity, Judaism and Islam, and therefore hopefully of little offence to any.

In the Book of Exodus, we are introduced to the character of Moses, a child of Israel by birth who was reputedly born in Egypt at a time when the Israelites were enslaved by the ancient Egyptians. Hatred of the Israelites by the Egyptians, resulted in the death of thousands of children, but Moses was saved by being hidden in reeds that lined the banks of the River Nile. On being discovered the child was taken to the palace of an Egyptian princess where, according to the Jewish philosopher Philo, he was educated as an Egyptian prince, which resulted in his being taught the concepts of knowledge that, during the era in which Freemasonry was formalised, would have been embodied in the *Seven Liberal Arts and Sciences*.[59]

Moses was educated in the mysterious cycle of life, in arithmetic and geometry.

Thus, when later in his life he was instrumental in a rebellion of his people, leading them out of Egypt in an effort to establish a separate tribal homeland, he drew on his earlier education in the construction of the *Tabernacle* and the geometrically intriguing wooden box known as the *Ark of the Covenant* as constructed by two very clever men, Aholiab/Oholiab and Bezalel.[60]

The Tabernacle was aligned on an East-West orientation, so that, when the sun rose over the horizon at dawn, the first rays of light it emitted shone through the length of the tent. Other details recorded in the Old Testament reflect knowledge about the solar and lunar years, and these same concepts were later incorporated into Solomon's Temple. In consequence, all churches in the Medieval period were aligned in a similar fashion, orientated like of all Lodge and Chapter rooms.[61] Moses, Aholiab/Oholiab and Bezalel are the main characters mentioned in a Royal Arch ceremony.

The sun rises each day, bringing light to an otherwise darkened world. In the Craft Lodges, the Master sits in the East, directing his Lodge in its learning; this is defined as bringing light to esoteric subjects associated with Freemasonry, which is a reflection of the knowledge used by the operative mason. As previously mentioned, within the Lodge structure, the Master is assisted by two Wardens who create a management group of three individuals. In the Royal Arch, the three most senior roles are occupied by three Principals, who represent three biblical characters from Israelite history: Zerubbabel, defined as a Prince of Jerusalem, Haggai, the Prophet, and Jeshua, the High Priest.

According to biblical tradition, a few hundred years after Solomon had built the Temple, an army from the Assyrian

Empire ruled by Nebuchadnezzar invaded Jerusalem, stole its most valuable treasures, destroyed the Temple and most of the city, and took many of the inhabitants into captivity as slaves in Babylon. There they lived and worked for a period of 70 years, dreaming of a time when they might return to Jerusalem. During their captivity, Cyrus, the ruler of the Persian Empire, defeated the Babylonians and encouraged the Israelites to return to their former home. The main characters in the biblical text are Zerubbabel, who re-established the laws of Moses; Nehemiah, who oversaw the construction of the city walls and access gates; Haggai, who did much to encourage the exiled Israelites to leave the life they had in Babylon and return to Jerusalem. As some 70 years had passed, most of the Israelites in Babylon were descended from the original captives but, while they were conversant with life in the country of their birth, they would have had very little affinity with the home of their forebears, so persuading them to travel to a place they had never actually known would have been an enormous task in itself.

Jeshua was the head of one of the main tribes that followed Zerubbabel in the first wave of returning peoples. Having done so, the Israelite rulers, Zerubbabel, Haggai and Jeshua decided to rebuild the Temple of Jerusalem. In some of the early versions of the Old Testament used in the King James Authorised Version of the Bible, the translation of the name Jeshua was incorrectly noted as Joshua. Many such translation problems were only corrected in the 1960s/1970s with the result that a number of the older Royal Arch Chapters still refer to this character by the original translated name.

The first few verses of Ezra Chapter Three, state:

1   And when the seventh month was come, and the children of Israel were in the cities, the people gathered themselves together as one man to Jerusalem.

2   Then stood up Jeshua the son of Jozadak, and his brethren the priests, and Zerubbabel the son of Shealtiel, and his brethren, and builded the altar of the God of Israel, to offer burnt offerings thereon, as it is written in the law of Moses the man of God.

3   And they set the altar upon his bases; for fear was upon them because of the people of those countries: and they offered burnt offerings thereon unto the LORD, even burnt offerings morning and evening.

4   They kept also the feast of tabernacles, as it is written, and offered the daily burnt offerings by number, according to the custom, as the duty of every day required;

5   And afterward offered the continual burnt offering, both of the new moons, and of all the set feasts of the LORD that were consecrated, and of every one that willingly offered a freewill offering unto the LORD.

6   From the first day of the seventh month began they to offer burnt offerings unto the LORD. But the foundation of the temple of the LORD was not yet laid.

7   They gave money also unto the masons, and to the carpenters; and meat, and drink, and oil, unto them of Zidon, and to them of Tyre, to bring cedar

trees from Lebanon to the sea of Joppa, according to the grant that they had of Cyrus king of Persia.

8 Now in the second year of their coming unto the house of God at Jerusalem, in the second month, began Zerubbabel the son of Shealtiel, and Jeshua the son of Jozadak, and the remnant of their brethren the priests and the Levites, and all they that were come out of the captivity unto Jerusalem; and appointed the Levites, from 20 years old and upward, to set forward the work of the house of the LORD.

9 Then stood Jeshua with his sons and his brethren, Kadmiel and his sons, the sons of Judah, together, to set forward the workmen in the house of God: the sons of Henadad, with their sons and their brethren the Levites.

10 And when the builders laid the foundation of the temple of the LORD, they set the priests in their apparel with trumpets, and the Levites the sons of Asaph with cymbals, to praise the LORD, after the ordinance of David king of Israel.

The foundations of the new Temple at Jerusalem were laid, but all did not run smoothly, as surrounding nations complained about the rebuilding of the city and the Temple, which impeded work. The complaints were eventually resolved, however, allowing Zerubbabel and Jeshua to proceed with their objectives. Thus the key characters in the Chapter adopt similar names to those found in the biblical account of the return of the Israelites to Jerusalem, after their Babylonian captivity, as recorded in the Book of Ezra.

There are a series of elaborate historical standards which decorate the central area of the Chapter room. Each banner bears a symbol associated with one of the twelve tribes of Israel, and their position follows the location of the tribal groups relative to the cardinal points of their settlements. Thus in the East there are emblems representing Judah, Issachar and Zebulun; in the South are Reuben, Simeon and Gad; in the West are Ephraim, Manasseh and Benjamin; and in the North, Dan, Asher and Naphtali.

*For image, see colour section plate 31.*

It is highly probable that the twelve tribes may also signify the 12 constellations of the Zodiac. Monitoring the movement of the constellations across the sky at dawn provided a virtual calendar for predicting the arrival of the seasons, and thereby the times for growing and harvesting of various foods, along with the seasonal variations in climate. Precession of the Equinox was a means of noting the passing of *ages,* as the earth, having a slight wobble in its rotation, causes the axis to turn very slowly, taking around 26,000 years for it to make one full revolution. This was monitored by the ancient peoples, although they may not have known the cause, by watching the sky at dawn on the day of the Spring Equinox, which in our current calendar is 21 March. Very slowly, the twelve constellations that appear to encircle the earth, drift down the horizon as the sun rises, taking it roughly 2,160 years for each constellation to complete such a cycle. In the days when Solomon built the Temple of Jerusalem, the dominant constellation was Aries, the ram. If, as biblical scholars suggest, the Temple was built around 950 BCE, then Aries was around halfway through its cycle as the dominant precessional constellation. The accuracy of measuring devices used at this time may well have led the priests – the watchers – to believe that Aries was at the central point in its transit, and that Solomon's Temple was built as a marker for that occasion. After Aries, the next precessional constellation in the chain to become dominant, was Pisces, the fishes. It has therefore been suggested that the first year CE was the point in time when priests agreed that the precessional age should change; Aries was left behind and they entered the age of Pisces.[62] Within the next few hundred years, we will move into the precessional age of Aquarius and are therefore at the dawning of a new era. Using the processes of astro-archaeology, a range of scholars have concluded that the tribes of Israel correspond to each of the constellations as follows:

Ten of the twelve tribes and associated constellations are mentioned in 'Genesis' chapter 49, wherein Ephraim and Manasseh are substituted for Jacob and Joseph. In 'Genesis' chapter 48, Jacob is introduced to his grandsons Ephraim and Manasseh. Manasseh was the eldest, but Jacob denoted Ephraim to come before his brother. This has been interpreted to mean that in the cycles of precession – which are often defined as starting with Leo, which had precessional prominence around 10,000 BCE – a constellation for Ephraim would come first.

Simeon is associated with Gemini and the twins as Simeon and Levi were brothers (probably twins). They had a sister who was abducted and raped, so the brothers went to the rescue, killing her abductors and thereby obtaining justice. Hence, in some schedules Levi is used in place of Manasseh for the constellation of Libra.

| Tribe of Israel | Constellation | Astro-sign |
|---|---|---|
| Asher | Virgo | Lady wheat bearer |
| Jacob/Manasseh/Levi | Libra | Scales of Justice |
| Dan | Scorpio | Scorpion |
| Gad | Sagittarius | Archer on horseback |
| Benjamin | Capricorn | Goat |
| Reuben | Aquarius | Water carrier |
| Zebulun | Pisces | Fish |
| Naphtali | Aries | Ram |
| Issachar | Taurus | Bull |
| Simeon | Gemini | Twins |
| Joseph/Ephraim | Cancer | Crab |
| Judah | Leo | Lion |

The twelve tribes in Royal Arch, therefore seem to point out not only the period of the rebuilding of Jerusalem after the enslavement of the Israelites in Babylon, but the geographical positioning in the land of the tribal communities, and the significance of the seasonal orbits and precessional rotation of the earth which govern and affect every aspect of life on the planet.

*This purpose-built Temple (Lodge room) is used for both Craft Lodge and Royal Arch Chapter meetings. It has a magnificent circular Zodiac painted on the ceiling. At the far end is the Master's chair, usually referred to as the Chair of King Solomon. The Zodiac has been rotated so that the constellation of Aries sits directly above the Master's chair, denoting that when Solomon's Temple was built the dominant precessional constellation was Aries.*

# Regalia of the Royal Arch

The regalia of the Royal Arch, comprises three separate elements: apron, sash (although perhaps more correctly referred to as a *riband*), and jewel.

As with the Craft Lodge regalia, the Royal Arch includes an apron, of similar size to that of the Master Mason, and while the underlying colour for the Craft is blue, that of the Royal Arch is a dark red/scarlet. With the base of the apron being white, there is a band around the outer edge comprising a series of scarlet and blue triangles. These triangles, by virtue of their dual colouring, symbolise three aspects: regal dignity, union and benevolence (charity). To understand how these two colours can have several meanings, one needs to study the structure of a typical Chapter, to understand how the colours are a reflection of the three main offices.

*For image, see colour section plate 25.*

As previously noted, blue is the predominant colour of Craft Masonry, while scarlet is the colour of the Royal Arch; therefore the interspaced colours are a symbol of the union between the two degree formats.

The three Principals are a reflection of the Israelite leaders who returned to Jerusalem and commenced to build the Second Temple, indicating the senior position they held in their society. To emphasise that position, the three Principals of a chapter are clothed in robes while in office: the First Principal wears a scarlet robe; the Second Principal is purple; the Third Principal is blue, all colours are derived primarily from the Book of Exodus, concerning the construction of the Tabernacle which influenced the design of Solomon's Temple.

Moreover thou shalt make the tabernacle with ten curtains of fine twined linen, and blue, and purple, and scarlet: with cherubims of cunning work shalt thou make them.

*'Exodus' 26:1, King James Version*

Make the tabernacle with ten curtains of finely twisted linen and blue, purple and scarlet yarn, with cherubim woven into them by a skilled worker.

*'Exodus' 26:1, New International Version*

It should be noted that the middle colour is purple because this is the result of mixing the two colours on either side, scarlet and blue, while purple is a colour long associated with royalty. Two of the colours are mentioned elsewhere in the Old Testament, associated with the building of Solomon's Temple, while the third colour is crimson, very close to scarlet. When Huram-Abi was sent by Hiram King of Tyre, to assist King Solomon in the construction of the Temple, he chose a man of great skill:

And now I have sent a cunning man, endued with understanding, of Huram my father's, the son of a woman of the daughters of Dan, and his father was a man of Tyre, skilful to work in gold, and in silver, in brass, in iron, in stone, and in timber, in purple, in blue, and in fine linen, and in crimson; also to grave any manner of graving, and to find out every device which shall be put to him, with thy cunning men, and with the cunning men of my lord David thy father.

*2 Chronicles 2 :13 and 14,*
*New International Version*

I am sending you Huram-Abi, a man of great skill, whose mother was from

Dan and whose father was from Tyre. He is trained to work in gold and silver, bronze and iron, stone and wood, and with purple and blue and crimson yarn and fine linen. He is experienced in all kinds of engraving and can execute any design given to him. He will work with your skilled workers and with those of my lord, David your father.

*2 Chronicles 2 :13 and 14, New International Version*

Depending on which version of '2 Chronicles' is used, some of the colours changed, although in the King James and New International versions they are as stated above.

From the 'Chronicles' text, it seems that Huram-Abi was knowledgeable about the production of dyes and fine linen; Crimson dye, being described as a reddish purple colour, would in the times of Solomon have been extracted from worms. By the Middle Ages, an insect found on evergreen oak trees in the Mediterranean area was harvested by local inhabitants and became the source of the dye until it was overtaken by cochineal. Scarlet is a much brighter red, which is believed to have originated in Persia about 3,000 years ago and, being close to the colour of blood, was seen as symbolising life. Blue dyes were developed sometime after the reds and purples, but were used in the funerary dressing of some Egyptian kings. Evidence suggests it was in use on the island of Crete in the Minoan culture, before 2,000 BCE. The base for the blue dye of that time seems to have been a mineral shipped from the area now known as Afghanistan. But it is the regal colour of purple, that is most worthy of comment.

At the time of King Solomon, purple dye was extremely expensive, quoted by Aristotle as being 10 or 20 times more so than gold. It was produced from a sea snail known as *trunculus murex,* and some 50,000 such snails needed to be harvested in order to produce just one pound (450 grams) of the dye. The result was a light purple colour that did not fade in the sun, so this characteristic, together with its rarity, meant it was a dye that only the wealthy elite of ancient society could afford to buy – in consequence of which, it became a regal colour.

Thus, although the Second Principal is the one who wears the purple robe, his two colleagues are equal in the final equation and are therefore all associated with *royal* dignity. Hence one can deduce that the colours on the apron are not only an allegorical symbol of unity, but also of the regal dignity associated with the Order.

In the foregoing consideration of the apron, we have looked at several issues associated with the colours of the regalia. There is another possibility that should not be overlooked.

We have already noted the probable connection between the colours of the Craft Lodges and those of Oxford and Cambridge Universities, therefore the colours used in the Royal Arch have a close relationship with those of the Master of Arts degrees and doctorates. As confirmed by information available through Oxford University, it seems that Doctors of Divinity (DD) wear a full scarlet dress gown and a scarlet convocation habit, while those of a Master of Philosophy (MPhil) are dark blue, silk-edged and lined with white silk. Both blue and scarlet are the colours employed in Royal Arch regalia.

It is also interesting to note that, just as the Master Mason apron had two sets of seven tassels, so too has the Royal Arch regalia, although the emphasis is probably very different. In former epochs, a young man fortunate enough to go to university probably started his primary studies at around 14 years of age, the same as for an apprentice. Thus he is likely to have concluded a course of study and been awarded a Bachelor of Arts (BA) degree some seven years later. In respect of the Master of Arts (MA) degree, Oxford University literature makes the following observation:

> The degree of Masters of Arts is granted to BA graduates at a degree ceremony no sooner than 21 terms after [University] matriculation.

This seems to have been the tradition that existed even in the late Middle Ages, and if we assume that the university year comprised three terms – autumn, spring, summer – then the full period would be a further seven years. Thus the tassels on the Royal Arch aprons would represent the two seven-year periods culminating in the award of a BA and MA degree. In the Craft ceremonies there is frequent encouragement to study the liberal arts, to the point that, on reaching the ceremony for the Installation of the Master, reference is made to a Master of Art and Science. From this, it is easily concluded that when the regalia was designed at the time of the Union, the Master Mason degree was perceived as a reflection of a course of study equating to a Bachelor of Arts with the Master/Past Master as the Master of Arts and the completion of the Royal Arch as being bestowed with a doctorate, especially in divinity. Just as a Doctor of Divinity wears a scarlet gown, so the holder of the highest office in a Royal Arch Chapter also wears a scarlet robe, and the number of years it usually takes to achieve the Chair is a further seven years.

The sash, or riband, is quite a different matter and has been the subject of much written discussion in the past, primarily because our forebears could not positively ascertain why it is part of Masonic regalia. In the absence of positive proof one way or another, speculation has ranged across many notions. One of the most highly respected Masonic writers of the mid-20th century devoted very little comment to this important item of regalia, instead making observations on various instances of use around the 1770s.[63]

Indeed, the lack of comment regarding this item of regalia could well infer that a much more interesting provenance is involved.

The current constitutions dictate that the sash/riband is worn over the left shoulder and hangs down at the right hip, at the end of which an emblem of the Royal Arch is affixed, comprising a triangle incorporating a Triple Tau and tassel. The word *sash* is believed to have been of Arabic origin, describing a length of cloth that was wound around the body to hold flowing clothing together. During the religious wars of the Crusades, knights in body armour would find that the heat retained by the metal was very draining, and to shield themselves from the sun they wore a light cloth cape which they could remove when going into battle. An additional observation can be made from the reign of Charles I, when it apparently became fashionable for military commanders to tie a sash around the waist, fastened on the opposite side to the sword to hold the weapon firmly in place when riding, a fashion which extended through the time of the Civil War. By the early 1700s, it seems the sash was being worn predominantly from the right shoulder to left hip as a symbol of honours that may have been bestowed, especially emblems of a chivalric Order of Knighthood which would be placed at the end of a sash. Even today the sash plays an important role in royal and military ceremonial regalia. The colour may denote the highest award of a particular country, with the emblems of honour being attached to them. Some British Army ceremonial dress codes incorporate a scarlet sash being worn around the waist during daylight hours and across the body for evening receptions, while representatives of official government office may wear a sash containing the adopted colours of the nation when performing ceremonial functions as part of their duty. For some Scottish ladies, they remain a treasured item of clothing to indicate the clan or family with which they are connected. It can therefore be summarised that, for the past two centuries at least, the sash has been a symbol of authority and honour.

Irrespective of its use, it will be seen that for at least the past few centuries, the sash/riband has had a close connection with royalty and chivalry. Throughout most of Europe – 'the old world' – the sash is usually worn from the right shoulder to the left hip. Some countries in Africa and the Far East that have recently adopted the sash as an emblem of authority, wearing it from the left shoulder to right hip. As far as the Royal Arch is concerned, noting that the royal families of Europe usually wear the sash/riband from right shoulder to left hip, and the close connection with royalty that the Order enjoyed at the time of the union, it may have been deemed appropriate to use the sash/riband to indicate the honour with which the Order had been bestowed, but worn from left to right so as not to conflict with (or be confused with) official state regalia, despite imitating it. Noting that the sash is used in some countries for fastening the insignia of state, it is also interesting to note that, in Royal Arch, medals indicating honours bestowed within Freemasonry are attached to the left breast, in very close proximity to the sash, further underlining its connection with state honours.

The third item of regalia is the jewel.

The main visual component of the jewel is the circle within which are the interlaced triangles. This symbol is often called *Solomon's Seal*.

*For images, see colour section plate 26.*

*Author's note:*
*In an earlier chapter about the Master/Past Master degree, I noted that one needs to understand the knowledge conveyed in those two levels if one is to understand the Royal Arch. I have included some of the following text and images in earlier books, and will add them here for completeness.*

This symbol, or variations of it, appear not only in the Royal Arch but also in many of the great cathedrals of Britain and Europe. One of the most evident of these is a window in the north face of Chichester Cathedral, but it also appears regularly in stained glass windows such as Notre Dame Cathedral in Paris.

**Above:** *The image comprising a circle and interlaced triangles in Chichester cathedral.*

**Top right:** *A similar illustration in a south-facing stained-glass window at Notre Dame.*

We have already touched on the subject of the Vesica/Mandorla in earlier chapters. There is only one way that Solomon's Seal can be constructed using the square and compasses, the symbols of Freemasonry, as the square provides a straight edge like a ruler. It is by using the two circles and the Vesica to create equilateral triangles that the interlaced symbol is derived from a simple development of geometric principles outlined by the philosopher Euclid, the father of geometry, that of dividing any straight line of unknown length into two equal parts.

But, the influence of Vesica Piscis goes even deeper into Royal Arch symbolism – via the double cube.

This appearance in churches and cathedrals is unlikely to be by coincidence, especially when there is almost no evidence of it across Europe prior to the Gothic building boom that started in the 12th century. Canterbury cathedral was the first in England to undergo, what in its day was a revolutionary building style. In the stained glass windows of that cathedral, we not only find Solomon's Seal, but it is also linked to Vesica's built in the glass below.

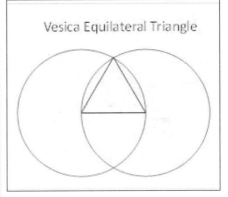

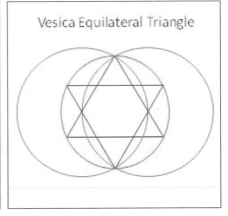

## The double cube and altar of incense

In the layout of the Chapter room is a white pedestal in the shape of a double cube. It stands on its end and is described as being *in the form of an altar of incense*. This is described in 'Exodus' 30 verses 2–19:

Make an altar of acacia wood for burning incense.

It is to be square, a cubit long and a cubit wide, and two cubits high, its horns of one piece with it.

Overlay the top and all the sides and the horns with pure gold, and make a gold moulding around it.

Make two gold rings for the altar below the moulding – two on each of the opposite sides – to hold the poles used to carry it.

Make the poles of acacia wood and overlay them with gold.

Put the altar in front of the curtain that shields the ark of the covenant law – before the atonement cover that is over the tablets of the covenant law – where I will meet with you.

Aaron must burn fragrant incense on the altar every morning when he tends the lamps.

He must burn incense again when he lights the lamps at twilight so incense will burn regularly before the Lord for the generations to come.

Do not offer on this altar any other incense or any burnt offering or grain offering, and do not pour a drink offering on it.

Once a year Aaron shall make atonement on its horns.

This is the only detailed reference to an altar of incense in the whole of the Old Testament, although it is mentioned again in 'Leviticus', referring to the same device. Intrinsically, this is a small wooden box in the shape of two cubes merged together as one, and covered in gold. Another allegory perhaps?

From a geometrical point of view, keeping in mind that Freemasonry is allegedly derived from operative masons using practical means to solve problems, the double cube as described posed a huge problem to the Greeks and Egyptians. Both sought a way of geometrically taking a cube and doubling its volume, and the means to determine the lengths of the sides that would achieve this. They were looking for a constant such as pi = 3.142, or phi = 0.618 and 1.618, but they sought in vain. This is the only major geometrical problem that cannot be solved easily by only using a pair of compasses and a square or straight edge. In many books on mathematics and geometry, it is described as the *Delian problem* which, according to tradition, arose in ancient Greece when the Oracle of Delphi demanded that the cube-shaped altar should be doubled in size. Over the years, centuries and millenia, several solutions were developed but none produced the magical constant that they all sought. Sir Isaac Newton developed a solution, but like all the others it could not be solved by the compasses and square alone. It requires that the line providing the solution must be adjusted so that the length (1) to the right of it, is pivoted to and fro, until the length of the original cube side dimension is achieved. Sir Isaac apparently only achieved this by sliding a piece of paper on which he had

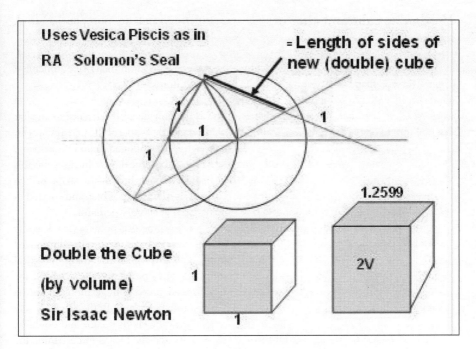

made appropriate markings along one edge. Because the construction centres around an equilateral triangle and circle, it lends itself to the versatility of Vesica Piscis.

Sir Isaac Newton devised his solution at Cambridge University, where he also lectured. He had a considerable respect for the geometrical processes evolved by the ancient Greeks, and while he left the University in 1696, by 1714, as the Wars of Spanish Succession drew to a close, his reputation as a philosopher had grown immensely across Europe. During his time at Cambridge, James II had sought to make both of the universities in England into Catholic-based institutions, which Newton vehemently opposed. Newton died in 1727, just 10 years after the formation of the Premier Grand Lodge.

Links between Solomon's Seal, Gothic architecture and the double cube/altar of incense do not cease there, as it can be linked to yet another Royal Arch symbol involving a circle and the so-called Triple Tau.

*Author's note:*

*I am firmly of the opinion that, following the death of Sir Isaac Newton, a man who made an enormous contribution to the world of knowledge in the Age of Enlightenment through his understanding of the forces of gravity, the spectrum of light and the development of Calculus to name but a few, the reference to the altar of incense became a means of honouring him in an allegorical fashion. It also provided a means of establishing the ratio that operative masons could use in defining the proportional relationship between the diameter of a classical column and the size of the base on which it would be mounted. This inclusion of the altar would have been the sort of allegorical ceremonial development that may well have taken place in the mid-1700s. It would therefore explain why there is a double cube in the Chapter room, a decoration that is out of context with the ceremonial background of rebuilding the temple in Jerusalem, 2,500 years ago, although, as we will see later in the next chapter, a column in a vault is related* to a fourth-century fable. As such, it seems to represent another symbol illustrating an allegory – the celebration of the life of Sir Isaac Newton and a solution to the Delian problem that so tested the ancient philosophers.

## The Triple Tau symbol in the Royal Arch

The so-called Triple Tau is a major feature of Royal Arch symbolism, as it appears as a decorative triangle on regalia. In nearly every Chapter room, behind the thrones of the Three Principals or adjacent to them, a large image of the Triple Tau encased in a circle is usually displayed. Depending on the production technique employed, it is sometimes presented with the Triple Tau resting on the base of the triangle or sometimes centred within the triangle.

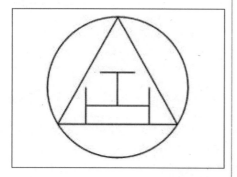

*Author's note:*
*Over a period of some months, I regularly showed the above diagram to a number of Royal Arch members of long standing, including some of the most senior ranks of the Supreme Grand Chapter in England. I asked each one if they could explain what it was about, what it symbolised or where it came from. Not one single member approached could answer any of those questions. Some who had been members for many years even acknowledged that they* hadn't taken any interest in it but considered it just part of age-old decoration, while others acknowledged it but had never tried to understand why it was in place. I found it absolutely amazing that such senior members had no understanding of one of the most widely used symbols found in Chapters. Yet again, this underscores perhaps how hierarchy may have gradually increased in influence while the knowledge and wisdom behind some of the symbolism has diminished. The following is therefore this author's attempt to explain it.

The story starts with the Tau itself.

The tau –'T' – is acknowledged as being the 19th letter of the Greek alphabet. In Greek it is pronounced *taf* or *tof*, and in Hebrew as *tov*, while in the English Royal Arch it is pronounced *taw*. There seems to be no satisfactory explanation for this variance of pronunciation in England, as one would expect it to follow the Greek pronunciation as is the case with pi and phi, or alpha and omega. One can only assume that, as in the English language, the *au* is sounded *awe*, as in daughter, taught, caught, etc and someone started to use the *taw* pronunciation which has since become fixed, unless, of course, it does not symbolise the Greek character at all, but is an allegorical representation of something else.

To be a true Tau, it should be constructed on the ratios of the Golden Mean/Divine Proportion.

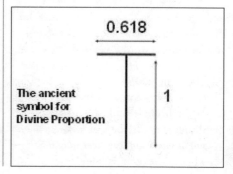

0.618

The ancient symbol for Divine Proportion

1

The Tau has a unique symbolism and features in the book of Ezekiel chapter nine on the subject of idolatry, when the symbol of the Tau was adopted as a device for protection. The following is the text that applies:

> And behold six men came from the way of the upper gate, which looks to the north: and each one had his weapon of destruction in his hand: and there was one man in the midst of them clothed with linen, with a writer's inkhorn at his reins: and they went in, and stood by the brazen altar. And the glory of the Lord of Israel went up from the cherub, upon which he was, to the threshold of the house: and he called to the man that was clothed with linen, and had a writer's inkhorn at his loins. And the Lord said to him: Go through the midst of the city, through the midst of Jerusalem: and mark *Thau* upon the foreheads of the men that sigh, and mourn for all the abominations that are committed in the midst thereof. And to the others he said in my hearing: Go after him through the city, and strike: let not your eyes spare, nor be moved with pity. Utterly destroy old and young, maidens, children and women: but upon whomsoever you shall see *Thau*, kill him not, and begin at my sanctuary.
>
> *Ezekiel 9, 2:6, King James Version*

The text of a more recent translation is similar but the word *Tau/Thau* is missing:

> Then the LORD called to the man clothed in linen who had the writing kit at his side and said to him, "Go throughout the city of Jerusalem *and put a mark on the foreheads* of those who grieve and lament over all the detestable things that are done in it." As I listened, he said to the others, "Follow him through the city and kill, without showing pity or compassion. Slaughter the old men, the young men and women, the mothers and children, *but do not touch anyone who has the mark*. Begin at my sanctuary." So they began with the old men who were in front of the temple.
>
> *New International edition*

It immediately becomes clear that in the 18th and 19th century, when the King James version of the Old Testament was probably the only version available to Lodges and Chapters, the word 'Thau' (for Tau) was relevant, but in more modern translations it is missing completely. We are merely left with a mark on the forehead and no indication as to what the mark would have been. Yet because of the interpretation in the King James version, a number of writers in earlier years described it as *an ancient symbol for life*. That would now seem to be a less reliable interpretation, as it is not the only terminology that has disappeared from biblical text.

From the middle of the 18th century the symbol seems to have been represented simply as 'T' over 'H', as in the simplified image below.

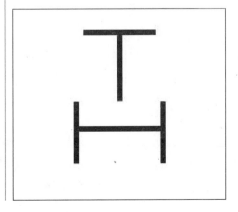

Depending on where the symbol was used in various regions of England, Ireland and Scotland, the presentation was more elaborate and seems to have had a variety of meanings. Various eminent writers previously cited the 'T' over 'H' symbol's use in Royal Arch at such dates as 1767, 1768 and 1792. As far as the Royal Arch is concerned, it is defined via the interpretation '*Templum Hierosolyma*', to mean the Temple of Jerusalem. Again, we must remember that religion was a major factor in life in the mid-18th century and the overriding source of reference was the King James Authorised Version of the Bible, and the works of Josephus, but, strangely, the term *Templum Hierosolyma* does not appear in either. There is only one reference to the Temple in any of the major versions of the Bible, and that is in the Latin Vulgate, and then only in a single verse:

Mark 11 Verse 15 (Latin Vulgate): et veniunt *Hierosolymam* et cum introisset *templum* coepit eicere vendentes et ementes in templo et mensas nummulariorum et cathedras vendentium columbas evertit.

Mark 11 Verse 15 (King James): And they come to Jerusalem: and Jesus went into the temple, and began to cast out them that sold and bought in the temple, and overthrew the tables of the moneychangers, and the seats of them that sold doves.

Mark 11 Verse 15 (New International): On reaching Jerusalem, Jesus entered the temple courts and began driving out those who were buying and selling there. He overturned the tables of the money changers and the benches of those selling doves.

There are many who have interpreted the phrase, *Temple in Jerusalem*, as referring to Solomon's Temple, because the Triple Tau featured on the Royal Arch jewel is sometimes known as Solomon's Seal. By virtue of this being quoted in the Book of Mark from the New Testament, and related to events that took place 2,000 years ago, it cannot be related to Solomon's Temple that was erected 1,000 years previously and destroyed after 400 years. Yet it does have a connection to Jerusalem, as we will see later. The 'T' over 'H' configuration does not necessarily create the Triple Tau, for according to the highly respected Masonic writer, Bernard E. Jones, it didn't appear in Royal Arch as such until around the 1820s.[64]

Yet maybe a link to Solomon's Temple was not intended at all. The Supreme Grand Chapter did not come into existence until 1817, and the ceremonies of Royal Arch are not believed to have *developed* until around 1845. This was an era when many of the most influential members of the organisation were well versed in classical languages. Thus, the 'T' over 'H' (T/H) symbol may again be a clever allegory.

The word 'over' could also be interpreted as 'above'; and in a period when religion was a driving influence in life, especially in the cohesion of the *establishment,* 'above' would have meant heaven as they understood it, the place where the deity dwelt and watched 'over' us. This being so, then the 'T' would be the deity, and the 'H' would be a reference to the people on Earth.

Ephesus was a major Greco-Roman city at the time of alleged events in Jerusalem, 2,000 years ago, and was a major trading centre in early Byzantium. A short distance from Ephesus is the town of Seljuk, a town in which John the Apostle, is believed to have settled after the crucifixion, and where he wrote the Gospel bearing his name which is included in the New Testament. Indeed, on the outskirts of Seljuk is the ruin of a once large and important basilica named after him. Between Ephesus and Seljuk is a hill, at the top of which is a small dwelling, a highly venerated shrine to Mary, Mother of the Christ. Tradition has it that after the crucifixion, John took Mary out of the Jerusalem area to Ephesus for safety, and the dwelling on the hill is presented as the place where Mary subsequently lived.

Ephesus at that time was in an area where the predominant language was Greek, and it is noted that the Gospels were originally translated from Hebrew into Greek prior to translation into Latin. Through the Roman and Byzantine periods, there had been a close association between all denominations of the Christian Church. When Charlemagne was crowned King of the Romans in the year 800 CE and declared Emperor, the Church in the West began to develop differences from that in the East. Friction occurred between the two cultures to the extent that, in 1054 CE, a great schism developed between them, resulting in the Roman Catholic Church in the West, with its language base of Latin, and the Eastern Orthodox Church in the East, which continued to use Greek. Thus the 'T' over 'H' symbol may well be an allegory for that split.

The Greek word for God is *Theos*.

The Latin word for man is *Homo*.

Thus the symbol would be a reflection of the two most common languages in which the Christian message was presented at the time of the Union, as well as symbolising *God* as being above *man*. Noting that the original texts from which the Latin versions of the Bible were translated were in Greek, it may also be a symbol to indicate the primacy of the Eastern Church over that of the Latin.

In the first chapter of this book, mention was made of the ceiling in the Banqueting House, Whitehall, London, which depicts, in allegorical form, the *apotheosis* of James I/VI. Within the Christian Church there is a concept that it should be the objective of every man, during his life, to become like God and thereby achieve a personal *apotheosis* – man rising to a god-like status by grace. This would perhaps give a far more credible interpretation to the T/H reference than any connection with Solomon's Temple.

The *Tau* symbol 'T', was apparently used by the monks of the Order of Saint Anthony as a symbol of their monastic community. Their patron was a holy man who lived around 300 CE, having spent his early life in the Nile Delta and reputedly died around 350 CE. He was one of the first Christians to adopt a hermetic existence, and it was in his honour that a series of monastic communities were established in Egypt and Eastern Europe. The Order seems to have achieved particular fame for assisting in the treatment of *St Anthony's fire,* a rather unpleasant affliction caused by a fungus that grew on rye which induced a disease afflicting a large number of the community. It apparently attacked limbs and extremities of the body, causing them to shrivel and fall off, and was recorded as being an extremely painful disease, usually resulting in death. *The Catholic Encyclopaedia* notes:

> Near the Church of St. Anthony at Saint-Didier de la Mothe they built a hospital, which became the central house of the order. The members devoted themselves to the care of the sick, particularly those afflicted with the disease - St Anthony's Fire…They wore a black habit with the Greek letter Tau - St. Anthony's cross – in blue.

An encyclopaedia definition of Saint Anthony's fire describes it thus:

> St Anthony's Fire – a disease caused by a fungus that grows on rye; causes sickness, diarrhoea; hits the central nervous system; convulsions and hallucinations.[65]

> (*A record for the year 857 CE notes that* 'a great plague of swollen blisters consumed the people by a loathsome rot, so that their limbs were loosened and fell off before death'.)

Not every reference to the Tau in scripture appears to have been accurate, for it seems that in some early translations it was confused with other words and meanings. Again, *The Catholic Encyclopaedia* notes:

> The interchanging of Hê and Hêth, of Yôdh and Waw, so easy with the new characters, is scarcely conceivable with the old ones; and the mistaking of Bêth for Caph is altogether excluded. Aleph and Tau on the other hand can easily be mixed up. Now in 'Chronicles', in itself recent and translated into Greek long after the Pentateuch, Waw and Tau, Yôdh and Hê, Caph and Rêsh have been mistaken for each other. This can be accounted for only when older forms of writing were employed.

So, despite the many pages written by eminent Masons of the past, compounded by further investigation, the only reliable information to be found indicates, that the Tau is the 19th character of the Greek alphabet, and in its correct form complies with the proportions of the Golden/Divine Ratio of 0.618 and 1.618, which are also commonly written as 0.6 and 1.6. This then raises the question as to how it is related to the circle and triangle which form the important symbol of the Royal Arch. The answer to that reflects the part played by Platonic theory in the relationship with the Triple Tau.

## The Triple Tau of Plato

Within the notes and instructions of Royal Arch ceremonial there is a rather obscure lecture, which forms no part of ceremonial activity within the Royal Arch in England (subject to the mode of working used) but is sometimes simply referred to as *Appendix C – An Explanation of the Jewel*. It attempts to deal with the subject associated with Platonic theory, of relationships between the Triple Tau and equilateral triangles. The language employed is not very helpful in terms of understanding what the subject is about, and the vast majority of members who have read it confess they are unable to grasp its meaning.[66] Yet the Triple Tau features in Royal Arch regalia and a range of other symbols; to explain why members experience such difficulty in comprehending the meaning, the following is a brief extract regarding the four elements of fire, earth, air and water, mentioned in Platonic theory:

> …Therefore, since the elements are bodies, and all bodies are solid and bounded by superficies which consist of triangles either equilateral or otherwise, the Platonic theory assigned to each of the four elements the form of a solid, bounded by plane surfaces constituted of triangles; for although one of these solids is bounded by squares and another by pentagons, yet it will be evident that equilateral rectilineal figures may be resolved into many triangles as the figures have sides united by their vertices in a common centre…

Keeping in mind that the text above represents just a few short sentences from eight pages of ceremonial detail, it is hardly surprising that many members of the Royal Arch have considerable difficulty comprehending it.

Historically, Platonism and Platonic theory were subjects taught in many independent public schools of Britain as part of their curriculum of classical studies, until around the mid-20th century, and was also associated with a university degree in Philosophy, and is probably extant. Therefore, remembering that 200 years ago, many senior members of Lodges were well educated at a time when the greater portion of the population was not and had been schooled in Platonic theory as part of their classical studies, it is not difficult to perceive how it may have found its way into Masonic ceremonies, the Royal Arch in particular. Yet there is surely a story to tell and one can see abundant evidence of its influence even today. Essentially, what this obscure Royal Arch lecture achieves, is to interpret Plato's idea: one of the first rules of geometry is that in a right angle triangle (90 degrees) then all the angles will add up to 180 degrees. If we take an equilateral triangle, all the angles are 60 degrees, so the total is 180 degrees. If we cut the equilateral triangle in half, two right-angle triangles result and we have 90+60+30 = 180 degrees.

The Triple Tau has eight right-angles of 90 degrees, therefore the total angular value is 720 degrees (eight x 90). This is the equivalent of taking an equilateral triangle and dividing the interior area such that four individual triangles emerge (four x 180 = 720); therefore four equilateral triangles = One Tau.

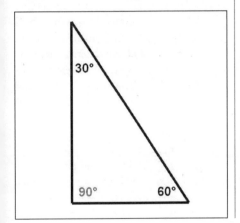

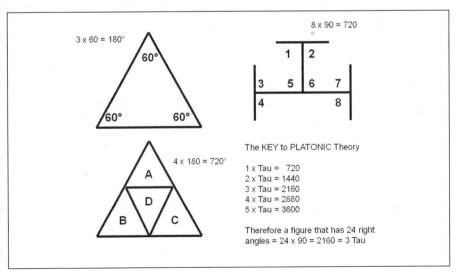

The KEY to PLATONIC Theory

1 x Tau =   720
2 x Tau = 1440
3 x Tau = 2160
4 x Tau = 2880
5 x Tau = 3600

Therefore a figure that has 24 right angles = 24 x 90 = 2160 = 3 Tau

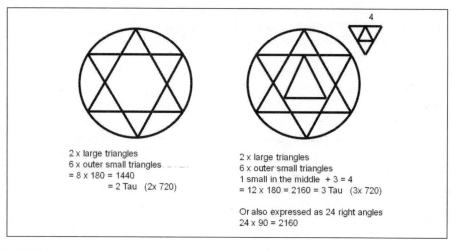

2 x large triangles
6 x outer small triangles
= 8 x 180 = 1440
= 2 Tau  (2x 720)

2 x large triangles
6 x outer small triangles
1 small in the middle  + 3 = 4
= 12 x 180 = 2160 = 3 Tau (3x 720)

Or also expressed as 24 right angles
24 x 90 = 2160

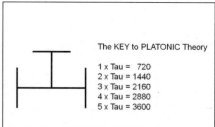

The KEY to PLATONIC Theory

1 x Tau =  720
2 x Tau = 1440
3 x Tau = 2160
4 x Tau = 2880
5 x Tau = 3600

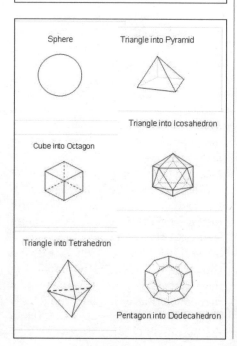

Sphere

Triangle into Pyramid

Triangle into Icosahedron

Cube into Octagon

Triangle into Tetrahedron

Pentagon into Dodecahedron

If we now take the image of Solomon's Seal, a key symbol of Royal Arch, one can see that it comprises the two larger overlapping or intertwined equilateral triangles and six smaller equilateral triangles around the outer edge, created by the overlapping lines. We therefore have eight equilateral triangles in total;

eight x 180 = 1440, which in turn is the equivalent of two tau (two x 720 = 1440).

If we now add the smaller triangle to the centre of the Solomon's seal configuration, we have the eight triangles of Solomon's Seal, plus the four smaller triangles, which makes 12 triangles in total: 12 x 180 = 2160; numerically this is equivalent to three tau (three x 720 = 2160); or 24 right-angles (24 x 90 = 2160). Thus we can create a simple table (*see above left*).

The next stage is to investigate what are known as Platonic solids.

If we now take a cube, one of the Platonic solids, we can determine that it has six faces and eight corners. Each corner is made up of three right-angles of 90 degrees. Therefore each corner is a total of three x 90 = 270. There are eight such corners so their total is eight x 270 = 2160. Thus, in Platonic theory, a cube is the equivalent of three Tau, which in turn is the equivalent of Solomon's Seal with the added small equilateral triangle at the centre.

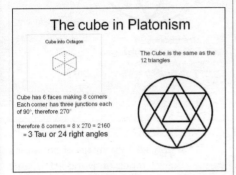

### The cube in Platonism

Cube into Octagon

The Cube is the same as the 12 triangles

Cube has 6 faces making 8 corners
Each corner has three junctions each
of 90°, therefore 270°

therefore 8 corners = 8 x 270 = 2160
= 3 Tau or 24 right angles

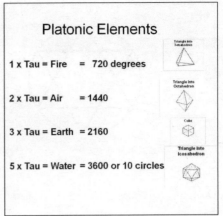

### Platonic Elements

| | | |
|---|---|---|
| 1 x Tau = Fire | = 720 degrees | Triangle into Tetrahedron |
| 2 x Tau = Air | = 1440 | Triangle into Octahedron |
| 3 x Tau = Earth | = 2160 | Cube |
| 5 x Tau = Water | = 3600 or 10 circles | Triangle into Icosahedron |

Platonism then takes this analogy a bit further, by suggesting that at the time of the creation of the world there were four primary elements: Fire, Air, Water and Earth. From this one deduces that a cube is a solid form and is therefore an equivalent of the Earth. Fire produces light, and it is obvious that one cannot see anything without light that illuminates and reflects from any object. As well as the solid Earth on which we walk and the light to see everything around us, for life to exist we require two other elements, Air and Water. To each of these elements the Platonists then assigned a geometrical solid to each, based on the Triple Tau numerical equivalent. Thus we get the Tetrahedron, Octahedron, Cube, Icosahedron and Dodecahedron. The five solids symbolise the Universal Sphere in company with the four elements.

This analogy has then been interpreted in a symbol that was very commonly used, particularly in the period of the Renaissance and the era following the creation of the United Grand Lodge.

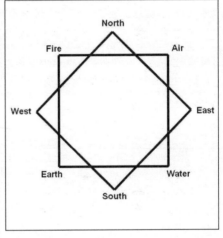

Resulting in an eight-sided or pointed figure, it is sometimes represented in the form of an *Octagram* and appears in many religious and stately buildings. The image above is embedded in the floor of the lobby at the Houses of Parliament in London, and in the Cathedral dedicated to the Knights Hospitaller, also known as the Knights of St. John and Knights of Malta, in Valetta, Malta. The same pattern is visible in a plate installed in the floor of St. Paul's cathedral, under the centre of the dome, but is only really noticeable when looking down on it from the *Whispering Gallery*.

*The Platonic Octagram symbol in a Buddist temple – Malaysia.*

*For other images, see colour section plate 29 & 30.*

There is another slight twist in the allegory. Within the ceremonies of the Royal Arch, there is one point when the members line up along the sides of the chequered pavement. Six long wooden staves are held on either side, so that the top of one touches that of the other directly opposite, with the other end of each stave resting upon the floor. In this way six equilateral triangles are created, as the staves actually create a tunnel, then by standing at each end one can also see two further equilateral triangles, making eight in all. Eight triangles have a Platonic Tau equivalent of two Tau (eight x 180 = 1440). Two Tau is the Platonic equivalent of the *Air* that we breathe. If we look at the Octagram image, created by the overlapping squares representing the cardinal points and the four elements, (*previous page*) there are eight equilateral triangles around the outer edge, the angles of which add up to 1440 = two Tau. Thus it can be argued, that this simple process of creating the eight equilateral triangles with the wooden staves is symbolising the eight points that create the Octagram, whilst the two Tau represent the duality of creation: heaven and earth.

Needless to note, in our highly developed technological and scientifically evaluated world of the 21st century, these ideas about the elements and creation as expounded by the Platonists have little credibility, but in the era when Freemasonry was being formalised and united it had a strong influence, which remained so until the mid-20th century. With such a strong connection with the religious views of creation, it is little wonder that it surfaces in Freemasonry, and particularly in the Royal Arch.

So much for the little understood Royal Arch lecture on Platonic theory. In attempting to comprehend the meaning, one can acquire a good understanding of the Royal Arch symbol shown earlier, comprising the circle, triangle and Triple Tau. And it is closely linked to another element of Royal Arch ceremony, known as the Mystical Lecture.

## The Mystical Lecture and the Royal Arch emblem

Again we should remember that most Masonic ceremonies were put together in their present form, in the 18th and 19th centuries, when the world was perceived in a very different way to the knowledge and understanding that developed in the 20th century. Thus the Mystical Lecture, delightfully presented as it is, is likewise a reflection of the religious interpretations that existed in a bygone era. In short, it points out that the Triple Tau is not only an illustration of the creation of the world as presented by the Platonists, but for Masonic purposes it also symbolises the three individuals that had a considerable influence over the building of the first Jerusalem temple: Solomon – King of Israel from whose kingdom most of the builders were recruited; Hiram – King of Tyre, who supplied a lot of the important materials and specialist skills; Huram Abi – the highly skilled craftsman specifically provided to assist with the construction. It also notes that the primary geometric symbols are the circle and the equilateral triangle.

The circle, in past eras, was closely associated with the symbol of a snake swallowing its own tail. By virtue of a circle having no starting or finishing point, but being a continuous line that exists without any interruption in its form, it is equated with the religious idea of eternity. The triangle is stated as having been long associated with various deities, but there is no actual evidence of this. It seems to have acquired this connection only when an eye is placed within it. The Egyptians used the symbol of an eye to represent their primary god, Horus, who was always watching over them. It then seems to have migrated to the eye being presented in a triangle to signify that the apex was the direction of heaven, where the deity resided, and hence became known as the all-seeing eye of God. (It is also found in Buddhism.) This really seems to be the only connection with the deity. So, based on these bygone ideas connected with symbols, the primary symbol of the Royal Arch could be interpreted as an eternal (circle) deity (triangle) who created the world and everything in it, based on the Platonist explanation of the elements (Triple Tau).

Amongst the ancient Jewish community however, the symbol of the triangle with apex uppermost represented the male, while the inverted triangle was a symbol of the female. It is widely believed that the symbol of the overlapping or intertwined triangles therefore became a symbol of a union through marriage. Thus, in Masonic allegory, the intertwined triangles of the Royal Arch can be construed as representing the *Union of the Grand Lodges*.

## The geometry of the combined symbol

Geometry, we are told, is at the core of Freemasonry. This suggests that it must be possible for the combined symbol to be produced in a defined manner geometrically, as indeed it can.

In an earlier chapter it was noted that without the knowledge contained in the Master or Past Master degree, and in particular that of the overlapping circles to create Vesica Piscis, it is impossible to understand the symbolism of the Royal Arch. This is where the reality of such statements is verified.

It starts by drawing the circles, and deriving the Vesica, then creating the overlapping equilateral triangles. Then add the central circle and the diagonal lines ensuring that the lines meet exactly in the centre of the Vesica.

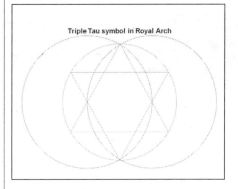

Triple Tau symbol in Royal Arch

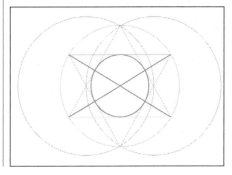

Next, draw a square that just touches the perimeter of the central circle.

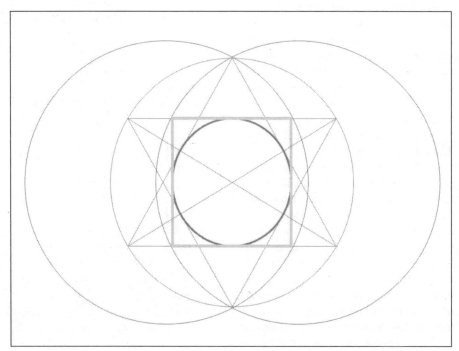

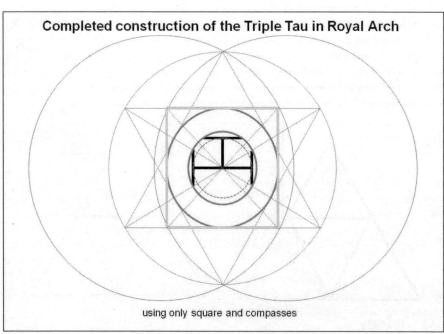

## Completed construction of the Triple Tau in Royal Arch

using only square and compasses

Complete the action by drawing a line through the centre to the two outer edges of the square and adding the outer lines to form 'T's', a perfect Triple Tau image is created, as used in Royal Arch symbolism, and using only a square and compasses, which comprises all the basic geometric symbols that feature throughout Freemasonry, viz. square, circle, triangle, Vesica Piscis and Mandorla.

Just one moment! Is it really a true Triple Tau? Answer - no.

Earlier in the chapter, it was pointed out that a true Tau is in the proportion of golden/divine ratio. In this symbol we have three 'T's'. If, however, one takes each of the 'T's' that are formed in the horizontal plane in turn, then the length of the horizontal line relative to the vertical end lines that create the cross of the 'T', are, when drawn accurately, of the rounded Golden/Divine Ratio of 0.6 and 1.6. It could therefore be argued that there are now two Tau. But the third leg is only half, and two and a half Tau is not three Tau, or a Triple Tau. What we do have however, are the three 'T's' that symbolise the religious concept of the *Trinity* – Father, Son and Holy Spirit. These are concepts connected with the biblical stories of the New Testament.

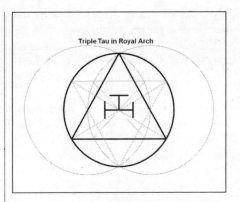

Triple Tau in Royal Arch

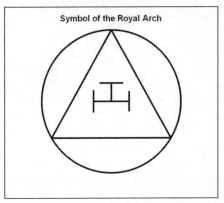

Symbol of the Royal Arch

It should also be noted that the triangle divided into four equilateral triangles, forms an association with Platonic theory and the Tau/Taw, often found in ecclesiastical circles as a symbol for the Trinity.

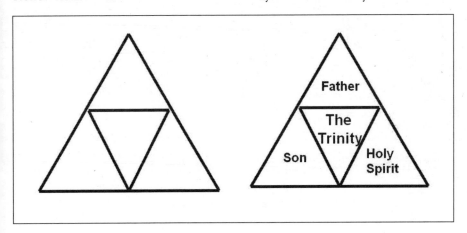

*Author's note:*

*The symbol of the circle, triangle and so-called Triple Tau are not presented in a single coherent manner across the spread of the Royal Arch. There are huge variances from Chapter to Chapter, or region to region. In some cases where a very old Chapter exists, the decoration that shows this symbol is handmade and the position of the Triple Tau is in the centre. In some more modern versions, the Tau image is larger and sits on the base line of the triangle. It seems reasonable to believe that the symbol should be constructed using the geometry that forms part of the knowledge contained in the former degrees. As such, there are numerous variants that can be achieved. During the preparation of this book, I wrote to the Supreme Grand Chapter/United Grand Lodge and asked if there was a corporate design for the symbol, that clearly showed the construction methodology. Despite prompting, there has been no reply, from which I can only conclude that no such defined design methodology exists. Therefore, I suggest that the actual solution is as follows:*

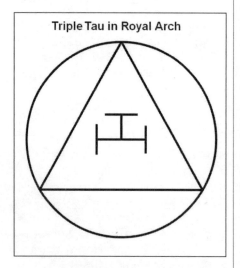

**Triple Tau in Royal Arch**

*It is the only symbol that can be brought together progressively using Vesica Piscis as the basis of the geometry.*

## The ox, man, lion and eagle

In addition to the 12 emblems indicating the twelve tribes of the Israelites, there are five others. They are so arranged that the image of the Triple Tau in a circle and the triangle, is placed centrally, while the other banners are arranged two on either side, showing representations of an ox, man, lion and eagle. Although each of the figures represented in the additional banners are mentioned in the Old Testament, they are usually referred to as symbolic representations of the four Gospels as defined by the Apostles Matthew, Mark, Luke and John. The Trinity and these four emblems therefore have a common ground.

Earlier in this chapter, in the description of the Master Mason's apron, mention was made of *The Book of Kells*, which is today housed at Trinity College, Dublin. Amongst the many wonderful Celtic illustrations from the sixth to the ninth centuries, there are two or three that depict the concept of the four Apostles and their Gospels with illustrations, the most impressive of which is known as MS58 *folio 129v.*

These symbols are derived from the Books of Ezekiel – starting at chapter one verse four, a book that forms part of Royal Arch ceremonies – and Revelations chapter four verse seven. These chapters mention winged figures with the appearance of a man, a lion, a calf, and eagle. These four symbolic representations, including wings, are illustrated in each of four panels that make up *folio 129v.*

*For image from the 'Book of Kells', see colour section plate 17.*

Other Masonic researchers may point out the slightly different order indicated by the illustration in *The Book of Kells* by comparison with the Chapter room layout described above. However, if we work from the centre, the Symbol of the Royal Arch, the Man, followed by Calf (Ox), and Lion followed by Eagle, is an entirely, allegorical representation of *folio 129v.*

The images are also displayed in a slightly different manner in another associated book, *The Book of Armagh.* They represent:

The Man ......... Homo ... Saint Matthew
The Calf (Ox) .. Vitulus .. Saint Luke
The Lion ........ Leo ........ Saint Mark
The Eagle ....... Aquilla .. Saint John

An interpretation of these figures is attributed to Pope Gregory I, defined as Gregory the Great, who became Saint Gregory I, having ruled around 600 CE. The time of his rule as Pope is contemporary to the period when the early illustrations in *The Book of Kells* were being created and Saint Columba was working as a missionary. Gregory identified the four evangelists by explaining them as the four stages of the life of the Christ, thus:

Man is the Christ at his birth.
Calf (Ox) is the death of the Christ.
Lion symbolises the resurrection of the Christ.
Eagle is the ascension of the Christ into heaven.

From this, one can conclude that the appearance of these four images in a Royal Arch Chapter room is a reference to the New Testament. With the emblem of the Royal Arch at the centre, we can now conclude an allegorical interpretation:

The circle (a symbol of eternity) represents the everlasting.
The triangle (a symbol of deity)

represents the Divinity of the Christ.
The Triple Tau/Taw represents the Trinity.

From this, we then have the combined emblems making the following possible statement:

Almighty and everlasting God, as father, son and spirit.

This being the case, it also implies that the symbol, attached to the end of the sash, and the apron worn by members of the Royal Arch, are a representation of a slightly shorter statement:

God, as father, son and spirit.

Furthermore, if the Royal Arch Triple Tau is slightly modified to add a further leg, then it becomes a representation not only of the four Apostles but also another symbol associated with the New Testament.

At the start of the religious and cultural wars of the Medieval period known as the Crusades, the Christian armies secured an early victory by seizing Jerusalem. One of the most important buildings for the Christian faith is the Holy Sepulchre, the shrine erected over the place where, traditionally, the Christ was buried. This site needed to be protected following the initial conquest and an Order of Knights, the Order of the Holy Sepulchre, was formed, which was pledged to protect the sacred site. Their symbol is the Royal Arch Triple Tau/Taw with the additional leg, creating a symbol known as the *Cross Potent*, or the *Jerusalem Cross*, although the latter is represented with four upright crosses in the centre of the area created by each leg. The *Cross Potent* has long been a symbol also associated with the Catholic Church. It could be argued that, in removing one leg and thereby creating the Royal Arch Triple Tau/Taw, it actually refers to a period some 200 years ago when tolerance of the Catholic faith was no longer a prominent feature of the British political landscape and the Holy Roman Empire had recently been abolished by Napoleon. It could have symbolically represented the break from the Catholic Church by the Protestants, and the resultant creation of the Churches of England and Scotland.

Thus we have the Knights of the Holy Sepulchre guarding a place where the body of the *son of God* was buried – the key personality at the core of the Trinitarian concept, together with the four main Apostles and authors of the Gospels featured in the New Testament. It could therefore be speculated that the reason why the Triple Tau of the Royal Arch is called a *Taw*, is that it symbolically represents the Triple Tau in Platonism, but used as an allegory for the *Trinity* and the creation of the Protestant religion, immortalised in the Church of England of which the reigning monarch is the head. Furthermore, at the time of the Union of the Grand Lodges, and the acknowledgement of the Royal Arch, the Grand Master was not only a man known to have a strong Christian faith but also a son of the then reigning monarch and therefore close to the head of the Anglican Church.

The story doesn't end there.

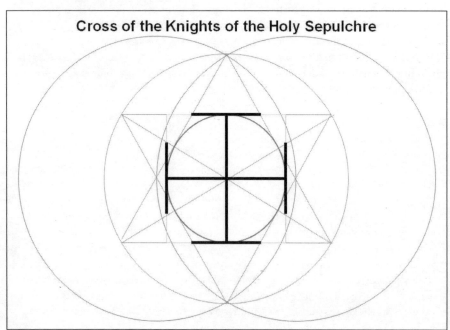

**Cross of the Knights of the Holy Sepulchre**

## Masonic Memory Review 9

We have noted how the geometry within the symbolism of the Royal Arch contains the knowledge that completes the understanding of the Master Mason.

That ability builds into esoteric knowledge contained within the former Master/ Past Master degree, which enhances an appreciation of the Vesica/Mandorla. Understanding the background to the equilateral triangle, together with that of the Vesica/Mandorla, enables the primary symbol of the Royal Arch degree – Solomon's Seal – to be constructed.

Once the geometry of *this powerful emblem* has been developed, it enables an understanding of Platonic theory and its link with the Triple Tau/Taw. This in turn relates to the ancient concept of the four primary elements associated with the creation of the world, Earth, Fire, Air and Water, which combine with the cardinal points to create another ancient symbol, that of the Octagram. They also combine to represent the Universal Sphere.

We have also seen that the sash, as a component of the Royal Arch regalia, has a connection with honours of state, while the colours of the robes of the three presiding officials in the chapter also have allegorical significance.

In addition, we have seen that the Triple Tau, so highly revered in Royal Arch ceremonial, may not be what is implied, and that biblical connections with the symbol, its interpretations and connections with the New Testament, seem to have long since ceased to be appreciated by some, if not most of the Senior ranks of the Royal Arch degree.

To heighten the problem, the double cube may have a relevance to the craft of the stonemason, as devised by Sir Isaac Newton as a solution to the *Delian problem*, and the emblems of the twelve tribes of Israel are linked to cosmology.

The range of allegorical interpretations implies cunning, yet highly developed logical and lateral thinking, on the part of those early forefathers of the institution.

But when it is understood, every brother is doubtless enlightened – what an education we receive.

*Chapter 14*

# Rebuilding the Royal Arch, the allegory of the legends

As PREVIOUSLY MENTIONED, THE main theme of the Royal Arch ceremonies, centre around the biblical account of the return to Jerusalem of the descendants of those Israelites taken into captivity in Babylon 70 years earlier. This followed the sacking of the city of Jerusalem by an Assyrian army, in which the original Temple built by Solomon was destroyed.

In other chapters of this book, mention has been made of the Roman engineer and *Father of Architecture*, Vitruvius, and his links with classical architecture. Likewise, mention has also been made of a man who was employed at the Vatican in the early 15th century, by the name of Poggio Bracciollini (Poggio). Vitruvius and Poggio lived in periods about 1500 years apart, but both have a profound effect on the ceremonial of the Royal Arch.

In the legend that accompanies one of the ceremonies, the Israelites have made their return to Jerusalem, and Zerubbabel, Haggie and Jeshua are setting about the task of rebuilding the Temple of Jerusalem on the site where the original stood. Whilst clearing away the fallen debris, the workmen, known in the ceremony as 'sojourners', reveal a vault below ground level. One of them descends into the depths and, whilst groping around in the gloom and dark, discovers a pedestal in the shape of a double cube and a long lost Volume of the Sacred Law. Yet there is only one event involving such a discovery recorded in the Old Testament. It takes place some years *before* the Assyrian army attacked and destroyed Jerusalem, and is related to Solomon's Temple. Depending upon which version of the Old Testament is used, King James or New International, the discovery was made when a priest was scurrying around in the dark recesses of the Temple:

> While they were bringing out the money that had been taken into the temple of the LORD, Hilkiah the priest found the Book of the Law of the LORD that had been given through Moses. Hilkiah said to Shaphan the secretary, "I have found the Book of the Law in the temple of the LORD." He gave it to Shaphan.[67]
> *2 Chronicles 34:14,15.*

So, by virtue of the fact that this text relates to an event that took place probably around 150 years prior to the Israelites return to Jerusalem, it can have no credible connection with the Royal Arch legend – unless it's an allegory for something else.

With regard to the origins of the Royal Arch legend, there has been much debate and millions of words written over the decades, devoted to the subject. By the late twentieth century, however, accepted opinion noted that the legend did not originate or become part of Royal Arch ceremonies until at least the year 1800. In the mid-20th century, the view about the origins of the legend, and widely accepted in the absence of any other plausible explanation, centres around one ancient fable that apparently originated in Byzantium in the fourth century. The theory presented to support this, is that in the late 1700s, Freemasonry had attracted a number of members who were well educated at the Universities of Oxford and Cambridge, and in this respect were well versed in the classics and Greek language. As such, they would have been aware of this fable as it was translated from the original Greek, and, at a time when Royal Arch ceremonies were going through a period of development, they introduced it as the legend we know today.[68] All of these connections seem entirely sensible, except they raise a few questions as to why an obscure fourth-century fable was taken and implanted into Royal Arch ceremonies, ostensibly a degree that was supposedly connected with Operative masons. Was it to pronounce their superior knowledge gained from studying the classics? Was it to win favour with their aristocratic hierarchical leaders? Or was it just a case of introducing something with a sense of drama and action as one might experience in a play at a theatre? Or, was it an allegory for something else?

The fourth-century origins of the fable are connected with a man named Philostorgius, who wrote an ecclesiastical history of the Church from 304 CE-440 CE. Encyclopaedias list him as being a church historian, who lived from circa 370 CE – 440 CE, and who apparently discounted the doctrine of the Trinity, seeming to sympathise with the views of Arius – *the Arian heresy* – and as such was branded a heretic by the church leaders of the day. (We might reflect that Whiston, of Josephus fame, had the same beliefs and endured the same punishment.) For some part of his life, Philostorgius lived in Constantinople, but it seems that none of his original manuscripts have survived the passage of time. Yet various copies and summaries exist, and it is from those translations that the text used in the legend is derived.[69]

The following is a word for word copy of the text that appears in *Freemasons' Book of the Royal Arch* by Bernard E. Jones.

Here is the legend as told in Walford's translation of *The Ecclesiastical History of Philostorgius:*

Chapter 14. When Julian bade the city of Jerusalem to be rebuilt in order to refute openly the predictions of our Lord concerning it, he brought about exactly the opposite of what he intended. For his work was checked by many other prodigies from heaven; and especially, during the preparation of the foundations, one of the stones which was placed at the lowest part of the base, suddenly started from its place and opened the door to a certain cave hollowed out in the rock. Owing to its depth, it was difficult to see what was within this cave: so persons were appointed to investigate the matter, who, being anxious to find out the truth, let down one of their workmen by means of a rope. On being lowered down he found stagnant water reaching up to his knees; and, having gone round the place and felt the walls on every side, he found the cave to be a perfect square. Then in his return, as he stood near about the middle, he struck his foot against a column which stood rising slightly above the water. As soon as he touched the pillar, he found lying upon it a book wrapped up in a fine and thin linen cloth; and as soon as he had lifted it up just as he had found it, he gave a signal to his companions to draw him up again. As soon as he regained the light, he showed them the book, which struck them all with astonishment, especially because it appeared so new and fresh, considering the place where it had been found. This book, which appeared such a mighty prodigy in the eyes of both heathens and Jews, as soon as it was opened shows the following words in large letters: 'In the beginning was the Word, and the Word was with God, and the Word was God.' In fact, that volume contained the entire Gospel which had been declared by the divine tongue of the (beloved) disciple and the Virgin. Moreover, this miracle, together with other signs which were then shown from heaven, most clearly showed that 'the word of the Lord would never go forth void,' which had foretold that the devastation of the Temple should be perpetual. For the book declared Him who had uttered those words long before, to be God and the Creator of the Universe; and it was a very clear proof that 'their labour was but lost that built,' seeing that the immutable decree of the Lord had condemned the Temple to eternal desolation.

In this text, mention is made of the *beloved disciple*. This is a reference often used when referring to Mary Magdalene. In the opening sentence there is reference to Julian. *The Catholic Encyclopaedia* gives his full name as Flavius Claudius Julianus, also called the Apostate. He was the Emperor of the Roman Empire based in Constantinople and succeeded his uncle, Constantine the Great, and is also recorded as being a philosopher. Whilst his uncle had promoted Christianity as the universal faith of the empire, Julian only outwardly supported the religion and is believed to have really been a supporter of the older pagan religions of Rome.

Bernard E. Jones makes the point that the legend attributed to Philostorgius has been restated in a range of forms, and draws particular attention to one by *Nicephorus Callistus* (Nicephorus Callistus Xanthopulus) who apparently lived around the 14th century in Constantinople, about one thousand years after Philostorgius. He is noted as having also been a compiler and writer of ecclesiastical history, his version of the fable being very close to that already stated above.

Bernard E. Jones also refers to a paper presented in Somerset in 1921 by A.E. Waite, wherein he draws on text from the Book of Enoch. In this article Enoch and his son, Methuselah, built a secret cavern with nine levels of vaults. The last sentence of the quoted extract reads:

> In the ninth, or undermost, Enoch placed a triangle of purest gold, on which he had inscribed that which was presumably the heart, essence and centre of the Sacred Tradition, the True name of God.[70]

Whilst these extracts provide a very good connection to indicate how and where the text of the ceremony may have originated, there is nothing to suggest why they are actually included, unless as suggested earlier, the fable is being used as an allegory. That being so, why this particular fable?

The Royal Arch ceremony is noted as being based on the rebuilding of Jerusalem after the Israelites had relocated from Babylon. The site of the city they would have encountered, would, no doubt, have been in ruins so it was akin to building a new Jerusalem rather than returning to one that already existed. This building activity would have required considerable manpower and materials. In addition, there is a record of a source of water, probably within the original temple facility, that is known as the Gihon Spring, and it is entirely reasonable to consider that the new temple built by Jeshua would have ensured that this spring was equally prominent. The spring still runs beneath Jerusalem.

Constantine relocated the centre of his administration away from Rome, and established a New Rome. Until his arrival, the location he chose was little more than a large fishing village, but no doubt there would have been a significant influx of new residents resulting in considerable building activity with the resultant need for manpower and materials. In his reign a large new basilica was constructed in the city. This original basilica is believed to have collapsed and was in ruins. Thus, the second basilica was raised, just as the Israelites had raised their second temple in Jerusalem. The second temple in Jerusalem was replaced by a third, the Herodian temple that was captured and destroyed by the Romans in 70 CE. Constantinople had a third basilica which today is known as the Hagia Sophia. Just as the Herodian temple in Jerusalem was destroyed, and the religion once practiced there ceased, later to become a centre of Islamic worship, so the third basilica in Constantinople was captured, and the original religion based there was replaced by Islamic traditions. Across the region there are a number of cisterns, large holes cut into rock beneath the surface of the surrounding ground, that were used to act as water storage facilities. A large cistern exists beneath the current Hagia Sophia, the third church built on the same site. It is believed that a cistern existed beneath the original basilica. So, where in the fable one of the builders was lowered into a cavern and found himself up to his knees in water, it would reflect being lowered into just such a cistern. Hence, we have water associated with the temples in Jerusalem and the basilicas of Constantinople. From all this, we can see that whilst the fable by Philostorgius provides us with a nice story, behind it we are drawn to the historic and religious parallels that exist between events that affected both Jerusalem and Constantinople.

Enlarging on the impact of Poggio, the Reverend W.M. Shepherd wrote a short book entitled *The Life of Poggio Bracciolini*, published in 1802 and printed in a later edition in Liverpool in 1837, just 20 years after the formation of the Supreme Grand Chapter of the Holy Royal Arch. In it he devotes one chapter to Poggio's discoveries of ancient manuscripts, including several that were copies of the works of the great philosophers that had lain undisturbed on the shelves of monastic libraries. The following text from the book by the Reverend Shepherd, gives a background to Poggio's discoveries:

…The vacancy of the pontifical throne still affording to the officers of the Roman chancery a considerable degree of leisure, Poggio about this time undertook an expedition of no small importance to the interests of literature. Having received information that many ancient manuscripts of classical authors were scattered in various monasteries, and other repositories in the neighbourhood of Constance, where they were suffered to perish in neglected obscurity, he determined to rescue these precious relics from the hands of barbarians, who were so little sensible of their value. He was not deterred from this laudable design by the inclemency of the season, or by the ruinous state of the roads; but with an industry and perseverance, which cannot be too highly applauded, he made several excursions to the places which were said to contain the objects of his research. These excursions he even extended to the city of Paris. For the fatigue and trouble which he encountered in these inquiries he was requited with the most signal success. A great number of manuscripts, some of which contained portions of classic authors, which the admirers of ancient learning had hitherto sought for in vain, were the reward of his literary zeal…in consequence of information which Poggio had received, that a considerable number of books were deposited in the monastery of St.Gall, he took a journey to that town, accompanied by some of his friends. There they found a large number of manuscripts, and amongst the rest a complete copy of Quintilian, buried in rubbish and dust. For the books in question were not arranged in a library, but were thrown into the lowest apartment or dungeon of a tower, 'Which', says Poggio, 'were not even a fit residence for a condemned criminal…'[71]

*The Catholic Encyclopaedia* makes the following observation in respect of Poggio's efforts in securing ancient documents:

An Italian humanist and historian; born in 1380; died at Florence, 10 October 1459. He studied at Florence and went to Rome about 1402. Boniface IX made him one of the Apostolic secretaries, which position he held under Innocent VII, Gregory II, Alexander V, and John XXIII.

The deposition of John XXIII and the delays of the Council of Constance afforded him leisure to search the libraries of the monasteries of Germany and France. In 1415 he discovered at Cluny a manuscript containing the following discourses of Cicero: *Pro Cluentio*, *Pro S. Roscio*, *Pro Murena*, *Pro Milone*, and *Pro Cælio*. This manuscript was sent to Florence where Francesco Barbaro deciphered it with great difficulty. Later Poggio discovered at St. Gall's the first complete text of Quintilian's *Institutio Oratoria*, of which Petrarch had known only fragments, a portion of Valerius Flaccus (I-IV, 317), commentaries on Cicero, among others that of Asconius, a commentary of Priscian on twelve verses of Virgil, and manuscript of Vitruvius. During another search through the monasteries, probably Einsiedeln, Reichenau on Lake Constance, and Weingarten, he discovered Vegetius, already known by Petrarch, Festus in the abridgment of Paul the Deacon, Lucretius, Manilius, Silius Italicus, Ammianus Marcellinus, the grammarians Caper, Eutyches, and Probus. It was during this journey or the next that Poggio discovered the "Silvæ" of Statius. In 1417 he went as far as Langres, France, where he recovered seven discourses of Cicero, three on the agrarian law, *Pro Rabirio*, *Pro Roscio Comœdo*, and *In Pisonem*. This journey also resulted in the discovery of a manuscript of Columella. …One in his own hand at Madrid (Bib. Nat., X, 81) contains Asconius and the first part of Valerius Flaccus.

After the Council of Constance Poggio accompanied Martin V to Italy and stayed with him at Mantua (1418). In 1423 he became his secretary. On his return from a journey to England Poggio discovered an incomplete Petronius at Cologne and Nonius Marcellus at Paris. Niccoli admitted him to his confidence with regard to the *History* of Tacitus, of which he made a secret. He shared in the discovery of the lesser writings of Tacitus by Enoch of Ascoli, in that of Aulus Gellius, of Quintus Curtius and the last 12 works of Plautus by Nicholas of Cusa. In 1429 he made a copy of the *De aquæ ductibus* of Frontinus. In 1429 he published his dialogue on avarice, in which he attacked especially the professors of law and the Mendicant Friars.[72]

The Reverend Shepherd also notes that Poggio made a trip to Britain after his time in Constance. On the subject of this visit, Poggio was most scathing, as it seems he had made the acquaintance of the Bishop of Winchester, 'Beaufort, a son of the celebrated John of Gaunt, Duke of Lancaster and uncle to the then reigning monarch, Henry V'.[73] Beaufort had succeeded to his position on the death of his predecessor, William Wickham, who in his lifetime had secured many masons from across the country to work on extensions to Windsor Castle, and retained them there on the threat of severe penalties should they abscond. The Revered Shepherd comments:

Nothing but some suddenly conceived dissatisfaction with his actual situation, or the prospect of some considerable emolument, could have induced Poggio to fix his residence in Britain, a country regarded by the Italians as the remotest corner of the globe, and as the abode of ignorance and barbarity. He was much chagrined

on observing the uncultivated state of the public mind in Britain, when compared with the enthusiastic love of elegant literature which polished and adorned his native country.[74]

The Revered Shepherd then adds:

The period of his arrival in England has been justly pronounced by one of our most accurate historians, to be in a literary point of view one of the darkest which occur in the whole series of British annals.[75]

Shepherd then continues to lament the state of literature at that time as if in support of Poggio's opinion.

Having made his manuscript discoveries at Constance, in conditions he described as a *dungeon – not even a fit residence for a condemned criminal*, Poggio sent the recovered documents to Florence, including that of the *long lost sacred law of architecture* – the works of Vitruvius. This one act could justifiably be termed, the start of the Renaissance architectural reawakening of the classical period.

*Author's note:*
*From the above I believe the allegory of the Royal Arch, uses the Philostorgius legend from the fourth century, as the allegory for the discovery of the Vitruvius manuscript. Bernard E. Jones suggested that the legend was probably not included in the Royal Arch ceremony until after 1800. Is it possible that the publication of Revered Shepherd's book about Poggio's life became the motivating factor that created the legend? That being so, then we can date the legend's inclusion to around 1837. Furthermore, the legend now has direct relevance to freemasonry rather than merely being a misplaced fable.*

By the end of the century in which Poggio made his trips of discovery, a series of wars had broken out in the area around the Abbey of St. Gall. The abbey had accumulated a vast collection of valuable manuscripts, some dating back to the ninth century; fearing for their safety, the monks rapidly moved the books to a safer location. In due course the abbey suffered great damage in battles that ensued, in consequence of which the old abbey was progressively demolished, including the tower and *dungeon* in which Poggio made his discovery, and rebuilt. Today, the Abbey of St. Gall is at the centre of the Swiss town of Saint Gallen, a short distance from the banks of Lake Constance. Standing on the Swiss side of the lake, one can look across the waters into Germany; not far to the right is Austria and Lichtenstein. The abbey church which stands out above the town was painstakingly rebuilt with the interior reflecting the beauty of the Baroque/Roccoco style, and also houses the abbey library, now declared a UNESCO World Heritage site, in which are located many of the oldest known surviving ecclesiastical books and manuscripts. The library also has on display a replica of a celestial globe, made in the lifetime of Mercator, by German-born astronomer/mathematician Jost Buri. The original globe is now in the Zurich Museum.

*For images, see colour section, plates 12, 14, 15*

In the past, there have been various eminent men who have suggested that the colours of the Royal Arch symbolise the light that shone from the revealed vault with the discovery of the book of the Sacred Law; because of the era in which they lived, they often represented a religious perspective. In another sense, the rediscovery of Vitruvius' manuscript, brought into the light by its translation and broad distribution, was another form of sacred law – the principles of architecture that have now long endured and been practised by the operative masons of Britain.

## Allegory of the Historical Lecture legend

One of the lectures within the Royal Arch deals with the subject of possible origins, the language being rather convoluted (as most of the lectures are), so the following contains paraphrased statements to outline the contents.

The lecture sets out three stages of the development of Freemasonry. An early paragraph states:

...there are three epochs in the history of Freemasonry which particularly merit your attention. They are the openings of the First, or Holy Lodge; the second, or Sacred Lodge; the Third, or Grand and Royal Lodge.

## Allegory of the First (or Holy) Lodge

The main body of the text surrounds the biblical story of the exodus from Egypt by the Israelites led by Moses, and their wandering in the Sinai desert during which his two companions, Aholiab and Bezaleel, designed and built the *Tabernacle* and the *Ark of the Covenant*.

There are two other paragraphs that may have an influence on the allegory:

...the Almighty had been pleased to reveal himself to his faithful servant Moses; when he commissioned him His High Ambassador; of wrath against Pharaoh and his people, but of freedom and salvation for the house of Jacob...

...And there, too, were dedicated, by His unerring wisdom, those peculiar forms of civil and religious polity which, by separating His favoured people from all other nations, consecrated Israel a chosen vessel to His service...

Throughout Freemasonry, it seems as if the biblical stories or records of events have been used as an education in the texts of the Bible, a moral lesson for life based on religious interpretation of the writings and as an allegory for conveying something else. There are two words used in this ceremonial text that few people today would consider using in everyday language, so we must be sure to understand their meaning. They are *epoch* and *polity.* The dictionary definition of these words is as follows:

Epoch – an extended period of time, characterised by a memorable series of events. A memorable event or date, a turning point.
Polity – a country or state regarded as a politically organised unit. A form of government or social organisation.

So on the basis of the opening few words of the first paragraph quoted above, it suggests that in looking for the allegory which may underpin this lecture, and the three periods of development of Freemasonry, we are looking at an extended period of time during which there was major change of some kind that affected the state and politics associated with it. We are, therefore, looking for other significant historical events that influenced the creation of something that has, for the purpose of edification, seemed worth recording. We have already seen how that was done with the historical knowledge embedded in the Second Tracing Board, by directing attention to the significance of St. Paul's Cathedral and the Wars of Spanish Succession. What is more, it should not be assumed that the titles given to these three periods are an indication that an actual Lodge of any kind existed during the period we may be dealing with. It is also worth noting, that biblical stories are used to provide a parallel set of circumstances and that a Lodge existed in the period when Moses was alive. Neither should we assume that whatever events we are seeking occurred in a progressive sequence, but were taken at random to satisfy the connection with the biblical story, each within the three periods of time that define each of the three Lodges.

In the reference to Moses and the exodus, the event records a breaking away of a group of people from the established state and political control of Egypt, and then spending a period of uncertainty in the wilderness. Moses recorded the Ten Commandments and thereby established a framework for religious devotion, as well as moral and physical character of a nation and the conduct of its people. Stability was provided when Moses, Aholiab and Bezaleel, constructed the *Tabernacle* and the *Ark of the Covenant,* in which to deposit the new laws that Moses had recorded. It was a series of events that swept away the old established customs that had framed life under the Egyptians and established a new beginning for the people of Israel.

If we assume that Israel is an allegorical reference to England, then there is only one epoch or sequence of events that offers a parallel with the biblical story. It started in the year 1534, when Henry VIII (Moses), assisted by Aholiab (Sir Thomas More ) and the cunning Bezaleel (Thomas Cromwell, Earl of Essex), led the people of England out of the Holy Roman Empire (Egypt) and Papal influence (Pharaoh). He then established the Protestant Church of England through the *Act of Supremacy* which was passed by Parliament (Polity) a few years later. In so doing, he established a new *Tabernacle* (church and centre for religious devotion) which was at variance with practises of Roman Catholicism that they had experienced whilst under their enslavement in the Holy Roman Empire (Egypt). Henry (Moses) separated his people from all the other nations, and for a time they were alone in the (Polity – political) wilderness. Two years after this separation, Henry (Moses) commenced the process of the *Dissolution of the Monasteries* in 1536, thereby removing any threat of possible Catholic revolution. In so doing, Henry (Moses) opened a new era (First Lodge) in the future development of the nation.

In respect of the sentence in the second paragraph quoted, it notes: '…But of freedom and salvation for the house of Jacob…'

The name Jacob is a Latin word for James.

In an earlier chapter, we saw that Henry VIII's sister, Mary Tudor, married James IV of Scotland of the Royal House of Stuart and thereby provided the basis of the future route for the Stuarts to rule England, when James VI of Scotland was crowned James I of England in 1603. Furthermore, it was during his reign that the Holy Bible was finally translated into English (the King James Authorised Version) and became the centrepiece of religion in England and its dependencies for the next 300 years, providing a means for citizens to read the scriptures in their own language without the interpretation of priests. Jacob (James I/VI) gained salvation by securing the freedom of the nation and the people from the yoke of an otherwise repressive religious regime.

This, it is suggested, is the background to what has been called the First, or Holy, Lodge.

## Allegory of the Second (or Sacred) Lodge

The text related to the Second Lodge, advances from the time of Moses, to the building of the First Temple of Jerusalem. It centres on the era and biblical account of David and Solomon, and how David had a vision to build a magnificent temple for which he devised plans that were ultimately implemented by his son. The key elements of the text are noted in the following paragraphs:

> Solomon, King of Israel, Hiram, King of Tyre, and Huram Abi, presided over the Second Lodge, which was opened in the bosom of the holy Mount Moriah, on the very centre of the ground on which the Solemn Sanctuary of the Sanhedrim[n] was afterwards erected…
>
> … Abraham had proved his intuitive faith by not refusing to offer up his beloved son Isaac as a destined victim on the altar… when it pleased the Almighty to provide an acceptable sacrifice…

... David offered up the mediatorial sacrifice by which the plague was stayed...

The opening few words of the paragraph referring to the three individuals becomes a first point of focus. We have two kings; Solomon who is resident in Israel, and credited with taking the plans conceived in the vision by his father, David, and building the temple and a second king, Hiram of Tyre, who resides in an entirely different country but is supportive of Solomon's efforts and agrees to supply materials. Huram Abi, a highly skilled craftsman, assists by taking those plans and bringing the building of the magnificent temple to completion.

If we refer back to the First Lodge, it seemed reasonable to assume that the reference to Israel might be an allegorical substitution for England. So the King of Israel would therefore be the King of England. This leaves us with a foreign king that supplies materials in support. There is only one period of time that fits the scenario: that of Mary II (Stuart; Solomon, King of Israel) and William III (House of Orange in the Netherlands; Hiram, King of Tyre). Mary, as a daughter of James II, was a legitimate claimant to the throne of England, and she and her husband William ruled jointly. William also provided the materials (landed in England with an army). On this basis, the second paragraph above might be interpreted as a reference to the abdication of James II (Abraham), when his son, James Edward Stuart (Isaac) by Mary of Modena, became a source of great political tension in England (Israel) because he presented potential for a future Catholic king and the return to the unwanted influence of the Pope. William was James' son-in-law, and was aware of his plan to escape to France, and making no attempt to prevent him doing so (mediatorial). The abdication by James II (Abraham) and coronation of Mary II (King Solomon) and William III (Hiram, King of Tyre), brought an end to the Catholic threat (plague) and political crisis.

It was during this time that the bulk of the construction of St. Paul's cathedral was undertaken, when the foundation stone was laid in 1675 and the construction phase completed by 1710. The reference to building a new temple and visionary plans is probably a reference to Sir Christopher Wren (Huram Abi), while it was Charles II (David) who visualised the rebuilding of a section of the cathedral before the Old St. Paul's was burnt down in the Great Fire of London of 1666. Two years later, he gave Wren (Huram Abi) the commission to prepare designs for a replacement.

The Bishop of London oversees the Diocese of London, of which St. Paul's cathedral is a part, and if we assume that *Mount Moriah*, as stated in the first paragraph, is the hill on which St. Paul's was built, then the *bosom* would mean in close proximity to the heart of it but not within the actual heart. In the area known as St. Paul's Churchyard, at a public house named The Goose and Gridiron, a Lodge is alleged to have existed in 1693, having been formed in 1691.[76] This same public house became the place where the first meeting of the Premier Grand Lodge was held in 1717, and thus the *Solemn Sanctuary of the Sanhedrin* (the Sanhedrin was a Council of Elders) would be a reference to the Grand Master, Wardens and senior members of the Grand Lodge who met there.

This, it is suggested, is the allegorical significance of the Second/Sacred Lodge.

## Allegory of the Third or Grand and Royal Lodge

The text of this section primarily notes the return to Jerusalem of the Israelites after their captivity in Babylon. As well as the three primary characters mentioned in the Biblical text, viz. Zerubbabel, Haggai and Jeshua, two others, Nehemiah and Ezra, are also mentioned. Nehemiah was the High Priest who accompanied Zerubbabel with the first group of Israelites that left Babylon. *Ezra the Scribe* was a High Priest and had a special understanding of the Hebrew laws.

Nehemiah was an official in the Persian Court, and carried letters and messages to Jerusalem. He had become concerned that the city walls of Jerusalem had been destroyed, and stayed on in the city, supervising their reconstruction rather than return to Persia.

*The Catholic Encyclopaedia* notes that the two biblical books of Ezra and Nehemiah were originally one scroll, but the later Jews divided it into two individual books.

The paragraphs that are worth noting from the ceremony are:

...Then was the kingly power restored [by a prince of the people] to the royal house of David and the princely tribe of Judah.

... nor was all vestige thereof effaced until after the destruction of Jerusalem by the Romans under Titus, in the seventieth year of the present era...

...The two scribes were lectors and expounders of the Sacred Law and attendants on the Grand Sanhedrim[n]...

If we assume that the royal house of David, is a reference to Charles II as per the deduction made in the Second, or Sacred, Lodge, then the princely tribe of Judah is the Royal House of Stuart. As may be remembered from the history previously noted in an earlier chapter, when Queen Anne died, the line from Charles I through James II was also terminated. To resolve the line of succession, there was a need to go back to James I of England and a second line that had evolved through his daughter into the House of Hanover. Thus, if we refer to the House of Hanover as a restoration of the *tribe of Judah* then we are referring to the reign of kings that started with George I, and a descendant from that line was the Duke of Sussex, a son of George III.

*The Romans under Titus in the 70th year,* refers to the period of the Jewish uprising against Roman rule. Titus was a Roman General and led the campaign against the Jews. In the year 70 CE he laid siege to Jerusalem, ultimately seized control of the city and destroying the Jewish Herodian Temple that was allegedly built on the site of Solomon's Temple. In searching for a link that might equate to such an event, there seems to be only one candidate: the American War of Independence, a revolt against rule by a king in London (Jerusalem) led by General George Washington (Titus). George I was crowned King of England and Scotland in 1714. The American war commenced in 1775–1783, and therefore ended in the 70th year in the reign of the House of Hanover.

The extract of the last paragraph above rather seals the suggestion. There were the five individuals principally associated with the formation of the United Grand Lodge, and in particular the process of putting the ceremonials together following the merger of the two Grand Lodges and the Grand Chapter:

Duke of Sussex
William White – Grand Secretary
William Williams – Provincial Grand Master, Dorset.
H.J. da Costa - Provincial Grand Master, Rutland (unofficial secretary/scribe to the Duke of Sussex)
Reverend Dr Samuel Hemming

Dictionaries define the *lector* as being derived from a Latin word of similar spelling that means a reader of sacred texts who speaks them aloud, such as in a church. Thus the *lectors and expounders* would have been the primary individuals involved with the Lodge of Reconciliation and the Lodge of Promulgation. In the above group, there are two scribes, William White – the Grand Secretary – and H.J. da Costa – unofficial secretary to the Duke of Sussex, while the 'expounders' may well be a reference to the Reverend Dr Samuel Hemming and William Williams.

From the analysis that has been compiled above, it seems that the *Historical Lecture* that forms part of the Royal Arch ceremonies is an allegory for the periods over which Freemasonry in England was formalised, or during which developments took place that influenced it in the epoch between the reign of Henry VIII and the formation of the United Grand Lodge of England under the Grand Master, Prince Augustus Frederick, the Duke of Sussex.

In addition, the decoding of the Royal Arch ceremonial contents demonstrates that it comprises a series of carefully selected elements of knowledge coherently bound together that provide an education in history, architecture, philosophy and religion, once the allegory has been understood.

Rebuilding of *the Holy Royal Arch of Jerusalem* is now complete.

## Masonic Memory Review 10

Through the pages of this chapter, we have seen how a wide array of influences from history, religious culture, ancient philosophy and royal interface have been deliberately fused together to create a culminating degree in regular Freemasonry. It is built upon part of the knowledge that is presented in allegorical form in the three formal degrees of the Craft Lodge system, plus the Master or Past Master degree.

Much of the geometry and philosophy mentioned or illustrated in the Royal Arch came to the fore through Giovanni Francesco Poggio Bracciolini, who by his diligence in the early 15th century rediscovered many of the works of the ancient philosophers, on the bookshelves and in the dungeons of some of the oldest monastic houses in Europe. More particularly, he discovered a copy of the manuscript of Vitruvius – the father of architecture. With this discovery the era of Renaissance architecture began, and the craft and skill of the stonemason was amply displayed through the many stately edifices built throughout Britain and Europe, based on the ancient design concepts linked to the natural world, as illustrated by Vitruvius. The ceremonial legend in the Royal Arch seems to have been based on another legend derived from a fourth-century citizen of Byzantium, Philostorgius, which in turn is probably an allegorical reflection of the rediscovery of the works of Vitruvius at the Abbey of St. Gall's, near Lake Constance.

Referring back to the comment made earlier:

> … Although Count Goblet d'Alviella suggests a union between the medieval masons and philosophers, most students (the present writer [Bernard E. Jones] among them) cannot see even the slightest possibility that the Royal Arch has developed from operative masonry…[77]

It may be partially right, as we have seen how the works of the philosophers appear in Freemasonry together with the practical knowledge that an operative Freemason would have possessed. It was the craftsmen that used the knowledge that they gained in respect of executing the primary designs of the Gothic and Renaissance periods, that enabled them to build such wonderful structures as the many cathedrals and large churches across Europe, or buildings of state copied around the world. The connection with the Triple Tau/Taw and the Trinity would possibly have originated within monastic communities, and the most likely place of origin is probably Ireland. To enable us to envisage how this may have come about, the three illustrations of the political, religious and philosophical maps of development in Britain that follow provide a possible route as to how the various ceremonial elements actually arrived.

Finally, the elusive *key* that is *wanting* is actually buried in ceremonial text about the Triple Tau/Taw that few Royal Arch members actually read, let alone understand. When understood more thoroughly, it points out the value of the Triple Tau/Taw in Platonic theory, but also draws attention to the second volume of the Holy Bible – the New Testament.

*For images, see colour section plate 32, 33. 34.*

*Chapter 15*

# The Closing

OH, WONDERFUL FREEMASONRY. PERHAPS it should be viewed as the world's first virtual university and encyclopaedia of wisdom and knowledge for mass education.

In the opening pages, mention was made of how Freemasonry is sometimes believed to be connected with conspiracies. From the information contained in the pages of this book, most right-minded people will have some difficulty locating evidence of any such conspiracy. Knowledge, and the conveying of such knowledge, albeit in a somewhat bizarre fashion, has been at the heart of Freemasonry for at least 300 years.

We have now completed a journey of discovery of the knowledge and wisdom that appears to be contained in Freemasonry, albeit obscured by allegorical presentation of biblical references and geometric symbols. It is also clear that every degree in mainstream Freemasonry is created by several separate strands of knowledge, neatly packaged, to create a single ceremony that progressively builds to the impressive array which adorn the Royal Arch.

One can only admire the great skill in purposeful deception, and the many hours spent by groups of our forebears in deliberating and packaging the ceremonies we now have, to preserve information and pass it down through the centuries. It provides us with an ancestral link to them and enables us to reach back to the turbulent times in which they lived, for they are not forgotten.

Having completed the process of researching the allegorical connection with the ceremonies and symbols of Freemasonry indicated in this book, one thing suddenly emerged that had not previously seemed obvious. It was as if a template for the organisation of Freemasonry had been drawn, probably at the Union of the Grand Lodges in 1813, into which various categories of events could be allocated, thereby enabling the process of the Union to be undertaken in a systematic manner, as shown below. The most likely person to have developed such a template and first acted upon it was the Reverend Dr Samuel Hemming. Yet this hard-working school master obtains little recognition in any Masonic literature of the past.

| Beginning | Middle | End |
|---|---|---|
| Birth | Life | Death |
| Old Testament Text | Life of the Christ | Gospels, New Testament |
| Craft freemasonry | Master P/Master | Holy Royal Arch |
| University, BA degree | Masters Degree | Doctorate degree, PHD |

Perhaps the time has come for Hemming to receive greater recognition.

Through Masonic ceremonial, one is urged to undertake a study of the Seven Liberal Arts and Sciences, which along with religion were the primary subjects of study at Oxford or Cambridge Universities at the time Freemasonry was formalised in 1717, while the Union of 1813 clearly indicates when the allegorical code now in place was deciphered:

Grammar, Rhetoric, Logic, Arithmetic, Geometry, Music, and Astronomy.

In the foregoing chapters, it has been noted that the Triple Tau/Taw of Platonic theory is regarded as the key to understanding the allegorical meanings of Freemasonry, and this author would suggest that perhaps the theory should now be revised to highlight the significance of at least two of those Liberal Arts: *Geometry* and *Logic*.

Also buried within the ceremonies of our ancient institution is a level of philosophy, history, knowledge of two significant forms of architecture, the tools of the stonemasons of the medieval period, the outline structure of the guild of the Company of Masons, all as they were understood in the era preceding the Union of the Grand Lodges in 1813, prior to the restructuring of the institution that followed over the subsequent decades. Study any branch of the Liberal Arts that have so far been mentioned in a meaningful way, and many others that have not, and one receives an intense education comparable to any formal study. When fully understood, it reveals *Freemasonry Decoded*.

At the start of this book, a series of questions were raised, to which we now have answers. Although not conclusive due to the lack of positive evidence that was lost in the mists of time, we can obtain a very objective perception of the way in which events may have unfolded and led to the Freemasonry that now exists. In particular, it seems to be a product of a long period of political and religious turmoil that resulted in a number of discrete strands of wisdom and knowledge. This was variously reflected in the practical knowledge needed by the stonemasons of the late Middle Ages; philosophical wisdom embedded in religion; a reawakening of the wonders of the world that had been suppressed by centuries of intolerant religious dogma and power mongering; an acceptance of new discoveries and ideas that developed in the Age of Enlightenment, and historical events that were landmarks in the development of the British Empire which reached its ultimate geographical extent in the late Victorian era.

Eminent researchers and writers of previous ages, tell us that the ceremonies were *developed* during the first half of the 18th century, added to in the latter part of the same century, and re-organised in the early 19th century. In the early years after 1717, members of Lodges were not all extremely wealthy merchants and aristocrats but often men of modest upbringing who were shopkeepers, traders, craftsmen, clergymen or from a range of professions. Yet, somewhere in this mix of human spirit there seem to have been groups of like-minded individuals who took this hidden, and sometimes controversial knowledge, understood it and repackaged it in allegorical form beneath a layer of acceptable religious reference, which in itself also provides a moral education. Furthermore, the allegorical packaging has proved to be so secure that it has been passed down a succession of generations and remains available in the 21st century.

There were four questions raised in the opening chapter. Perhaps now we have sufficient information to provide possible answers:

1. *Why is the Installation Ceremony of a Master ignored and not seen as a degree?*
   Possible answer: it contains knowledge that was an illustrative connection with the Roman Catholic Church and its brand of religious conviction. This occurred in an age when Catholicism, and its allies were considered a threat to the stability of the British nation. Therefore, it was expunged from the rule of the country and large sections of social responsibility, and national and colonial administration in the era of empire. The ceremony for the installation of the Master is still retained and the esoteric knowledge can still be deciphered, but its role has become more associated with administration and hierarchy and it is by-passed as a link to the *degree* of the Holy Royal Arch. Yet it seems to be virtually impossible to understand Royal Arch ceremonies without the vital element of ancient wisdom that the Master or Past Master degree contains.

2. *What were the differences in the ceremonial contents practised by the Antients and Moderns?*
   Possible answer: in the reign of Henry VIII the connection with the Holy Roman Empire was severed, the Protestant religion embraced and the religious guilds abolished, although some reinvented themselves as *societies and fraternities*. It was also an era when the development of Gothic architecture came to an abrupt halt, for in England after 1600 a new architectural phase was adopted known as the *Renaissance*. It had been motivated by the discovery of manuscripts on the works of various philosophers, but particularly Vitruvius by Poggio at the Abbey of Saint Gall on Lake Constance. The Renaissance led to a revival of interest in the knowledge that had existed in the ancient classical world of the philosophers, such as Plato, Euclid and Pythagoras, a knowledge which became known to the *Moderns* – the Premier Grand Lodge, whose members were mainly based in the Southeast of England. In the North of England, and possibly in the main cities of Scotland and Ireland, residual knowledge essential for the application of geometry relative to Gothic architecture, was retained by the operative masons. After the creation of Great Britain in 1707, men who were members of Masonic fraternities in Scotland and Ireland, moved to London and tried to join local Lodges. They were refused and consequently established their own Lodges, bringing with them the knowledge of Gothic geometry, apprenticeship structure and organisation. Aware that this knowledge had been prominent in the days of the great cathedral builders and thereby predating the start of the *Renaissance,* they became known as the *Antients*. Within this new entity was also knowledge and symbolism still associated with the Catholicism which linked with the Gothic era, and the rediscovered philosophers of the early 12th century. Perhaps it also contained some Celtic fables from the period of religious devotion known as *Celtic Christianity*.

3. *Where did the concept that was the basis of the Royal Arch degree ceremonies originate, and what does it mean?*
Possible answer: exactly where it came from is still a mystery because, to date, no definitive proof or positive evidence has come to light that can confirm the origins. Perhaps the assertion that it came from Ireland may not be too far from the truth, as it has retained its strong Catholic traditions despite being ruled from England for most of the past 1000 years. As a result, priests retained a bond of contact with other Catholic sources, including France, and would therefore have been very aware of the connection with the Mandorla and the goddess worship encouraged by St. Bernard and his veneration of the Virgin Mary. Thus they would have known of the Mandorla/ Vesica geometrical connection with the symbol of the *Trinity*, which in England became the *Triple Tau/ Taw* to provide distance between the Protestant religion and Catholic symbolism. (See diagrams at the end of Chapter 13. This is an attempt to illustrate the changes in religious influence in Britain over a period of 1000 years, along with the changes in national political development, and the paths of knowledge that combined to create the United Grand Lodge of England.) The legend is a dramatisation of the rediscovery of the works of Vitruvius, and the knowledge and wisdom of ancient philosophers which evolved in the same period.

4. *Why is the Royal Arch Degree considered to be the completion of the Master Mason Degree?*

Possible answer: the Craft Lodge structure to the level of a Master Mason contains the requisite elements of knowledge which were required by the operative masons when setting out foundations, laying the first foundation stones and making sure that the structure was erected square and vertical, so as to withstand the test of time. The additional knowledge contained in Vesica Piscis enabled the creation of angles including 30, 60 and 90 degrees, and an equilateral triangle. During the classical architectural period of the Renaissance, Sir Isaac Newton devised a means of calculating the size of the base of a column relative to the diameter, thereby ensuring visual harmony, which was based on an understanding of the Vesica. All this knowledge was embodied in the Royal Arch degree, because it amply illustrates the powerful use and symbolism of Vesica Piscis. It represents the completion of knowledge that operative masons of the Gothic era possessed and the insight necessary to complete the acumen of a Master Mason. Although the core knowledge of the Vesica really resides in the Master or Past Master Degree, the bypass to the Royal Arch was devised simply for the convenience of hierarchical expediency, perhaps with the unintended consequence that the power of the Vesica, and its relationship with the symbolism of the Royal Arch, was eroded.

What also becomes apparent is that the ceremonial contents of the Royal Arch is not one story, but a series of separate elements of esoteric knowledge, wisdom and history moulded together to create the perception of a continuous story that fits with a particular aspect of scripture.

In addition to the four main questions posed, there were four illustrations that each may have provided a link with the knowledge and wisdom contained in Masonic ceremony.

*Could the design of the bishop's mitre (Image A), provide a connection with a discarded ceremony and a lost symbol of Freemasonry which now form the basis of the Installation of the Master?*

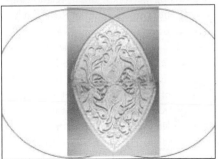

Possible answer: yes. When the mitre is inverted and two halves of the same shape are joined together, it closely resembles the Vesica. One half, when placed on the head of a bishop, locates the head/brain around the centre of the Vesica, the womb of all knowledge and understanding.

*Is it possible that the building (Image B), a once proud monastery now in ruins, is the basis for the knowledge of the Antients contained in allegorical form?*

Possible answer: yes. Tradition has it that in the early 12th century, the Abbey of Morienval in France was the place where the knowledge of Vesica Piscis was first used in the construction of a cloister, and therein the concept of the Gothic arch was understood before being deployed in the reconstruction of the ancient abbey church of St. Denis, Paris. With the knowledge of the Vesica being possibly that of the *Antients*, this would be the site which became the prototype proving ground of their ceremonial knowledge.

*Then there is the doorway (image C). Does it open into the world of the Moderns?*

Possible answer: yes. It is the Dean's Door in the south face of St. Paul's Cathedral, London. Behind that door is a winding/spiral staircase that leads to the upper level where Sir Christopher Wren and his colleague, Robert Hooke, had their surveyors' office and resolved many of the construction problems that arose. Prior to the Old St. Paul's being destroyed by fire. Inigo Jones, the man who had introduced Renaissance architecture to England through the construction of the Queen's House at

Greenwich, proposed partial redesigns, but the plan coincided with the English Civil Wars and was set aside. Sir Christopher Wren also studied the architecture of the Renaissance, much of which was embodied in the new style called English Baroque. It was also the era when the London Company of Masons received their Charter – the basis of the Freemasonry we now know was probably established in 1691, and interest in the philosophers of the ancient world was rekindled with the advent of the Enlightenment. It therefore justly deserves to be regarded as the doorway to the world of the *Moderns*.

*Could it be that the old church (Image D) provided the basis for the ceremonies, contained in allegorical form, of the Holy Royal Arch?*

Possible answer: yes. If we can accept that the legend of the Royal Arch is an allegorical representation of the discovery of the works of Vitruvius, by Poggio, in 1415, then it was on this site, at the Abbey of St. Gall's, near Lake Constance in Switzerland, where that discovery was made. Thus the discovery and the site represent the basis for the legend contained in the ceremony of the Royal Arch.

Assuming that only half of the conclusions illustrated in this book are valid in any way, then it is sad to note that so much of this knowledge has been permitted to decline into obscurity by the quest for hierarchical control and the glorification of individuals. Perhaps that was not intended, but the result has been to condemn Masonic ceremonies to become mere empty shells devoid of meaning. Perhaps the time has come to reverse that trend.

There may be many in our society who will view the information contained in this book as old fashioned and irrelevant to our modern world, and therefore worthy of being ignored and cast aside. It represents, in some instances, knowledge that has been gathered together by generations of thousands of years ago, and deemed important to be retained as a key for the organisation of a well-disciplined society, a storehouse of knowledge and wisdom, and tools crucial for survival. Man has faced many periods when natural events have led to his near-extinction, let alone his own warlike follies. Freemasonry is unique as a vessel for projecting knowledge into the future, as our forebears have projected their understanding to us over the past 300 years. Maybe the time has come to not only preserve what we now have and know, but also to collate new ceremonies that contain, in allegorical form, some of the highlights of recent generations; the survival of St. Paul's Cathedral in the Blitz bombing of London in the 1940s; man landing on the moon; high-rise architecture of steel, glass and chrome; the discovery of DNA; the invention of the Internet, and the advent of stem cell technology.

The last time a complete reorganisation of Freemasonry occurred was 200 years ago, and as we enter the fourth century of formal organisation it is our duty, like that of our forebears, to ensure that we leave behind a progressive institution of which future generations will be rightly proud, and that they, in turn, will readily embrace the avowed principles of Brotherly Love, Relief and Truth.

# Appendix 1

## Masonry Dissected (copy)

THE FOLLOWING PAGES ARE a copy of the text of *Masonry Dissected* by Samuel Pritchard, as published for public consumption, in the year 1730. It should be remembered that this was the first major insight to the form of Masonic ceremony as it is believed to have been at that time. In the description attached by Pritchard to this disclosure, he notes that no regular communications existed in 1691. We could therefore make the reasonable assertion that the ceremonial contents at around the start of the 1700s, and prior to the formalisation of Freemasonry in 1717, followed closely with those shown in this publication. As such, it suggests that much has subsequently been lost or omitted, but also that a reasonable proportion has traversed the past 300 years.

In transcribing the text of this publication, I have endeavoured to provide a reasonable representation of what was published, including some spelling that is at variance with today's standard. Some of the formatting has also been changed, in order to provide a level of clarity.

In this transcription, all three Craft degree ceremonies are published, as they apparently were at that time.

KLG.

MASONRYDISSECTED:
Being a Universal and Genuine
DESCRIPTION
of All its B R A N C H E S from the
Original to this Present Time.
As it is deliver'd in the
*Constituted Regular Lodges*
Both in C I T Y and C O U N T R Y,
According to the Several Degrees of A D
MISSION.
Giving an Impartial A C C O U N T of
their Regular Proceeding
in Initiating their New Members in the
whole Three Degrees of M A S O N R Y.
*By* SAMUEL PRICHARD, late Member
of a
*CONSTITUTED LODGE*
*L O N D O N*
Oct 1730

THE ORIGINAL Institution of Masonry consisteth on the Foundation of the Liberal Arts and Sciences; but more especially on the Fifth, *viz. Geometry.* For at the Building of the Tower of *Babel,* the Art and Mystery of Masonry was first introduc'd, and from thence handed down by *Euclid,* a worthy and excellent Mathematician of the *Egyptians,* and he communicated it to *Hiram,* the Master-Mason concern'd in the Building of *Solomon's* Temple in *Jerusalem,* where was an excellent and curious Mason that was the chief under their Grand-Master *Hiram,* whose Name was *Mannon Grecus,* who taught the Art of Masonry to one *Carolos Marcil* in *France,* and from thence was brought into *England* in the Time of King *Athestone,* who order'd an Assembly to be held once every Year at *York*, which was the first Introduction of it into *England*, and Masons were made in the Manner following.

    *Tunc unus ex Senioribus tencat Librum, ut illi vel ille pponant vel ponat Manus supra Librum; tum Praecepta debeant legi.* i. e. *Whilst one of the Seniors holdeth the Book, that he or they put their Hands upon the Book, whilst the Master ought to read the Laws or Charges.* Which Charges were, that they should be true to one another without Exception, and should be obliged to relieve their Brothers and Fellows Necessities, or put them to labour and reward them accordingly.

    But in these latter days Masonry is not composed of Artificers, as it was in its primaeval State, when some few Catechetical Questions were necessary to declare a Man sufficiently qualified for an Operative Mason.

    The Terms of Free and Accepted Masonry (as it now is) has not been heard of till within these few Years; no Constituted Lodges or Quarterly Communications were heard of till 1691, when Lords and Dukes, Lawyers and Shopkeepers, and other inferior Tradesmen, Porters not excepted, were admitted into this Mystery or no Mystery; the first sort being introduc'd at a very great Expence, the second sort at a moderate Rate, and the latter for the Expence of six or seven Shillings, for which they receive that Badge of Honour, which (as they term it) is more ancient and more honourable than is the Star and Garter, which Antiquity is accounted, according to the Rules of Masonry, as delivered by their Tradition, ever since *Adam*, which I shall leave the candid Reader to determine.

    From the Accepted Masons sprang the Real Masons, from both sprang the *Gormogons*, whose Grand-Master the *Volgi* deduces his Original from the *Chinese*, whose Writings, if to be credited, maintains the *Hypotheses* of the *Pre-Adamites*, and consequently must be more antique than Masonry. The most free and open Society is that of the *Grand Kaihebar*, which consists of a select Company of Responsible People, whose chief Discourse is concerning Trade and Business, and promoting mutual Friendship without Compulsion or Restriction.

    But if after the Admission into the Secrets of Masonry, and new Brother should dislike their Proceedings, and reflect upon himself for being so easily cajoled out of his Money, declines the Fraternity or secludes himself upon the Account of the Quarterly Expences of the Lodge and Quarterly Communications, notwithstanding he had been legally admitted into a Constituted and Regular Lodge, shall be denied Privilege (as a Visiting Brother) of knowing the Mystery for which he has already paid, which is a manifest Contradiction according to the Institution of Masonry itself, as will evidently appear by the following Treatise.

## *Entr'd Prentice's* **DEGREE.**

Q    From whence came you?

A    From the Holy Lodge of St. *John's.*

Q    What Recommendations brought you from thence?

A    The Recommendations which I brought from the Right Worshipful Brothers and Fellows of the Right Worshipful and Holy Lodge of St. *John's*, from whence I came, and Greet you thrice heartily well.

Q    What do you come here to do?

A    Not to do my own proper Will, but to subdue my Passion still; The Rules of Masonry in hand to take, and daily Progress therein make.

Q    Are you a Mason?

A    I am so taken and Accepted to be amongst Brothers and Fellows.

Q    How shall I know that you are a Mason?

A    By Signs and Tokens and perfect Points of my Entrance.

Q    What are Signs?

A    All Squares, Angles and Perpendiculars.

Q    What are Tokens?

A    Certain Regular and Brotherly Gripes.

Exam.    Give me the Points of your Entrance.

Resp.    Give me the first, and I'll give you the second.

Exam.   I Hail it.
Resp    I Conceal it.

Exam.   What do you Conceal?
Resp    All the Secrets of Secrecy of
        Masons and Masonry, unless to
        a True and Lawful Brother after
        due Examination, or in a just and
        worshipful Lodge of Brothers and
        Fellows well met.

Q   Where was you made a Mason?
A   In a Just and Perfect Lodge.

Q   What make a Just and Perfect Lodge?
A   Seven or more.

Q   What do they consist of?
A   One Master, two Wardens, two Fellow
    Crafts and two Enter'd 'Prentices.

Q   What makes a Lodge?
A   Five.

Q   What do they consist of?
A   One Master, two Wardens, one Fellow
    Craft, one Enter'd 'Prentice.

Q   Who brought you to the Lodge?
A   An Entr'd 'Prentice.

Q   How did he bring you?
A   Neither naked nor cloathed, bare-foot
    nor shod, deprived of all Metal and in a
    light moving Posture.

Q   How got you Admittance?
A   By three great Knocks.

Q   Who receiv'd you?
A   A Junior Warden.

Q   How did he dispose of you?
A   He carried me up to the North-East
    Part of the Lodge, and brought me back
    again to the West and deliver'd me to the
    Senior Warden.

Q   What did the Senior Warden do with you?

A   He presented me, and shew'd me how to
    walk up (by three steps) to the Master.

Q   What did the Master do with you?
A   He made me a Mason.

Q   How did he make you a Mason?
A   With my bare-bended Knee and Body
    within the Square, the Compass extended
    to my naked Left Breast, my naked Right
    Hand on the Holy Bible; there I took the
    Obligation (or Oath) of a Mason.

Q   Can you repeat that Obligation?
A   I'll do my Endeavour. *[The candidate
    then repeats an obligation not to reveal the
    secrets of Freemasonry that may be conveyed
    to him. The nature of the wording is very
    similar to that still in use.]*

Q   What form is the Lodge?
A   A long Square.

Q   How long?
A   From East to West.

Q   How broad?
A   From North to South.

Q   How high?
A   Inches, Feet and Yards innumerable, as
    high as the Heavens.

Q   How deep?
A   To the Centre of the Earth.

Q   Where does the Lodge stand?
A    Upon Holy Ground, or the highest
    Hill or lowest Vale, or in the Vale of
    *Jehosaphat*, or any other secret Place.

Q   How is it situated?
A   Due East and West.

Q   Why so?
A   Because all Churches and Chappels are
    or ought to be so.

Q   What supports a Lodge?

A    Three great Pillars.

Q    What are they called?
A    Wisdom, Strength and Beauty.

Q    Why so?
A    Wisdom to contrive, Strength to support, and Beauty to adorn.

Q    What Covering have you to the Lodge?
A    A clouded Canopy of divers Colours (or the Clouds.)

Q    Have you any Furniture in your Lodge?
A    Yes.

Q    What is it?
A    *Mosaick* Pavement, Blazing Star and Indented Tarsel.

Q    What are they?
A    Mosaick Pavement, the Ground Floor of the Lodge, Blazing Star the Centre, and Indented Tarsel the Border around about it.

Q    What is the other Furniture of a Lodge?
A    Bible, Compass and Square.

Q    Who do they properly belong to?
A    Bible to God, Compass to Master, and Square to Fellow Craft.

Q    Have you any Jewels in the Lodge?
A    Yes.

Q    How many?
A    Three Moveable, and three Immoveable.

Q    What are the Moveable Jewels?
A    Square, Level and Plumb-Rule.

Q    What are their Uses?
A    Square to lay down True and Right Lines, Level to try all Horizontals, and the Plumb-Rule to try all Uprights.

Q    What are the Immoveable Jewels?
A    Trasel Board, Rough Ashler, and Broach'd Thurnel.

Q    What are their Uses?
A    Trasel Board for the Master to draw his Designs upon, Rough Ashler for the Fellow Craft to try their Jewels upon, and the Broach'd Thurnel for the Enter'd 'Prentice to learn to work upon.

Q    Have you any Lights in your Lodge?
A    Yes, Three.

Q    What do they represent?
A    Sun, Moon and Master-Mason.
N.B.  *These Lights are three large Candles placed on high Candlesticks.*

Q    Why so?
A    Sun to rule the Day, Moon the Night, and Master-Mason his Lodge.

Q    Have you any fix'd Lights in your Lodge?
A    Yes.

Q    How many?
A    Three.
N.B.  *These fix'd Lights are Three Windows, suppos'd (tho' vainly) to be, in every Room where a Lodge is held, but more properly the four Cardinal Points according to the antique Rules of Masonry.*

Q    How are they situated?
A    East, South and West.

Q    What are their Uses?
A    To light the Men to, at and from their Work.

Q    Why are there no Lights in the North?
A    Because the Sun darts no Rays from thence.

Q    Where stands your Master?
A    In the East.

Q    Why so?
A    As the Sun rises in the East and opens the Day, so the Master stands in the East [*with his Right Hand upon his Left Breast being a Sign, and the Square about his Neck*] to open the Lodge and to set his Men to Work.

Q   Where stands your Wardens?
A   In the West.

Q   What's their Business?
A   As the Sun sets in the West to close the Day, so the Wardens stand in the West [*with their Right Hands upon their Left Breasts being a Sign, and the Level and Plumb-Rule about their Necks*] so close the Lodge and dismiss the Men from Labour, paying their Wages.

Q   Where stands the Senior Enter'd 'Prentice?
A   In the South.

Q   What is his Business?
A   To hear and receive Instructions and welcome strange Brothers.

Q   Where stands the Junior Enter'd 'Prentice?
A   In the North.

Q   What is his Business?
A   To keep off all Cowans and Eves-droppers.

Q   If a Cowan (or Listner) is catch'd, how is he to be punished?
A   To be plac'd under the Eves of the Houses (in rainy Weather) till the Water runs in at his Shoulders and out at his Shoos.

Q   What are the Secrets of a Mason?
A   Signs, Tokens and many Words.

Q   Where do you keep those Secrets?
A   Under my Left Breast.

Q   Have you any Key to those Secrets?
A   Yes.

Q   Where do you keep it?
A   In a Bone box that neither opens nor shuts but with Ivory Keys.

Q   Does it hang or does it lie?
A   It hangs.

Q   What does it hang by?
A   A Tow-Line Nine Inches or a Span.

Q   What Metal is it of?
A   No manner of Metal at all, but a Tongue of good Report is as good behind a Brother's Back as before his Face.
N.B. *The Key is the Tongue, the Bone Bone Box the Teeth, the Tow-Line the Roof of the Mouth.*

Q   How many Principles are there in Masonry?
A   Four.

Q   What are they?
A   Point, Line, Superfices and Solid.

Q   Explain them.
A   Point the Centre (*round which the Master cannot ere*) Line Length without Breadth, Superfices Length and Breadth, Solid comprehends the whole.

Q   How many Principle-Signs?
A   Four.

Q   What are they?
A   Guttural [sic], Pectoral, Manual and Pedestal.

Q   Explain them.
A   Guttural the Throat, Pectoral the Breast, Manual the Hand, Pedestal the Feet.

Q   What do you learn by being a Gentleman-Mason?
A   Secresy, Morality and Goodfellowship.

Q   What do you learn by being an Operative Mason?
A   Hue, Square, Mould-stone, lay a Level and raise a Perpendicular.

Q   Have you seen your Master to-day?
A   Yes.

Q   How was he Cloathed?
A   In a Yellow Jacket and Blue Pair of Breeches.

N.B. *The Yellow Jacket is the Compasses, and Blue Breeches the Steel Points.*

Q   How long do you serve your Master?
A   From Monday Morning to Saturday Night.

Q   How do you serve him?
A   With Chalk, Charcoal and Earthen Pan.

Q   What do they denote?
A   Freedom, Fervency and Zeal.
[*There then follows an examination similar to that of today.*]

Q   How old are you?
A   Under Seven. [*Denoting he has not pass'd Master.*]

Q   What's the Day for?
A   To See in.

Q   What's the Night for?
A   To Hear.

Q   How blows the Wind?
A   Due East and West.

Q   What's a Clock?
A   High Twelve.

*The End of the Enter'd 'Prentice's Part.*

## Fellow Craft's **DEGREE.**

Q   Are you a Fellow Craft?
A   I am.

Q   Why was you made a Fellow Craft?
A   For the sake of the Letter-G.

Q   What does that G. denote?
A   Geometry, or the fifth Science.

Q   Did you ever travel?
A   Yes, East to West.

Q   Did you ever work?

A   Yes, in the Building of the Temple.

Q   Where did you receive your Wages?
A   In the middle Chamber.

Q   How came you to the middle Chamber?
A   Through the Porch.

Q   When you came through the Porch, what did you see?
A   Two great Pillars.

Q   What are they called?
A   [*The names given in response are those that appear in the Old Testament Books of Kings and Chronicles.*]

Q   How high are they?
A   Eighteen Cubits.

Q   How much in Circumference?
A   Twelve Cubits.

Q   What were they adorn'd with? *Vide I Kings Chap. 7.*
A   Two Chapiters. Chap. 7.

Q   How high were the Chapiters?
A   Five Cubits.

Q   What were they adorn'd with?
A   Net-Work and Pomegranates.

Q   How came you to the middle Chamber?
A   By a winding Pair of Stairs.

Q   How many?
A   Seven or more.

Q   Why Seven or more?
A   Because Seven or more makes a Just and Perfect Lodge.

Q   When you came to the Door of the middle Chamber, who did you see?
A   A Warden.

Q   What did he demand of you?
A   Three things.

Q    What were they?
A    Sign, Token, and a Word.
[*The member is then examined to demonstrate
    that he is aware of each.*]

Q    How high was the Door of the middle
     Chamber?
A    So high that a Cowan could not reach to
     stick a Pin in.

Q    When you came into the middle, what
     did you see?
A    The Resemblance of the Letter G.

Q    Who doth that G denote?
A    One that's greater than you.

Q    Who's greater than I, that am a Free and
     Accepted Mason, the Master of a Lodge?
A    The Grand Architect and Contriver of the
     Universe, or He that was taken up to the
     top of the Pinnacle of the Holy Temple.

Q    Can you repeat the Letter G?
A    I'll do my Endeavour.

*The Repeating of the Letter G.*

Resp.    In the midst of *Solomon's* Temple
         there stands a G,
         A Letter fair for all to read and see,
         But few there be that understands
         What means that Letter G.

Exam.    My Friend, if you pretend to be
         Of this Fraternity,
         You can forthwith and rightly tell
         What means that Letter G.
Resp.    By Sciences are brought to Light
         Bodies of various Kinds,
         Which do appear to perfect Sight;
         But none but Males shall know my Mind.

Exam.    The Right shall.
Resp.    If Worshipful.

Exam.    Both Right and Worshipful I am,
         To Hail you I have Command,
         That you do forthwith let me know,

         As I you may understand.
Resp.    By Letters Four and Science Five
         This G aright doth stand,
         In a due Art and Proportion,
         You have your Answer, Friend.

Exam.    My Friend, you answer well,
         If Right and Free Principles you
         discover,
         I'll change your name from Friend,
         And henceforth call you Brother.
Resp.    The Sciences are well compos'd
         Of noble Structure's Verse,
         A Point, a Line, and an Outside;
         But a Solid is the last.

Exam.    God's good Greeting be to this our
         happy Meeting.
Resp.    And all the Right Worshipful
         Brothers and Fellows.

Exam.    Of the Right Worshipful and Holy
         Lodge of St. *John's.*
Resp.    From whence I came.

Exam.    Greet you, greet you, greet you thrice,
         heartily well, craving your Name.
Resp.    Timothy Ridicule.

Exam.    Welcome, Brother, by the Grace of
         God.
         [N.B. *The Reason why they Denominate
         themselves of the Holy Lodge of St.* John's,
         *is, because he was the Fore-runner of our
         Saviour, and laid the first Parallel Line
         to the Gospel (others do assert, that our
         Saviour himself was accepted a Free-
         Mason whilst he was in the Flesh) but
         how ridiculous and profane it seems, I
         leave to judicious Readers to consider.*]

*End of the Fellow Craft degree*

## *The Master's* DEGREE

Q    Are you a Master-Mason?
A.   I am; try me, prove me, disprove me if
     you can.

Q    Where was you pass'd Master?
A.   In a Perfect Lodge of Masters.
Q    What makes a Perfect Lodge of Masters?
A.   Three.
Q    How came you to be pass'd Master?
A.   By the Help of God, the Square and my own Industry.
Q    How was you pass'd Master?
A.   From the Square to the Compass.

Exam.   An Enter'd 'Prentice I presume you have been.
Resp.   *Jachin* and *Boaz* I have seen. A Master-Mason I was made most rare, With Diamond, Ashler and the Square.

Exam.   If a Master-Mason you would be, You must rightly understand the Rule of Three. And *M.B.* shall make you free; And what you want in Masonry, Shall in this Lodge be shewn to thee.
Resp.   Good Masonry I understand; The Keys of all Lodges are all at my command.

Exam.   You're an heroick Fellow ; from whence came you?
Resp.   From the East.

Exam.   Where are you going?
Resp.   To the West.

Exam.   What are you going to do there?
Resp.   To seek for that which was lost and is now found.

Exam.   What was that which was lost and is now found?
Resp.   The Master-Mason's Word.

Exam.   How was it lost?
Resp.   By Three Great Knocks, or the Death of our Master *Hiram*.

Exam    How came he be his Death?
Resp.   In the Building of *Solomon's* Temple he was Master-Mason, and at high 12 at Noon, when the Men was gone to refresh themselves, as was his usual Custom, he came to survey the Works, and when he was enter'd into the Temple, there were Three Ruffians, suppos'd to be Three Fellow Crafts, planted themselves at the Three Entrances of the Temple, and when he came out, one demanded the Master's Word of him, and he reply'd he did not receive it in such a manner, but Time and a little Patience would bring him to it: He, not satisfied with that Answer, gave him a Blow, which made him reel; he went to the other Gate, where being accosted in the same manner, and making the same Reply, he received a greater Blow, and at the third his *Quietus*.

Exam.   What did the Ruffians kill him with?
Resp.   A Setting Maul, Setting Tool and Setting Beadle.

Exam.   How did they dispose of him?
Resp.   Carried him out at the West Door of the Temple, and hid him under some Rubbish till High 12 again.

Exam.   What time was that?
Resp.   High 12 at night, whilst the men were at rest.

Exam.   How did they dispose of him afterwards?
Resp.   They carried him up to the brow of a hill, where they made a decent grave, and buried him.

Exam.   When was he miss'd?
Resp.   The same day.

Exam.   When was he found?
Resp.   Fifteen days afterwards.

Exam.   Fifteen loving brothers, by the Order of King Solomon, went out of the west door of the temple, and divided themselves from right to left, within call of each other; and they agreed that if they did not find the Word in him, or about him, the first word should be the Master's word. One of the brothers, being more weary than the rest, sat down to rest himself, and taking hold of a shrub, which came easily up, and perceiving the ground to have been broken, he hailed his brethren, and pursuing their search, found him decently buried in a handsome grave, six foot east, six foot west, and six foot perpendicular, and this covering was green moss and turf; which surprised them; whereupon they replied *Muscus Domus Dei Gratia*; which, according to Masonry, is, *Thanks be to God, our Master has got a Mossy House*. So they cover'd him closely and, as a farther Ornament, placed a Sprig of Cajsia at the Head of his Grave, and went and acquainted King Solomon.

Exam. What did King Solomon say to all this?
Resp. He order'd him to be taken up and decently buried, and that 15 Fellow Crafts, with white Gloves and Aprons, should attend his Funeral [which ought amongst masons, to be perform'd to this Day.]

Exam. How was Hiram rais'd?
Resp. As all other Masons are, when they receive the Master's Word.

Exam. How it that?
Resp. By the five Points of Fellowship.

Exam. What are they?
Resp. Hand to Hand, Foot to Foot, Cheek to Cheek, Knee to Knee, and Hand in Back.
N. B. *When Hiram was taken up, they took him by the Fore-fingers, and the Skin came off, which is called the Slip; the spreading the Right Hand, and placing the middle Finger to the Wrist, clasping the Fore-finger and the Fourth to the Sides of the Wrist, is called the Gripe, and the Sign is placing the 'thumb of the Right Hand to the Left*

*Breast extending the Fingers.*

Exam. What's a Master-Mason nam'd.
Resp. Cassia is my Name, and from a Just and Perfect Lodge I came.

Exam. Where was Hiram interr'd?
Resp. In the Sanctum Sanctorum.

Exam. How was he brought in?
Resp. At the West Door of the Temple.

Exam. What are the Master-Jewels?
Resp. The Porch, Dormer, and Square Pavement.

Exam. Explain them.
Resp. The Porch the Entering into the Sanctum Sanctorum, the Dormer the Windows or Lights within, the Square Pavement the Ground Flooring.

Exam. Give me the Master's Word.
Resp. Whispers him in the Ear, and supported by the five Points of Fellowship before-mentioned, says [M.B.], which signifies, The Builder is smitten.
N. B. If any Working Masons are at Work and you have a Desire to distinguish Accepted Masons from the rest, take a Piece of Stone, and ask him what it smells of, he immediately replies, neither Brass, Iron, nor Steel, but of a Mason, then by asking him, how old he is, he replies above Seven, which denotes he has pass'd Master.

*The End of the Master's Part.*

There then follows a list of some of the Lodges, known to Pritchard, that were operating in the London area at the time he wrote his outline of the ceremonies.

The closing observations suggest that, for whatever reason, he has become somewhat disaffected with Freemasonry, hence the reason for his implied revelations about the ceremonies.

# Appendix 2

## Other books by the same author

IN FREEMASONRY THE SUBJECTS of *what are we doing?* and *where did it come from?*, have resulted in three previous books, taking a different approach and progressive step forward each time.

## The Secrets of Solomon's Temple.

'...a remarkable book.....a definite textbook on the subject.' – *MQ magazine*

Because Solomon's Temple features in Craft Freemasonry, I set out to explore just about everything we know about this mythical building, and the religious doctrine that surrounds it. By drawing on recent archaeological and historical evidence, and piecing this together with knowledge involving *geometry, astronomy, logic* and other aspects of the *Liberal Arts and sciences* that had been amassed over a considerable time, I presented a thesis which was considerably at variance with previous ideas about what the temple was used for, what it looked like, and how it worked. The work has been sufficiently well received that since publication it has been printed in other countries and distributed internationally.

## Chivalry: the origins and history of orders of knighthood

Every new Freemason is advised that Masonry is *older than the Golden Fleece and Roman Eagle, more honourable than the Garter or any other Order*

*in existence*, but very few Freemasons have any idea to what this statement refers, and it is never explained in Masonic ceremonies. Yet, this simple sentence ties Orders of knighthood together with families of wealth, power and influence from the medieval period to the present era. To place these in the appropriate context, the book also covers such institutions as the Order of St John of Jerusalem; Knights Templar; Knights of St. Thomas, Knights of the Holy Sepulchre, and many more that will be of interest to Freemasons and non-Freemasons, alike.

This book has also been translated into other languages and distributed internationally.

## The Mandorla and Tau

This book presents some of the possible origins of the Masonic movement through the little known *religious guilds* - organisations that provided charitable support and pensions to their members, some of which still exist under different names and structures; some of the ancient knowledge and wisdom likely to have been known by the ancient stonemason guilds, and contained in Masonic ceremonies, and passed on through medieval apprenticeships. It also uncovers how the Virgin Mary rose to prominence as a figure adored within the Christian religion, together with links to gothic architecture and the alleged founder of the Knights Templar – St. Bernard.

This book too, has been distributed internationally.

The above books are available through Lewis Masonic at: http://www.lewismasonic.com

# Index

---

# Research and Bibliography

THE RESEARCH, SOURCES AND reference materials used for the background of this book were extensive over a prolonged period of fifteen to twenty years. The reference sources in the three previous books – *The Secrets of Solomon's Temple, Chivalry, Mandorla and Tau* – were all associated with development of this book, but not every reference to such sources used in this work was recorded separately. The following is a summary of the main sources:

*Antiquity of the Jews – Josephus, translated by William Whiston*
*Catholic Encyclopaedia, The*
Encyclopaedia Britannica
*Encyclopaedia of Religion*
*New Standard Jewish Encyclopaedia, The, Edited by G. Wigoden.*
*Holy Bible – King James Authorised Version.*
*Holy Bible – New International Version, Hodder and Stoughton.*

On-line version of *The Catholic Encyclopaedia* – New Advent – www.newadvent.org/encyclopedia
On-line encyclopaedia – Wikipedia – www.wikipedia.org
On-line Bible sources – www.biblegateway.com

*Vitruvius on Architecture* – Richard Schofield and Robert Tavernor,
*The Life of Poggio Bracciolini* – Reverend W.M. Shepherd, 1837
*The Invisible College* – Robert Lomas
*The History of Freemasonry in England* – John Hamill

*Freemasons' Book of the Royal Arch* – Bernard E. Jones
*Freemasons Guide and Compendium* – Bernard E. Jones
*The Early History of Masonry in England* – James Orchard Halliwell.
*The Genesis of Freemasonry* – Douglas Knoop M.A.
*An Introduction to Freemasonry* – Douglas Knoop M.A. and G.P. Jones (Lit.D)
*Illustrations of Freemasonry* – William Preston
Papers contained in the many volumes of *Ars Quatuor Coronatorum* (AQC).

Site visits (particularly for this work) includes those undertaken for previous books by the author, plus:
    Reims cathedral, France; Morienval, France; Strasbourg, France; Constance, Switzerland; St. Gallen, Switzerland; Verona, Italy.

Library and Archive resources used include:
    National Library, London;
    Guildhall Library, London;
    National Maritime Museum, Greenwich;
    Library of the Royal Institute of British Architects (RIBA);
    London Metropolitan Archives;
    Library of Freemasons Hall, London;
    Library of University of Sussex.
Special thanks to the *Friends* and librarians of: York Minster; St. Paul's Cathedral; the archivists at the State Library, Sydney, Australia, and Trinity College, Dublin.

# References

**(Endnotes)**

1   *Titbits* – week ending March 17th 1888.

2   *The History of English Freemasonry* – John Hamill.

3   *Catholic Encyclopaedia.*

4   Ibid.

5   A copy of Mercator's first book of maps of Europe is at the British National Library, London. Two of the earliest Mercator Globes, one terrestrial and one celestial, are on public display at the Ducal Palace in Urbania, Italy.

6   From a table noted in the online encyclopaedia Wikipedia – 'Style of the British Sovereign' at http://en.wikipedia.org/wiki/Style_of_the_English_sovereigns#Styles_of_English_sovereigns

7   In the National Trust property of Lyme Park, near Stockport, Cheshire, the former estates of the Legh family, is a letter signed by Mary Queen of Scots, thanking them for their hospitality.

8   Information received during a visit to Lyme Park.

9   *The Invisible College* – Robert Lomas.

10   *Freemasons' Book of the Royal Arch* – Bernard E. Jones.

11   Ibid.

12   Ibid.

13   Grand Lodge of Ireland.

14   *The History of English Freemasonry* – John Hamill.

15   Ibid.

16   *Freemasons' Guide and Compendium* – Bernard E. Jones.

17   *Freemasons' Book of the Royal Arch* - Bernard E. Jones.

18   For further background information see *Freemasons' Book of the Royal Arch* by Bernard E. Jones, sections four and five, published 1957.

19   *A Lecture by Andrew Prescott of the Centre for Research into Freemasonry*, University of Sheffield. Presented at the second international conference of the Canonbury Masonic Research Centre, 4-5 November 2000.

20   *The History of English Freemasonry* - John Hamill, Chapter Three – 'The Grand Lodge System'.

21   *A narrative of the persecution of Hippolyto Joseph da Costa Pereira Furtado* – Hipólito José da Costa, page 53.

22   Ibid. page 22.

23   Ibid.

24   *Encyclopaedia Americana* – Volume III.

25   *Encyclopaedia of Freemasonry* – Albert G. Mackey.

26   The information on Dr Samuel Hemming is derived from several documents in the Library of Freemasons' Hall, London and includes a paper in *AQC* – 1928 entitled 'Reverend Samuel Hemming SGW 1816, GC 1817 by W. Bro James Johstone'.

27   *Constitutions of Freemasonry* – Dr James Anderson.

28   *Masonry Dissected* – Samuel Pritchard UGLE No 14,798.

29   Based on a calculation table at *measuringworth.com*.

30   *Catholic Encyclopaedia* – Flavius Josephus

31   Considerable information about Charlemagne was researched for and contained in *Chivalry* by K.L. Gest

32 Further information about the Mandorla is contained in *The Mandorla and Tau* by K.L. Gest

33 Vitruvius – *On Architecture* – translated by Richard Schofield with introduction by Robert Tavernor.

34 *Catholic Encyclopaedia*.

35 The information about Brunelleschi was contained in the *Catholic Encyclopaedia*.

36 The text of this translation has been copied from an on-line version at http://www.vitruvius.be/boek4h1.htm.

37 Vitruvius – On Architecture – translated by Richard Schofield and with introduction by Robert Tavernor, pages 82 and 84.

38 The text of this translation has been copied from an on-line version at http://www.vitruvius.be/boek3h1.htm.

39 For more information on religious guilds, see *The Mandorla and Tau* – K.L. Gest

40 Ibid.

41 Ibid.

42 'Tracing Boards', see paper by Bro T.O Haunch, MA, AQC Volume 75 1963.

43 For details of Browns Master Key, see AQC Volume 105, 1992, 'The Third Man', by Douglas Vieler.

44 'Tracing Boards', see paper by Bro T.O Haunch, MA, AQC Volume 75 1963.

45 Paper published by William Ryan and Walter Pitman – 1997 – Columbia University.

46 *History of English Freemasonry*, John Hamill

47 Ibid.

48 Ibid.

49 Information obtained on a visit to Oxford University.

50 *History of English Freemasonry*, John Hamill.

51 *Freemasons' Book of the Royal Arch* – Bernard E. Jones.

52 Definitions taken from the Oxford Concise Dictionary.

53 *History of English Freemasonry* – John Hamill.

54 *Chivalry* – K.L. Gest.– see section about the Knights Templar – comments on information available in the small Italian town of Seborga.

55 *Freemasons' Book of the Royal Arch* – Bernard E. Jones.

56 Ibid.

57 *Freemasons' Guide and Compendium* – Bernard E. Jones.

58 *Freemasons' Book of the Royal Arch* – Bernard E. Jones.

59 *The Secrets of Solomon's Temple* – K.L Gest

60 Ibid.

61 Ibid.

62 Ibid.

63 *Freemasons' Book of the Royal* Arch – Bernard E. Jones, commencing page 256.

64 Ibid, section 22.

65 *Catholic Encyclopaedia* – 'Tau'.

66 Based on a verbal survey undertaken by the author.

67 Taken from Old Testament, new international version, '2 Chronicles' 34:14 and 15.

68 *Freemasons' Book of the Royal Arch* – Bernard E. Jones.

69 Ibid, section 11.

70 Ibid, section 11.

71 *The Life of Poggio Bracciolini* – Reverend W.M. Shepherd, commencing Chapter Three, page 97, eBook facsimile edition available at Googleplay.com.

72 *Catholic Encyclopaedia* – Poggio Bracciolini.

73 *The Life of Poggio Bracciolini* pp 111/12

74 Ibid, pp 112/13

75 Ibid, pg 113

76 *The History of Freemasonry in England* – John Hamill.

77 *Freemasons' Book of the Royal Arch* – Bernard E. Jones.